D1474306

FRANCES E. W. HARPER

Frances E. W. Harper

A Call to Conscience

Utz McKnight

polity

The right of Utz McKnight to be identified as Author of this Work has been asserted in accordance with the UK Copyright, Designs and Patents Act 1988.

First published in 2021 by Polity Press

Polity Press
65 Bridge Street
Cambridge CB2 1UR, UK

Polity Press
101 Station Landing
Suite 300
Medford, MA 02155, USA

ISBN-13: 978-1-5095-3553-8
ISBN-13: 978-1-5095-3554-5 (pb)

A catalogue record for this book is available from the British Library.

Names: McKnight, Utz Lars, author.
Title: Frances E. W Harper : a call to conscience / Utz McKnight.
Description: Cambridge, UK ; Medford, PA : Polity Press, 2020. | Series: Black lives | Includes bibliographical references and index. | Summary: "The first full account of a leading 19th century female writer and anti-slavery activist"-- Provided by publisher.
Identifiers: LCCN 2020015772 (print) | LCCN 2020015773 (ebook) | ISBN 9781509535538 (hardback) | ISBN 9781509535545 (paperback) | ISBN 9781509535552 (epub)
Subjects: LCSH: Harper, Frances Ellen Watkins, 1825-1911--Criticism and interpretation. | Harper, Frances Ellen Watkins, 1825-1911--Political and social views. | Social change in literature. | African Americans in literature. | Politics and literature--United States--History--19th century. | Antislavery movements--United States--History--19th century.
Classification: LCC PS1799.H7 Z73 2020 (print) | LCC PS1799.H7 (ebook) | DDC 818/.309--dc23
LC record available at https://lccn.loc.gov/2020015772
LC ebook record available at https://lccn.loc.gov/2020015773

Typeset in 10.75pt on 14pt Janson by
Servis Filmsetting Limited, Stockport, Cheshire
Printed and bound in Great Britain by TJ Books Limited

The publisher has used its best endeavors to ensure that the URLs for external websites referred to in this book are correct and active at the time of going to press. However, the publisher has no responsibility for the websites and can make no guarantee that a site will remain live or that the content is or will remain appropriate.

Every effort has been made to trace all copyright holders, but if any have been overlooked the publisher will be pleased to include any necessary credits in any subsequent reprint or edition.

For further information on Polity, visit our website: politybooks.com

Contents

Preface

Why does the general public today know so little about the life and writing of Frances Harper? She accomplished a great deal in her lifetime, and was a leading voice for African Americans in several national movements over the course of several decades. An abolitionist, temperance organizer, and suffragist, Frances Harper was also the most important Black poet in the country until the 1890s. She published many books of verse, four novels, numerous essays, letters, and newspaper reports, and several short stories. Her poetry readings and speeches were always sought-after events, well attended by the public.

Two book-length monographs on her literary and professional work have been published in the last three decades. Melba Boyd's *Discarded Legacy* (1994) and Michael Stancliff's *Frances Ellen Watkins Harper* (2011) give readers a thorough overview of her career and creative work, if from different perspectives. Frances Smith Foster's reader *A Brighter Coming Day* (1990) provides a handy resource that includes many of Harper's recovered poems, novels, speeches, and letters. Most of her recovered work has been the subject of academic articles, and also longer book chapters, by some of the most influential academics in the field of African American history and literary studies.

Frances Harper was by any professional measure one of the most successful individuals in the last half of the nineteenth century. She didn't, however, gain recognition by doing what was expected or easily achieved. As a Black woman, born free in the time of slavery, Harper sought above all to apply her creative talents to fighting for racial and gender equality in the US.

Frances Harper is at one level a formidable interlocutor. Her many poems, speeches, letters, short fiction, and novels make for a daunting engagement. There are some decisions that have to be made about the presentation and the argument about Frances Harper's contribution to Black intellectual thought, as a historical figure and for us today. I have chosen to present her writing and aspects of her professional life as a cohesive argument about how she thought of politics, equality, and the challenges of democracy. There are many different approaches possible with the study of the writing of someone so prolific and talented, as well as someone who was actively organizing politically throughout her life.

Frances Harper lived in interesting times, during which, after two centuries, a Civil War brought about the end of slavery. She spent 40 years fighting for voting rights for women, falling short of this goal in her lifetime. She witnessed the creation of a new regime of racial terror in the US, the collapse of the hopes and dreams of a newly freed people, at a time when industry was advancing rapidly. She traveled extensively, met thousands of people over her life, and was an astute observer of her environment and the living conditions of the people around her.

Frances Harper comforted John Brown's wife after the failed rebellion as he was waiting to be executed; she lectured alongside Sojourner Truth and Frederick Douglass; she was friends with Harriet Tubman; and she regularly had Ida B. Wells stay at her house in Philadelphia when she was traveling through. She was used to long hours on trains and coaches, and walking through the quarters of former slaves on plantations in Alabama and Georgia. She was raised in what was then the center of Black life in the US, Baltimore, Maryland, and so grew up surrounded by intense social activity. This is someone I would have loved to meet and talk politics with. Frances Harper was extremely talented and was always working on different projects of great importance and interest to many.

I have chosen to provide an overview of some of her writings, while ignoring the letters as private, and skipping some of the short pieces of fiction, and that comes at a cost. Frances Harper wrote and accomplished enough in her lifetime that no one series of poems, books, short stories, speeches, and letters can be thought to encapsulate her oeuvre. The closest we have to a comprehensive review of Frances Harper's work is the extensive study done by Melba Boyd in *Discarded Legacy*. Frances Smith Foster has – in collecting many of the available written works of Frances Harper in one volume, *A Brighter Coming Day* – not only provided useful commentary, but also organized the work chronologically so that the reader can follow the arc of Frances Harper's life in the written material. Stancliff, in his book, applies the work of Frances Harper to the study of rhetoric and pedagogy with superb results.

Acknowledging Frances Harper's genius and the incredible scope of her work, the fact that there are many very good studies to draw from, including articles written on specific works by Harper, is encouraging. I want us to read Frances Harper, and to do so as a call to a democratic politics that requires that race and gender be central to our understanding of this society. Her work is compelling and demanding, and without the research and recovery work of several amazing academic historians it would not be possible to read it. Frances Harper's works have not been adequately preserved, which in part accounts for her obscurity. For the last four decades, scholars have done the investigative work to find and restore her legacy to us.

I have chosen to use the name Frances Harper throughout to signal her authorship, even though this does interestingly coincide conceptually with the struggle that she experienced in her own life, where she wasn't accorded sufficient professional respect as a speaker on behalf of the Abolition of slavery until she had been married. As Frances Watkins prior to her marriage, she published poems and was active in public gatherings as a speaker, and the brief years of her marriage were a time of relative retreat from public writing. After her husband's death, the appellation "Harper" appended to her name allowed her the social cover afforded by the patriarchal tradition of the time. This distinction of social respectability, of having been married, in contrast to being an unmarried woman, was important in public, as a public speaker, and in the context of being a woman author of poetry and prose.

The reader should understand that there is a particular convention of names and naming, a politics of respectability with regard to women as authors, that remains accepted today, and that the social elements of this convention directly speak to a similar politics of race and gender that Frances Harper made the central part of her life's work. Names are not innocent, but full of portent and history, and few authors have been more aware of this than Frances (Ellen Watkins) Harper. I use the name Frances Harper here throughout not to conceal or suture over this politics, but to suggest that it matters that when she could have returned to using her maiden name of Watkins, after her husband's death, she did not; that, when she could choose, she kept the name of Harper, when as a child she could not choose anything but the name of Watkins. Harper was the family she chose.

It is through this representation of respectability, publicity, and personal ambition contained in what seems today marginal, even ephemeral, to a life of the writer and poet Frances Harper that we can begin to understand the challenge her work poses for us today. This was someone who – not only in her poetry and writing, but in her person, her speeches, and organizational activity – raised a challenge to the idea that Black women have not always been central to the development of the society. In this struggle against the social elision of Black women in society, Frances Harper is of course not unique. What she was able to do, however, was not only to overcome the social conventions of her time to publish, speak in public, and organize at the national level, but also to write about the problem of race and gender at a time when women couldn't vote, and for the first decades of her life she was a free Black person in a society where the enslavement of Black people was the social norm.

Frances Harper wrote, lectured, and organized while being active at the heart of the Abolitionist Movement, the Temperance Movement, and the Suffragist Movement. She traveled in the South immediately after the Civil War, and sent what today would amount to newsworthy dispatches north from the frontlines of the aftermath of the War. Frances Harper was one of the architects of the modern Women's Rights Movement, and she also was one of the first truly public intellectuals for Black Americans in the country. She spoke to and wrote for Black men and women at a time when the struggle to define the terms of Black life in America was both visceral and of immediate concern to everyone in the society.

It is important to understand that, though the sheer volume and contribution Frances Harper made to her public and the society during her lifetime are unappreciated today, certain pieces of her work have circulated widely. The claim in this book follows that of the researcher Frances Foster and others: that Frances Harper wasn't ignored, but instead diminished in importance. There is a particular politics, therefore, not simply of recovery, but of discovery, of developing a new description of the place of African Americans in this society, in working with the writing of Frances Harper. This book contributes to existing scholarship that seeks to make one of the most important thinkers and writers of the nineteenth century available to a wider audience. In doing so, it also provides a description of another America, a new society that we should aspire to become – one that acknowledges and understands the contribution of all members of the society to how we think of this nation.

The structure of the book is designed with, first, a biographical chapter. Chapter 2 discusses the novel *Iola Leroy*, in order to frame the oeuvre of Frances Harper and to provide an understanding of the themes of her earlier writings. Next, chapter 3 addresses *Trial and Triumph*, and then chapter 4 *Sowing and Reaping* and "The Two Offers." Chapter 5 considers *Minnie's Sacrifice* and the poetry of Frances Harper. Chapter 6 concludes the book with a discussion of her poetry.

Three considerations guide this approach to her work. The first and most important is that readers encounter the familiar first. If they have read anything by Frances Harper, it is usually *Iola Leroy*, and if not, it was one of the most popular novels in the last decade of the nineteenth century and should occupy pride of place for that reason. Second, I want the reader to get an understanding of the sophistication that determined the choices made by Frances Harper of genre, plot, and character in the novel, and to appreciate the overwhelming task with which she was faced in trying to establish a narrative of hope and progress for Black people in the 1890s in the US. The book was published the same year as Ida B. Wells' study of lynching, *Southern Horrors*.

Third, the reader today knows that what Frances Harper

tries to do in the novel with regard to her intended audience fails. I want the reader to understand that this is why the work of Frances Harper has been neglected until recently. In *Iola Leroy*, Frances Harper tried to gather the strands of a decaying set of political possibilities that were offered with the freeing of the slaves at the end of the Civil War. She tries to bind everyone up together. It is because she does this in *Iola Leroy* that we have in the novel her mature thinking about the politics of race as a societal idea. In the novel, she provides for the reader a vision of potential societal change, of what counts for political progress as a nation. It is here that she develops for us a radical egalitarian vision.

Chapter 3 takes up the novel *Trial and Triumph* to provide the reader with Frances Harper's perspective on community. What is required of the idea of equality to form a progressive and thriving community? Given the forces threatening to dissolve the relationships that the freed people had managed to develop after the War, what should the community do to resist its dissolution? In the novel, Frances Harper discusses the criteria for social community relations, how desire, avarice, fame, and modesty can be acknowledged so that the community can meet the challenges that it faces from a reconsolidating White authority in the society. The novel discusses many of the same problems of race and gender as we have today, and Frances Harper demonstrates a sophisticated understanding of the need for a description of equality that is always aspirational, external to the current conditions in the existing community.

In chapter 4, the reader is asked to think with Frances Harper about the demand for individual perfectionism and the problem of moral suasion in the society. The discussion considers the idea of individual, personal politics in the novel *Sowing and Reaping*, and includes also a study of the short story "The Two Offers." Frances Harper had the idea that the personal realizes concrete results in the community – a politics that then realizes change in the larger social world. She felt that, from personal decisions about morality and social practices, the necessary political changes could occur that would protect the community. The chapter addresses the struggle by the individual to determine how to positively contribute to the needs of the community.

The second through fourth chapters develop Frances Harper's description of how social change occurs and what is at stake in the period after the War for the society. Focusing on societal, community, and personal perspectives in her work allows the reader to grasp the complexity of her writing and activism. In chapter 5, the reader encounters the earliest of Frances Harper's novels in *Minnie's Sacrifice*; and the idea of what Frances Harper means by politics, and what her goals were in the work, are considered. The reader is brought into conversation extensively with her poetry for the first time. In doing this, we have come full circle to the reading of *Iola Leroy* in chapter 2. We can see the genesis of *Iola Leroy* in our study of *Minnie's Sacrifice* and the poems, and can ask the question of how we today should reconsider the challenges Frances Harper posed to her audience in the last half of the nineteenth century. In chapter 6, the conclusion, the conversation with the poems continues. The reader is asked to think with Harper about what is required to achieve progress toward racial and gender equality in the society.

1

Frances Harper's Poetic Journey

A life of consciences

We are always writing for the present, for those who share the concerns and anxieties of our lives. But, of course, we can't know how what we say and do today is measured by those who come after us, in spite of our desire to inhabit the thoughts and concerns of those who follow. Frances Harper – author, abolitionist, orator, political organizer, temperance activist, suffragist, mother, Black, American, woman – she dedicated her life to the politics of racial and gender justice.

Frances Harper was born in 1825 and lived an incredible life, sharing her ideas and her creativity with an American public until her death in 1911. She grew up a free Black person in a society where the majority of Black people were enslaved. The writer of the first short story published by an African American woman, Frances Harper also produced *Iola Leroy*, one of the most popular fiction novels in the US of the latter half of the nineteenth century. She was an accomplished and popular poet, and was able to make a living on the sale of her poetry at a time when it was not possible for a Black person to find a position at a university. An important orator and organizer for the Abolitionist Movement, the Temperance Movement, and the Suffragist Movement, Frances Harper was an activist – what we today call a public intellectual – with the tenacity and skill to remain at the center of the sweeping political changes that occurred in her lifetime. She was frequently published in the leading African American newspapers and magazines, contributing her ideas to a wide public in the society (Peterson, 1997).

What Harper couldn't know is that, by the latter part of the twentieth century, her own contributions would be largely obscured by the very forces of racism and sexism that she fought against all her life (Foster, 1990). Each discovery today of the wealth of contributions made historically by Black women in the society is a mandate to again center these voices integral to the American democratic project, who, because of the politics of their time, were obscured or have subsequently had their contributions largely erased. We can only wonder how much of what was achieved by those living before us is unrecoverable; how much of what was accomplished has been erased by disfavor, disinterest, simple neglect, and the prejudices of popular opinion. Our history is derived from the imagination of those who would silence and vilify certain persons, groups, and causes. What ideas and work remain available from our past? What should we think today in a time when racial and gender inequality still remain definitive of American society?

What we do know is that, until the work of Black feminist researchers in the last four decades, much of the writing of Frances Harper was unavailable and thought lost. It is only through the work of these scholars, the diligent work of recovery and preservation, that we now have access, as well as to her popular novel *Iola Leroy*, to Harper's three serialized novels, the work *Fancy Sketches*, many of her speeches, and the majority of her poetry. We owe a great debt to this research movement, by Black women working as established scholars, independent researchers, librarians, and activists. This dedication to recovering a Black past before the nadir in the late 1880s, and the decades of terror that described the time of lynching and Jim Crow, asks us as readers of Frances Harper's work to question how we consider race and the contribution of Black people today in this society.

Even if the proximate causes have changed, the general social concerns that occupied Frances Harper are shared by us today. She can serve as an inspiration for both creative writing and political engagement. She demonstrates what was possible to do as an individual in a society where Black community members were enslaved and where women were not able to vote. What would it mean for us to live alongside those who remind us of the terrible oppression possible for us as well, to interact with those who share the burden of social descriptions of racial inferiority, even as our political status differentiates us? We know.

Today more Black people are in prison than were enslaved in 1825, and one out of three Black male adults will be incarcerated at some point in their lives. With large numbers of African Americans living in poverty, and a perception of racial inferiority that persists, with significant pay differentials between men and women, and #MeToo a necessity, the words of and life led by Harper provide encouragement and an example of how we might also thrive. The timeline for Harper's life covers not only the last half of the nineteenth century, when the new nation sought to define its major institutions, but also the last decades of the centuries-long enslavement of Black people, the Civil

War, and Reconstruction. She was present as the Western US opened up to settlement, and in the period of national development that saw rapid industrial growth, and then the portion of the late nineteenth century that, because of the establishment of Jim Crow laws and lynching, many consider the nadir of the free African American experience in the US.

Frances Harper in the 1820s and 1830s

Born in 1825, in Baltimore, Maryland, Frances Harper was orphaned at 3 years of age and went to live with her uncle and aunt, William and Henrietta Watkins. The family had a library, and as a child Frances was, at a young age, given access to books and taught to read and write. This encouragement was to be her fortune, and words and their value would become her lifelong passion. In Baltimore, where the family was living, the social relationships of the family gave Frances conversational exposure to people with an interest in the major political causes of the day. Her uncle William Watkins was an abolitionist and public speaker, someone with social standing in the community of people, made up of free Blacks and Whites, advocating for social causes and racial equality. William Lloyd Garrison and many other activists were regular guests at the Watkins household.

Harper's upbringing among those who were were active in organizing against slavery and other social problems not only taught her the value of political activism but also provided her with an understanding of the importance of education and writing as tools to address social ills. The public critic – the person who would address an audience in speaking halls, living rooms, and in formal gatherings to advocate for changes in the society – was a fixture in the everyday lives of the inhabitants of the young nation. The first decade after

Frances Harper's birth saw the publication of *David Walker's Appeal*, the public work of Maria Stewart in Boston, and Nat Turner's Rebellion.

In Harper's day, there were established organizations that sought various types of reforms and social change in the society at large. And in Baltimore, where she grew up, free Blacks and Whites had long been able to establish a public audience ready to discuss a wide range of social causes and issues, through printing newspapers, adverts, and lectures (Foster, 1990). This public forum, a social space within which to publicly make statements and admonish fellow inhabitants and the government, was active throughout the mid-Atlantic seaboard and the East Coast in the 1820s. While, just as today, it was not clear how discussions in this public arena determined the definition of government interests, there is no question that the public intellectual in the nineteenth century had an importance beyond the imperatives of electoral politics. Much of this has to do with the place of this sort of public discourse in local politics – how independent town, city, county, and state politics are from the supervision of the federal government in the US. Electoral parties in the US are not an end in themselves, for a public is always engaged in discussion about the merits of a law, a policy, or the conditions in which local people live.

Unlike other Black women who became well-known public figures during her lifetime, Frances Harper did not have the financial means to remain at home throughout her childhood (Foster, 1990). Having established a school in 1820 – the Watkins Academy – her uncle William Watkins was able to provide the young Frances Harper with the vocational training necessary to succeed at those occupations conventionally available to her as a free Black woman. It was this training that allowed her to work, as a teenager, as a young servant in the household of a White family, and, eventually, to be the first woman hired as a faculty member to teach sewing at Union Seminary in 1850. When she later moved to Ohio with her husband to run a dairy farm and help raise their children, this practical experience as a servant was important, and necessary when she was shortly thereafter widowed and working to keep the farm. Frances Harper was raised with the best training available for someone Black who had no access to independent sources of income. This is a condition that most African Americans are too familiar with today, with a negative savings rate and few assets being the norm for too many families. She had to survive by the education that she received, opportunity, hard work, and the trust and assistance of those around her. This was a free Black person's life in the 1820s and 1830s, and is true today for us as well.

Harper's work as a servant paralleled the types of work done by those who were enslaved, but with the glaring distinction of being free – free to make use of her own life and time as she would, each day. As a servant, however, she came face to face with the consequences of a politics of race in the society whereby some Black people who worked were free, and some slaves. This experience undoubtedly transformed her thinking about how race defined the lives of Black people in America.

In the 1820s and 1830s, when Frances Harper was a child, the state of Maryland reflected many of the major forces for change in the new nation. Baltimore and surrounding areas were places where free Blacks could live alongside slaves in large numbers – enough to make the differences in status between Black people an explicit public issue that Whites sought to address. Whites did not generally suggest enslaving those who were free, but instead sought to reduce the number of free Blacks who lived in the state (Fields, 1985). The uneven economic development between the state's northern counties and southern counties was a source of great tension among politicians. The importance of slaveholding for agriculture and economic development that prevailed elsewhere in the South was not evident in Baltimore, even if true in the southern parts of the state. The importance of Baltimore as a growing industrial center on the mid-Atlantic seaboard meant it was a center for the political currents that were sweeping the young nation. For Frances Harper, growing up in Baltimore meant that she was regularly exposed to the social conditions of slavery, as well as given an insight into the value of schooling and literacy for effecting social change (Parker, 2010, p. 102).

Think for a moment of what Frances Harper's attendance at the Academy run by her uncle must have signaled for the slaves working around her, slaves who often were prohibited by their Masters from learning to read and unable to write. It is important not to make a false equivalence between what slavery and being free meant for Black people at the time. Slavery remains a terrible wound in our history today, but we don't need to think of Black people as always available to its constraints as a condition of living in the society, or as the limit to our political ambition. The necessary national conversation that we have today about reparations and reconciling the effects of slavery generations later should not prevent a discussion of how free and slave Black people lived alongside one another. What it meant to be Black at the time, and after the Civil War, should include such an understanding of the complexity of Black life.

Frances Harper's was a singular political awareness, if we consider the situation for a moment: to be free and yet to be exposed as a young child to those who were not; to be socially conscious of the aspiration toward racial equality derived from the attitudes and behaviors of those Whites who frequented the Watkins' home; to know that many Black people discussed the plight of those enslaved even as they wrote, spoke publicly, and organized for the welfare of those who had run away. She also came into constant contact with White slave owners, and those who perceived her free status as an impediment to her exploitation, even as they dismissed her capacity for constraining their desires with regard to their own slaves.

What would a White stranger have represented socially, politically, for Frances Harper? What would a slave have been for a young Frances Harper, if not a person to be pitied, and also an immediate existential threat, a literal symbol of the precarious nature of her own status in Baltimore (Fields, 1985, pp. 39, 79)? In the 1820s and 1830s, when the kidnapping of free Blacks to be sold as slaves further south was common, how did Frances Harper determine the motives and interests of the adults, White and Black, around her? I write this to have us consider how race was a factor in the young Frances' life, in contrast to how it is in our own lives. How would others have perceived this young woman, who was not only courageous and literate, but also independent? And though her situation with regard to opportunities for an education was unique, she herself, as a young free Black girl child, was not unique in Baltimore, or in the society as a whole.

How has our awareness of race changed, and what remains accessible to us of what she must have known? Answering this question requires a degree of reflective sophistication about the influence of race on our lives – an awareness that Frances Harper demonstrates throughout her work. It would be a rare person today who would have her degree of insight and courage. Thus, it is important to remember, when we read her poetry and books, how few of us have the same perspicuity, the determination that was required – when there were slaves present, and when women were unable to vote and were expected to be silent in most public fora – to confront the description of her own racial subordination in her public writing (Stancliff, 2011).

Today, when so many people write and publish works on race and society, it is simply too easy to remain within a narrative that sees progress in the fact that Black people can publish and find an audience for their work. Reducing the achievements of those like Frances Harper to a simple content analysis, or a discussion of literary form, reduces the achievements of those, like her, who succeeded at a time when there were substantial barriers to publishing and making a career as a public speaker and poet. Leveling the field of production in this way reduces the importance of the work that others have done to change how the society addresses race as a problem, and we tend to ignore the organizational and professional effort that this success took – how it was also a tremendous step in our progress toward the ideal of racial equality. To what extent is it possible to make sense of the types of commitments that are evident in the life of Frances Harper such that she would become the most successful Black poet of the mid nineteenth century, a writer of four novels – one of which was a bestseller – a public speaker, an essayist, and a leading organizer of social movements in the United States for almost 50 years?

In her letters, it is clear that Frances Harper led a life whose main ambition was to correct the racial and gender injustices that she perceived in the world around her. The activist and literary world in which she lived, as well as how she was raised when young, fostered an awareness of a politics of representation in her own person as a Black woman writer and social critic. This commitment to what we today call civil rights is ever present in her writing, her speeches, and her advocacy. I want to suggest that it is only now, with our complex theories that address the conjoining of the critical politics of race, gender, and sexuality, that there exists a public readership that can respect and understand how a Black woman could be one of the most important writers, poets, and activists of the last 50 years of the nineteenth century. Her story now can be brought to our attention as a difference of perspective that matters, her work given a place as an important component in a developing narrative of a diverse American democratic polity.

It is not a coincidence that, though Frances Harper was prolific and successful as a writer, her contribution to our understanding of the period in the nation's history has until very recently been obscured. Today we largely accept a description of the period of US history from 1850 to 1900 that has emphasized the story of the slave struggling for freedom, those valiant individuals who freed themselves through personal ambition and great adversity, and the successful heroic work of White people to emancipate the slaves who were unable to escape to freedom – the benighted and beleaguered, the self-emancipated, the savior and humanitarian. This is too easy a combination of roles to be true, to be the only description of what was possible for those who lived in the period. There are other narrative voices. Today, we increasingly include the claims of how slaves and free Blacks fought alongside their White compatriots for freedom during the Civil War, and how slaves were forced to fight in support of Confederacy.

But a story about American democracy that seeks to simply reconcile the fact of enslavement for Blacks with the ownership of other human beings by Whites is too easy and inaccurate, and accepts a problematic convention for slavery as a condition for some in the society. Thus, we have Harriet Tubman, who was a friend of Frances Harper, as well as Frederick Douglass, who worked often alongside Frances Harper over the years, in the Abolitionist Movement and later in the fight for voting rights for Black people and women. These two are thought to represent today in the collective imagination a necessary and particular depiction of what it meant to be Black and American in that time in US history.

We ask the questions of the past that provide the answers we need in our own lives. The runaway slave, the slave who confronts and defeats the ambition of mastery by the owner, the slave who goes on to free others, who publishes and speaks in public about their successful emancipation, make us think about what it means to live in a society where slavery was possible. Both those whose ancestors owned slaves and those whose ancestors were enslaved can supposedly find a form of reconciliation, a foundation for going forward together, if the history of slavery is viewed as a mistake, reproduced over many generations – one corrected through righteous struggle by those whose morality and personal conviction overcame greed. Sacrifice and suffering finally came together for the cause of freedom: to free the benighted Black slave, to educate and lift up those least fortunate.

Frances Harper represents a different voice from that of Harriet Tubman or Frederick Douglass, as well as that of Sojourner Truth or William Wells Brown. Instead of seeking to establish her equality to a White person who is not a Master, as a concession to a personal emancipation, Frances Harper embodies in her writing and public speaking the always free Black person who also represents the democratic aspirations of the society. To constantly measure racial equality with a claim to having once been enslaved – as being less than human perhaps in the eyes of some – retains in the new conception of race after slavery the condition, the possibility, of an enslavement to come. Such an argument suggests that the baseline of the Black experience is always slavery, and not a freedom that is suborned or taken away. This difference in perspective matters today, as we seek a description of how racism thrives in spite of our effort to create conditions of equality socially, economically, and politically.

Imagine instead if a person had always been free, if someone Black in America had never been a slave. Should we then make the story of slavery their definition, rather than accept that for many Black people in the US slavery and freedom were more complicated, requiring a description of racial equality beyond that of asking Whites for justice in the form of allowing Black people to be free? The end of legal slavery occurred concurrently with the argument about what constraints could exist for free Black equality in the society, a conversation centuries old, about the definition of political equality between racial groups in the society. Frances Harper is an important voice in this tradition of exploring the definition of racial equality within the Black community – someone who left a legacy of published work for us to consider.

The kidnapping of free Black people and their sale into slavery caused a furor in the society in the decades leading up to the Civil War not solely because the sale of Black people was thought by many to be morally wrong, but because it suggested that all Black people were potentially slaves, in ways that had not previously been true in the US. This idea of slavery as a natural state of Black life in the US not only is incorrect historically, but also allows for an erroneous description of the racial justice to be achieved today. It is very important to understand the contribution of Frances Harper to how we think of race today, in terms of her being a free Black woman writing during the last two decades of legal slavery, and then for several decades after the Civil War. There was no one else in the period, no other free Black writer or poet, who addressed the problem of both race and gender, and what these ideas meant for the society, with such success. Frances Harper is singular, unique, and I want to suggest her work is central to a consideration of how we should think of race and gender in the US from the 1840s to the 1890s, and therefore also how we describe a critical race and gender politics in the US today.

Frances Harper's work disturbs a desire to return today to a conversation about what race requires as a supposedly natural condition – the desire to engage in this as a question, rather than to reject its assumptions as fundamentally flawed. It is important to understand how important this counter-argument to slavery was in her lifetime, and how in the 1840s and throughout her life she wrote about the intersectional politics of race and gender as an aspiration of democratic society. Her life and work represents a very different description of racial reconciliation for the society than is often offered when thinking only about the concerns of the White male slave owner, the permission given through a definition of Whiteness for the ownership of human beings, over many generations in the society. That she spent her entire adult life writing, speaking, and campaigning on behalf of racial and gender justice is a fact that should add weight to our assessment of her legacy, and should make us think twice about the current tradition of reducing her contribution to American letters and society in her lifetime to a few short poems and one major novel, *Iola Leroy*.

Frances Harper in the 1840 and 1850s

If we take the newly rediscovered volume of verse, *Forest Leaves*, as having been published sometime between 1846 and 1849 (Ortner, 2015), Frances Harper was between 21 and 24 when she published her first volume of verse. She no doubt wrote poetry before this, but in the extant letters from the period there is evidence of some reluctance on the part of publishers to publish the poems. Her childhood education at the Academy and experience as a servant in a household with an extensive library that she was given permission to peruse in her free time, and the exposure to poetry readings and public speeches in the abolitionist social community of which her uncle and aunt were a part, provided the opportunity for Frances Harper to develop her craft. In this, but for the material differences in our lives today from hers, Frances Harper had what many today would think of as those influences necessary to create a poetic muse.

Her uncle William had been at the center of the development of the Abolitionist Movement in Baltimore for decades, and was an active contributor to the publishing of writings in support of the Movement. His house was a frequent location for meetings with other central figures of the growing Abolitionist Movement, such as Willian Lloyd Garrison. One of William's sons, a cousin of Frances Harper, was also involved in the Abolitionist Movement and a public speaker on this issue. He would later facilitate her introduction to abolitionists in the Northeast (Washington, 2015). But another influence on the life of the young Frances Harper was the work of women writers and poets, and public speakers in the Abolitionist Movement, such as Jarena Lee, Zilpha Elaw, and Elizabeth Margaret Chandler (Washington, 2015, p. 69). Even as a young child, she was brought into contact with the work and persons of women who were able to publicly declare their ideas about slavery, racism, and gender.

This publicity was at odds with the prevailing gender social norms whereby women were expected to be silent in public gatherings where men were present, and not engage in public speaking to an audience comprised of both men and women. This early exposure to women writers, poets, and speakers was definitely important to the young Frances Harper's sense of what was possible. She would go on to be only one of several Black women to speak regularly as part of the Abolitionist Movement (Peterson, 1995).

African American print culture

It was from Sojourner Truth that Frances Harper saw first-hand the difficulty of making a living as a public speaker. To raise sufficient money for her travels and sustenance while on the speaking circuit, Truth would sell small commemorative items related to herself and her story at her talks. Truth's image on sale, in the pamphlets, was for everyone present a natural extension of the tradition of printing and public newspapers in the free African American community throughout the Northeast at the time. Instead of ignoring the growth of print culture in the African American community, we should consider how important this must have been for Harper, as an aspiring poet and writer – someone who sought to reach an audience with her written word (Peterson, 1995, pp. 310–12).

The Liberator, a newspaper published first in the 1830s by Garrison, was constantly seeking submissions from African Americans, for example, as was *The Colored American*. Once Douglass started publishing the newspaper *The North Star* in 1847, Harper and other aspiring African American writers were given a ready forum in it. *Frederick Douglass' Paper* and *Douglass' Monthly*, his other two newspaper publications, also published their work (McHenry, 2002, p. 116; Washington, 2015, pp. 61–6). While certainly there was an eager White American readership for this work, there was also an extensive African American audience for these newspapers and for literary magazine content. African American literary societies had been an important mainstay of the free African American community since their inception, and before the founding of the new nation. The newspapers that circulated within the free African American communities empha- sized the importance of reading and education as a means of moral and political progress. It was in *Freedom's Journal*, published from 1827 to 1829, that African American literary societies and their participants, such as David Walker and Maria Stewart, were able to find a larger audience for their writings. In 1837, *The Colored American* began publishing work dedicated to the audiences from these literary societies (McHenry, 2002, p. 102).

Always free

It is very important today to understand what the erasure in our collective memory of the presence of a larger, engaged African American reading public prior to the Civil War means for us (McHenry, 2002, p. 137). This erasure serves, in this period, to elevate the struggle for Emancipation and the plight of the slave as a condition of African American life, over the reality of a free Black population that was con- sidered already literate, and engaged in the emancipation of their brethren in bondage. And it makes it too easy to suggest that education and reading have not always been an element of African American life. It allows us to think, there- fore, that the problem of race today is simply that suggested by Booker T. Washington toward the end of Harper's life at the turn of the nineteenth century, to cultivate well- meaning charitable White interests to advance the education of the race. It is not a coincidence that the two literary Black women figures who were well known prior to the Civil War, Maria Stewart and Frances Harper, have had their contri- bution to our development of ideas about race and society eclipsed by the images of Black women who could not write, such as Sojourner Truth and Harriet Tubman (Connor, 1994, pp. 74–5; Painter, 1996).

This traditional narrative of erasure truncates the true relationship between Black people and slavery in the US, ignoring that the nation always also contained a free population and that the idea of enslavement is therefore artificial and wrong. This narrative was only true for those seeking to propagate a politics of racial subordination that seeks to reconcile the fact of slavery historically with the need to claim that Black people are always unequal. We can see the development of this racist polemics in how Harper responded to the history of the aftermath of the Civil War in her book *Iola Leroy*, published in 1892.

Prior to the Civil War, however, Black people had already achieved equality in their literary pursuits – if not materially – with Whites, alongside the presence of slaves in the society. Frances Harper, and all other free African Americans in the society in the 1840 and 1850s, were well acquainted with the importance of literacy and print culture. Periodicals and newspapers formed an important part of the sense of community, as these allowed for news, public debates, and literary works published by Black people to be available to the larger Black population (Peterson, 1995, p. 310).

In the 1850s, the newspapers the *Christian Recorder* and the *Weekly Anglo-African* were published, and magazines dedicated to African American literary works began to be published: the *Repository of Religion and Literature, and of Science and Art* and the *Anglo-African Magazine*. It was in the first issue of the *Anglo-African Magazine* in 1859 that Frances Harper began serializing her short story "The Two Offers," and Martin Delany began serializing his novel *Blake; or, the Huts of America* (McHenry, 2002, p. 131). And the *Christian Recorder* was where Frances Harper would publish three novels serially from 1868 to 1888, in addition to the short piece *Fancy Sketches* (Peterson, 1995, pp. 307–8; Robbins, 2004, p. 179).

In the 1840s and 1850s, when Frances Harper was beginning to find her poetic and literary voice, there was a public ready for her, an audience of African Americans and White Americans willing to carry around her small books and portable newspapers and magazines for further distribution. There was a public that would meet in salons and dining rooms, in literary circles, and read and discuss her poems. It was to this public that Frances Harper became visible in her early twenties with her first book of poetry *Forest Leaves*, and it is this that partially explains the phenomenal publishing success of her book *Poems on Miscellaneous Subjects* in 1854.

This book of poems would go on to be reprinted 5 times over the next 17 years, and over 10,000 copies were printed. As Michael Bennett points out when comparing the popularity, and therefore public importance, of Frances Harper to that of Walt Whitman at the time, fewer than 100 copies of *Leaves of Grass* were sold when it was published in 1855. There was no interest in Whitman reading his poetry in public akin to that for Harper. She was, in contrast to Whitman, "the poet of democracy" (Bennett, 2005, p. 48).

In the 1850s, Frances Harper was considered an important poet in the society – one whose poems spoke to the immediate social and political concerns of the population. By the time of the publication of "The Two Offers," the first published short story by an African American woman, Frances Harper was a well-known and important literary figure, not only in African American society, but in abolitionist circles and the White literate public. By the late 1850s, Frances Harper was a very popular public speaker, and sold her books of poetry to successfully support herself, as Sojourner Truth did with her images.

The question we have to ask ourselves today is how

committed we are to the idea of a description of Black women as available to caricature and stereotype, as unequal partners in the democratic polity, meaning that we resist understanding the place of Frances Harper and other Black literary women in developing a response to the challenges of race in the society (Harris, 1997, p. 93). By the 1850s, Frances Harper had begun to establish a literary reputation, not as a former slave but as a quintessential American poet, someone whose writing addressed the major fault lines that existed in the fledgling democratic society. As someone who had always been free, Harper could not be looked upon by White Americans with that particular mix of charity and condescension, the disdain due to having been perceived as less than or differently human, that was reserved for the former slave.

That Frances Harper became a poet and writer, a public speaker, a national organizer should be understood for what it represents for us today, in our perspective on the history of race in America. It is not slavery that defines Black life today, but the need to equate Black people with slavery, with a capacity to be enslaved, unlike White people. Eschewing the idea of slavery as the description of a possible Black life, Frances Harper did not see herself as categorically less than human.

This perspective should not immediately be contrasted with a description that obviates or erases the terrors of slavery, which remained the most important social and political problem in US society in the 1840s and 1850s. Instead, a consideration of Frances Harper's life should disturb the equation we have today of racial uplift with the convergence of White largesse and moral clarity that we often use to explain Black life after the prohibition of slavery. Not all Black people required an education by Whites in the obligations of citizenship and equality, and White people in the

1840s and 1850s understood this, if they were not too preju-
diced to even entertain the fact of a free Black reading and
literary public.

A private life

The Baltimore where Frances Harper was raised in the
1840s was rife with racial tensions, and the economy was
growing rapidly due to the trade in cotton and industri-
alization (Fields, 1985). This meant that ideas about racial
equality, and ideas of economic and political development
that were of importance elsewhere in the country, were
of great interest locally. The Abolitionist Movement had
been gathering more adherents throughout the 1830s and
into the 1840s with increased publicity, and William Lloyd
Garrison and others were frequent visitors to Baltimore.
The Movement as a political and therefore public force, in
newspapers and magazines, in lectures and speeches, was
an established part of Baltimore public culture. Frederick
Douglass, who had been enslaved in Maryland, published
his first autobiography in 1845, and became a celebrity
public presence amongst those in the Movement. He was
only seven years older than Frances Harper, and therefore a
social contemporary, unlike Sojourner Truth, who was born
in 1797.

Frances Harper, because of her family's involvement in the
Movement, would have had contact with both noted Black
abolitionists by the 1840s. She would work extensively with
both in the decades to come. Frances Harper would also
come to work with Harriet Tubman from the 1850s, from
whom she was only three years apart in age. It is important
to give readers a sense of the activist environment that surrounded Frances Harper in her teen years and twenties, as

she began to form her ambition for a vocation beyond that traditionally available to her as servant and housewife.

I want the reader to resist the compression of generations, particularly when considering the life of someone such as Frances Harper, whose work reflected the different political forces at work in different decades. It does matter that, when Frances Harper was a young child, the organization of anti-slavery efforts in Boston led to the publication of *David Walker's Appeal* and then Maria Stewart's writings. It matters that decades of Black women's efforts to organize in literary circles and social groups to address the problem of slavery had already become a factor in the definition of free Black life in the North (Jeffrey, 1998, pp. 64–5). Frances Harper's uncle William was at the center of the debate between anti-slavery activists, between colonization and becoming a new category of former slave and a free Black community (Sinha, 2016a; Washington, 2015, pp. 63–7). What should the larger goal of a necessary emancipation be in the context of a heightened public conversation about the Abolition of slavery, a conversation that was also active in Europe at the time?

By the 1840s and 1850s, the Abolitionist Movement was represented by several journals and regularly published newspapers, public-speaker fora in cities across the Northeast, and discussions in the living rooms and salons of the very civil society that had birthed the nation some 80 years earlier (Sinha, 2016a). It was in this same period that efforts toward establishing an American university and college system of higher education were accelerating, and as a result the development of social spaces for learning about, discussing, and organizing around specific concerns that were both local and national in focus was an acceptable activity for many in the society. The Black community as a political force within this public – what today is sometimes referred to as a new counter-public – was well established by the 1840s and 1850s, with the first Black student graduating from Oberlin College in 1844. That Frances Harper attended a local academy in the 1830s can be attributed to the fact that her uncle had helped found the institution, as academies and schools were not yet regularly accessible to young Black women (Baumgartner, 2019).

For reasons not clear to historical researchers, Frances Harper was not provided the support by her family expected by a young Black woman in a middle-class household such as the Watkinses'. At 13, she was forced to make her living as a servant for a White family in town, which was not something that would be expected of a child in a Black middle-class home. While the Watkinses had many children of their own, their income and social status were sufficient to have maintained Frances Harper at home throughout her schooling years (Washington, 2015, p. 70). In her later writing, Frances Harper does not speak glowingly of her childhood, and in fact describes those years as ones lacking in the affection and love that a mother would have provided. Something to remark on in this context is that it is unusual that someone as prolific as Frances Harper did not pen an autobiography. If we think of the slave autobiographies written by those who she worked alongside in the period leading up to the Civil War, hers would be a remarkable and expected document for us today from the pen of a free Black woman. That such a text does not exist is perhaps a testament to the pain and emotional difficulties that Frances Harper may have experienced as a young girl. As several researchers have opined, there is much to suggest that her childhood was fraught and wanting in affection (Foster, 1990; Still, 1872; Washington, 2015). At the same time, this exposure to service work as a young teenager must have been formative and important to her own intellectual development. It also meant she was outside what otherwise would have been a very restrictive Black middle-class household.

There is no doubt this relative freedom, no matter how arduous in its requirements, allowed Harper access to the gendered experiences of African Americans who were of a different social class than her own family. In the household where she worked, she was granted permission to take her service breaks in the White family's extensive library, an opportunity that she was encouraged by her employer to take advantage of. From the perspective of the contemporary reader, the experience with differences of class and social station, racial inequality, and the gender politics to which the young Frances Harper was exposed both at home, in Academy classes, and in her work as a servant provided the environment expected of someone who would later achieve the incredible public and literary success she would acquire in her lifetime. What was missing as a young child was only a commitment – the personal conviction to contribute to specific political goals in her lifetime. This she would acquire in the 1840s and 1850s, as events in the larger society defined the opportunities available to her as a teacher and poet. Her first publication, *Forest Leaves*, shows little evidence of the political journey that Frances Harper would undertake in later decades, but also should warn readers against assuming that her poetry in later decades arose solely as a function of a description of political activism. Frances Harper was a poet before she became active as a public speaker, and so I think we should consider Frances Harper as a poet who found her muse in the social and political events of her time. That she was also a writer of prose, an important nationally recognized activist, and a phenomenal and famous public speaker reveals the tremendous force of intellect and will she was to carry throughout her life.

The problem of her work for the contemporary reader is

that Frances Harper in fact developed what would be considered at the time – and today – four very successful careers simultaneously. If we acknowledge this fact, we must concede that Frances Harper was in her day one of the most important figures of the last half of the nineteenth century. Without taking away from the perception we have of the contributions of, for example, Sojourner Truth, Harriet Tubman, and Ida B. Wells, or Frederick Douglass, William Wells Brown, and Martin Delany, Frances Harper produced a variety of work, and was so important to the many political events of the time that, today, we should recognize how her ideas and presence gave to the society something both exceptional and enduring. She should be a household name for us, and that she isn't represents a tremendous loss.

That Frances Harper was able to publish *Forest Leaves* in the mid to late 1840s is an accomplishment not to be ignored, as she did not have the expectation of publicity, and the vocation of the poet affirmed, beyond her immediate circle of friends and family. For a Black person to publish poetry was still not a common occurrence, and Black women were not encouraged to publish by a public that discouraged their participation in social spaces where organizational activities sought a hearing. There exists no evidence of support for her poetic ambitions as a Black woman from within Frances Harper's family, and, as Washington points out, one of the most important abolitionist journals of the period, *The Colored American*, in 1838 had published an editorial critical of Black women engaging in public speaking and protests on behalf of the goals of the Movement (Washington, 2015, p. 69). What we do not have from the period is a description of her friends, her personal interlocutors, and researchers instead are reduced to analyzing the early volume of poetry for clues as to her intimate and personal life (Ortner, 2015). *Forest Leaves* contains poems centered on themes of personal conviction, intimacy, and loss, in addition to being a study of the place that religious faith should hold in the thoughts of her audience.

The combination of independence and education evident in the childhood of Frances Harper led to her being hired as a faculty member in 1850 at Union Seminary in Ohio, which later provided the institutional foundation for Wilberforce College. Hired to teach sewing, Harper was the first woman faculty member at the Seminary. She was 25 years old. If we consider this in the context of that time period, rather than of our own time in which many Black people claim firsts, in sports, in the media, and in politics, we can imagine how difficult and precocious it must have been to seek and gain employment at the Seminary. This was a novel and important achievement, when the idea of the Black exception proving the rule of racial equality as it does today was not yet discovered. She was, instead, someone who refused to accept the limitations placed upon her, not as a matter of freedom, but as a statement of equality. There is ample evidence in her later writings that her professional ambition was always described in both gendered and racial terms, just as she was always aware of the class politics that circumscribed her choices.

Harper left Ohio in 1852, and instead moved to Little York, Pennsylvania, and began teaching young children. From her letters, it is clear that she soon became disenchanted with the job. It is hard to reconcile her disenchantment with teaching in this instance with her enthusiasm for teaching young children in the South some 15 years later, immediately after the Civil War, unless we think about the fact that the early position offered no obvious outlet for her personal ambitions to address the larger issues of injustice in the society. There is no one personal event that obviously defined the sense of political commitment for Frances Harper, with the exception of her exposure to the conditions in which people lived around her, and her access to those in the Abolitionist Movement at the time. However, there is one political event that many researchers attribute as the turning point in Harper's professional direction (Still, 1872, p. 758).

In 1853, Maryland passed its fugitive slave law, which stated that any free Black person who had left the state could be enslaved if they returned. The law was perceived as an answer to the problems of the growth of the free Black community in Baltimore, of the relationship between the free and the enslaved typified in the personal experience of Frances Harper, and of the appeal of Maryland as a destination for runaways, which heightened tensions between North and South (Fields, 1985). Suddenly, at 28, Harper lost legal access to the state of her birth, and this new status, coupled with the highly publicized kidnapping and sale of a free Black man in the state upon passage of the law, is thought to have radicalized her and emboldened her to write and protest in public for the Abolitionist Movement (Still, 1872, p. 757).

Frances Harper moved to Philadelphia in 1853, and lived at the home of William and Letitia Still, one of the centers for the Movement in Pennsylvania. At this time, she sought to become an active member of the Underground Railroad, but was discouraged by those participating in the Anti-Slavery Society of Philadelphia – largely, it seems, due to her being a single woman, and the precarity of her own free status because of the new law in Maryland (Parker, 2010, p. 103; Still, 1872, p. 758). She faced the likelihood of being enslaved if she were to assist runaways in Maryland to escape north. Women were also openly discouraged from representing their opinions in public, and only two Black women, of the many engaged in organizing in the Abolitionist Movement, were regular public speakers up to the Civil War. The two were, in fact, Sojourner Truth and Frances Harper.

When we think about this rejection of her application to become a conductor on the Underground Railroad, we should take a step back from this study of her life and think about how, today, we reduce the experiences of Black people in the immediate pre-Civil War period to the problem of slavery. Frances Harper had never been a slave, and so the idea of the new law was perceived by her and other free Blacks as an insult to their own categorical status; even though they had not been described as citizens, they were still, in their own social standing, equal to the Whites around them. The idea of being available to enslavement must have seemed ridiculous in its reduction of social and legal capacity, something beyond intimate understanding, and at the same time an explicit attack on their person.

The rejection of this idea of being a natural slave on a personal level would have propelled most free Blacks to the barricades, so to speak, on behalf of their humanity, alongside many Whites who had, of course, lived alongside free Blacks (Spires, 2019, p. 221). In fact, we should consider the fugitive slave law in this context as a partial catalyst for the collapse of the regime of slavery in the United States. The law thought necessary to safeguard the system of enslavement by slave owners was also perhaps the instrument of its defeat. It created an enormous problem for how race was defined in the society. We should think of the fugitive slave laws as an attempt to change the practice of racial difference – as an extension of a particular dehumanization of Black people that even some of those in the South who were accepting of the slavery must have found problematic.

For someone with the intellectual gifts and creative impulses of Frances Harper, the idea of her being subject to enslavement if she returned to Maryland, where she was born, must have felt like a violation of the very idea of her person and the capacity she had to write and reason. It is important to disabuse ourselves also of the contemporary notion that slavery was a thing of the Southern states and not also present, under different economic conditions than the large-scale plantation economy in the South, in the form of domestic, farm, and factory labor in the North. Frances Harper had grown up in Baltimore with slaves working and living in her neighborhood, and the differences between her social standing and theirs would have been painfully obvious, and politically salient to Frances Harper as an adult. Sojourner Truth, for example, had been a slave in the North.

In 1854, Frances Harper published her second book of poetry, *Poems on Miscellaneous Subjects*, which was an immediate success and gained her considerable attention. In the same year, at the age of 29, Frances Harper gave her first speech, in Massachusetts, and shortly thereafter began lecturing regularly for the cause of Abolition in Maine, despite public hostility expressed by those who felt it was not respectable for women to speak in public (Foster, 1990, pp. 11–12; Logan, 1999, p. 49; Painter, 1996, p. 139).

The Maine anti-slavery women's organizations were very active, and Frances Harper was their only Black woman public speaker, a fact that must have been important to her own personal development as someone who would later become a central figure in post-Civil War Women's Rights movements (Logan, 1999, p. 2; Still, 1872). She was also a talented seamstress and so was able to contribute directly to the sewing circles raising money for the Movement (Salerno, 2005, pp. 128–31).

The space of the public in which lectures and political speeches occurred was deemed the province of men, and women were to be granted access only exceptionally. Frances Harper was determined to become a regular public speaker, and she succeeded, but not through the direct intervention of her cousin William Watkins Jr., who was involved in the Abolitionist Movement in the New York area (Washington, 2015, p. 71). She participated in the Movement through the organizational efforts of women. She negotiated her moral stance with her audience as she lectured – as a single woman, later when married, and then as a widow after 1864 – and constantly answered for her erudition, as some accused her of not being Black simply because they lacked experience of Black people with an education (Still, 1872, p. 772; Yee, 1992, pp. 112–14).

Andreá Williams argues that Frances Harper, in her capacity as a single woman for much of her public speaking career, modeled the idea of "single blessedness" (Williams, 2014). Alongside the traditional characterization of single women in public as pernicious and immoral was a social capacity to define the single woman as contributing to the sanctity of marriage, through the single woman's labor in support of this ideal. As Williams points out, the single woman could also be thought of along a continuum from the "kind Aunt who assists her overwhelmed married sister to the unwed church-goer who masters fundraising" (Williams, 2014, p. 101). The single woman could in this conceptual frame justify in public their assistance of an anti-slavery cause and organization, in support of the moral probity that this political activism represented; they had found a community that, from this perspective, could make positive use of their single status (Williams, 2014, p. 113). As Williams points out, the support that Frances Harper provided for the widow of John Brown after Harpers Ferry falls within this category of the single woman providing assistance to support marriage, where her status as single allows her to aid the widow unconditionally (Still, 1872, p. 763; Williams, 2014, p. 111).

This narrow capacity for social acceptance in public did

not obviate the social force of the description of the immorality of single women speaking in public, and the historical
record demonstrates that Frances Harper experienced public
criticism for her status, as did all single women who were
public speakers in the Movement (Jeffrey, 1998, p. 208). In
her letters from the early period of her public speaking, we
get a sense of how difficult it must have been to be a single
Black woman abolitionist speaker in Maine, sleeping in
houses owned by Whites, and traveling with White women
(Still, 1872).

Reports suggest, however, that Harper was quickly able to
become a poised, organized, and charismatic speaker, forthright and learned in her delivery (Jeffrey, 1998, p. 207). The
evidence of this that we have today is in the praise lauded upon
her speeches in letters and published newspaper accounts, as
well as the record of the speeches themselves in later decades at national conferences and conventions (Still, 1872,
pp. 775–6, 779–80; Yee, 1992, pp. 117, 119). That Frances
Harper often spoke extemporaneously and responded to her
audience with alacrity and respect, entertaining them as well
as providing listeners with unconventional thoughts and
ideas, made the announcements of her impending lectures
something of a local occasion, after her first years in the field.
She was paid very little, if anything, for these lectures, which
meant that she needed to offer something to her audience
that incentivized them to purchase the poetry books that she
would sell alongside each event. Often, she would recite her
poetry as a part of her lecture.

That Harper sold thousands of copies of the book *Poems*
in this fashion should, by today's economic calculations,
earn our respect for her speaking talent. Her talks were sufficiently valuable for her also to be at the forefront of the
developing public-speaking profession in the country, sharing the stage with everyone from Lucretia Mott and Susan

B. Anthony to Fredrick Douglass and Sojourner Truth, and conducting sometimes two lectures a day, several days a week, for decades. She was a rare individual as a speaker, but also someone who did not trade on her own exceptionality by accepting social advancement and acceptance. For Frances Harper, what mattered was not her own person, but what she could do for other Black people. This perspective on the nature of her own contributions to the causes of her day held true throughout her life.

It is this profession of speaking on behalf of the anti-slavery cause that provided the impetus for the collection of her poetry in this period of her life, determining the type of sentimental poetry that she produced, so that it would be legible to, and meet the needs of, those without an extensive education beyond the capacity to read the Bible. These requirements defined its published form as well, in small inexpensive books that people could carry away from the lectures.

In what would today be considered chapbooks, the audience could enjoy the poems in the privacy of their own homes, and consider the ideas of which she would speak publicly. These small books contained poems on the subjects dear to those to whom the Abolitionist Movement sought to appeal, but also addressed the problem posed by the conditions whereby gender, race, and class intersected within the lives of everyone in the society. Frances Harper's poetry in the 1854 *Poems*, and later work in the period before the Civil War, was drawn from the experiences she had with self-emancipated refugees, the needs of the people she encountered in her travels and on the lecture circuit, as well as her personal knowledge of events such as the protests at the recapture of the former slave Burns in Boston in 1854, the death of Nat Turner, and the many examples of militancy by abolitionists in the 1850s leading up to the Civil War.

Because of the distance with which many think of racial politics in their daily lives, and the limits to which we allow poetry on this subject to impact us today, it is difficult to understand how powerful these books of poems and her recitations must have been for her audience. An audience without access to social media and the steady stream of video information with which we are constantly inundated would have been enthralled by the charisma and confidence she displayed. They would have welcomed the opportunity to listen to her readings and lectures.

That Harper was also usually accompanied by other lecturers, and the speaker events were advertised through the auspices of a well-known anti-slavery society, meant that there was usually a large public in attendance, as the issue of slavery was considered one of great controversy in the 1850s. We should also consider that there were few universities to serve as centers for public conversation about controversial topics or specific ideas, at the time. These lectures were held in meeting halls, churches, and public gathering places. In this historical sense, we should think, then, of Frances Harper as participating in a quintessential American democratic public politics, as the speaker in the town square and church hall.

Frances Harper describes her first successes as a public speaker thus:

> Last night I lectured in a White church in Providence. Mr. Gardener was present, and made the estimate of about six hundred persons. Never, perhaps, was a speaker young, or old, favored with a more attentive audience . . . My maiden lecture was Monday night in New Bedford, in the Elevation and Education of our People. Perhaps as intellectual a place as any I was ever at of its size.
>
> (Still, 1872, p. 758)

A month after this occurred, Frances Harper was employed by the State Anti-Slavery Society of Maine as a regular lecturer, giving scheduled talks three times a week (p. 759). In 1853, the narrative *Twelve Years a Slave* by Solomon Northup had been published, and after reading it Frances Harper began advocating for the Free Products or Free Labor boycott movement, whereby those in the North should refuse to purchase goods made in the South by slave labor. This movement was more honored in the breech, and was never successful as an economic boycott (Gordon, 1997, p. 47; Still, 1872, p. 760).

By 1856, Frances Harper had left Maine and was lecturing regularly throughout Ohio, Pennsylvania, New York, and Massachusetts to great acclaim. As an agent for the Western Anti-Slavery Society, Frances Harper gave speeches in Kansas and Nebraska. After the passage of the Kansas–Nebraska Act of 1854 violated the 1850 Missouri Compromise to not permit slavery in new territories, the Movement realized that slavery as an institution would continue to grow in importance in the nation. Thus, fiery and popular speakers such as Frances Harper were sent to agitate for the anti-slavery cause. She toured Canada in this period as well (Washington, 2015, p. 77). She did this for the next three years, while also writing poetry and prose. This was when she would have traveled with Sojourner Truth, selling her books of poetry alongside the copies of the narrative and images of Truth, to support their labor.

There is no evidence that Frances Harper acted personally as a conductor in the Underground Railroad, but she donated financial support and her own time to assist those who did. At the same time, we can say today, with what we now know about the Railroad, that we wouldn't expect her activities if she had been a conductor to become public or the activity of a conductor to become known unless, as in the case of Harriet Tubman, the person was a former slave risk-ing recapture by assisting those still enslaved.

When Margaret Garner was captured in 1856 in Ohio, after killing her daughter rather than allowing the child to be returned to slavery, Frances Harper was deeply affected. She writes in a letter to William Still, "Ohio, with her Bibles and churches, her baptisms and prayers, had not one temple so dedicated to human rights, one altar so consecrated to human liberty, that trampled upon and down trodden innocence knew that it could find protection for a night, or shelter for a day" (Still, 1872, p. 764). Frances Harper also wrote a poem published in 1857 about the ordeal: "The Slave Mother: A Tale of the Ohio" (Graham, 1988, pp. 28–30).

The 1850s was a time when the fugitive slave laws were testing the accommodation that the North had made with the slave South in response to the Missouri Compromise of 1850. As a free Black woman, Frances Harper had to moti-vate her audience with the idea that she faced the legal threat of enslavement if she were to return to Maryland. This was a different approach than that of the former slave testifying to the horrors of their captivity. Instead, Frances Harper spoke to the audience's capacity to imagine how someone like her could be thought of as enslaved. Erudite, poised, socially capable, and genteel, Frances Harper the poet stood before her largely White audiences and asked the question of how Black people could be thought of as naturally, instead of capriciously and immorally, enslaved by others. This was not a statement of racial difference from Whites first, but rather a question of what the audience thought being Black should require of the nation. What was the category of the human to which race should apply? Would they countenance the reduction of her status to that of a slave because of the eco-nomic needs of the slavers, or respond to her poetic genius, her ability to articulate many of the same personal ambitions and desires as her audience, regarding the meaning of freedom and faith?

Accepting the injustice of the fugitive slave laws did not require that a White person admit to social equality with Frances Harper, but rather that the audience accept that a shared description of racial difference did not encompass the necessity of slavery. In her person, Frances Harper was advocating for political equality, the idea that, once free, a Black person was considered a person with certain inalienable rights due from the government, and with rights with regard to the desires of all other persons, even if these were White. In this sense, the social mores against women speaking in public must have emphasized and focused her message, rather than detracted from its impact.

Harper would have been perceived as courageous and unusual, representing as a Black woman how a Black person who had never been a slave could be thought of as someone with rights that all should respect. But public speaking in this way by Frances Harper must have required enormous courage and fortitude – the crowds were often not respectful or polite, and it was sometimes dangerous (Jeffrey, 1998, p. 208; Washington, 2015, p. 72). What called her to lecture? Since we have little direct autobiographical information about her experiences when young, we can only speculate. Yet offering herself as a speaker, to the skepticism of others in the organizations, and doing so against the social norms of the day must have been very stressful, and required determination.

Because of the focus of her writing and professional life, I suspect Frances Harper was someone who refused to be defined by the expectations of others. She was someone who wanted to establish in her person the equality, even superiority, of her own faculties, relative to those who would constantly have projected a social conviction of an innate racial superiority over her. This is an enormous weight to bear, this daily struggle against the pretentions of those who, being White, can rely on social norms of racial superiority to further their own desires. In a time when so many Black people were enslaved, the weight of what could be called "racial representation" must have been stifling for a young Black Frances Harper, who was both a poet and ambitious.

Frances Harper and Sojourner Truth were the only Black women who regularly lectured on the wider abolitionist speaker circuits. Sojourner Truth, a former slave, was much older and would sing and speak briefly of her former life as a slave in the North. Referring to printed copies of her narrative for sale, as well as her image, Truth therefore represented something different from the eloquent and literate poet Frances Harper, who would recite from her own poems and speak on the issues of Abolition as a moral imperative. The audience listening to both in one evening would have heard two converging ideas about Black life in the North: the former slave testifying as to the brutality of the experience, and the free woman poet declaiming on the merits of a faith whose moral probity would come with Black Emancipation. In encountering these discussions of what slavery was like and what freedom had wrought, the audience could equate the two as representing the political possibilities of Blackness.

In 1859, at the age of 34, Frances Harper published the short story "The Two Offers" (Foster, 1990). The same year, Harper spent the weeks leading up to the hanging of John Brown – sentenced for the failed rebellion at Harpers Ferry – offering material and emotional support to his wife (Parker, 2010, p. 109). This connection with Brown demonstrates the centrality of the young Frances Harper to the Movement, and suggests that she was more familiar with the organized struggle in the slave states involving the Underground Railroad than is evident from her letters and public writing.

Harper's relationship with Brown also hints at her understanding of the relationship between gender and race as important to the definition of the Emancipation being sought by the abolitionists. What role was she to be permitted in the Movement, if the wife of John Brown was not also implicated by law in the acts of her husband? Today, this complex assumption of a gender distinction of complicity in the work of the Movement may seem odd at first, but it should remind us that women could not vote, or own property, and were not perceived as public equals to men. They were expected to define their own ambitions through the men in their lives.

This expectation that women define themselves by the men around them would have been extremely difficult for a single woman such as Frances Harper to avoid as a social mandate, and so the absence of men in her life up until 1860 is an important question for future research to explore. At the same time, for Harper, involvement in the Movement came without obvious male attachments or relationships beyond those in the form of older patrons such as William Still. Harper's short story "The Two Offers" follows on this theme by providing a meditation on the choices available for women, in terms of marriage and professional life, while they did not have formal political rights in the society (Foster, 2010, p. 35). This story emphasized the importance of rights for Black women, as well as the need to develop moral certainty within the Black community. "The Two Offers" challenged the misogyny evident at the time in the Black community, and rejected the required dependence of Black women on the moral constancy of Black men. The publishing of this short story poignantly frames the personal choice that Frances Harper herself made to marry the next year, in 1860, and defines much of what we know about her life in the coming War years from 1860 to 1865.

Frances Harper in the 1860s and 1870s

Frances Harper married Fenton Harper in 1860, just as the Civil War broke out. The two of them and his three children moved to Ohio, bought land with the money that she had made from the sale of her poetry, and started a dairy farm. While taking a break from the speaker circuit, Frances Watkins Harper remained active as both a lecturer and an essayist during these years (Foster, 1990, p. 18; Still, 1872, pp. 764–6). In 1864, Fenton Harper died, leaving Frances Harper with four children to support and considerable financial debt. Since, as a woman, she was unable to secure the debt, after the bank repossessed her dairy equipment she was forced to lecture to generate income beyond the royalties from her books. It is not evident from biographical material what she arranged for the older children, but it is known that Frances Harper moved to Boston with her biological child, Mary, after she lost the farm.

Shortly after the end of the Civil War, in 1865, Frances Harper began her travels in the South, becoming one of many Northerners who sought to assist the newly freed slaves (Dudden, 2011, p. 115). She lectured and taught throughout the Southern states, often to audiences made up exclusively of Black women, but also to racially mixed audiences comprised of men and women, sometimes staying in the cabins of former slaves (Still, 1872, p. 772). Based upon these experiences, Frances Harper found it imperative to write about the difficult and impoverished circumstances of the newly freed people in her poetry and fiction.

Harper also participated in the new national organizational efforts by which activists in the North sought to secure political rights for the newly freed persons. That this effort was, by participants, increasingly connected organizationally with the rights of women is not a coincidence, as the issue of rights was one around which women had agitated since the founding of the nation (Brooks, 2018, p. 300). The success of this national organizational activity in the decades before the War was evident in the Women's Rights Convention in 1848 in Seneca Falls. The Civil War represented for the government an implosion of institutional norms, which brought with it a renewed organizational effort to secure rights for women.

In 1866, Frances Harper gave a speech at the Eleventh National Women's Rights Convention in New York. This speech represented her coming into national prominence for the post-War activist push for women's rights, work that would occupy her for the major part of the next few decades. For Harper, this transition from Abolition to Women's Rights after the War seems straightforward, given her personal and professional interests, and the relationships she had made through the success of her public speaking and published writing. She had always been a public advocate for political equality as a free Black woman, and the rights of women and free Black people were the major topic of the post-War period. She was also one of the most prominent public figures in the Abolitionist Movement, a nationally recognized poet and public speaker whose work was often in print in the newspapers and magazines of the Black community.

As she observes in her speech in 1866, "We Are All Bound Up Together," race after the Civil War remained a central concern for her vision of the country. In the speech, she describes how her friend Harriet Tubman, the last time she saw her, had swollen hands from having to fight a train conductor who had tried to eject her from the train. Calling Tubman "Moses," Frances Harper says, "The woman whose courage and bravery won a recognition from our army and from every black man in the land, is excluded from every thoroughfare of travel" (Harper, 1990f, p. 219). She goes on to ask whether White women need the vote to get them to care about the injustices done in their name (Dudden, 2011, pp. 84–5; Painter, 1996). This direct convergence of the issues of gender and race in the speech reveal how, for Harper, the idea of Black men supporting Tubman in her efforts to bring slaves to freedom could potentially lead to their improved understanding of the need to now support the rights of women. The importuning of Tubman as a woman in a physical altercation with the conductor should allow for the understanding by White women of the need for rights for Black people, as in their own struggle. Was not Tubman also a woman, yet having to physically fight to be allowed on a train as a Black person?

The provision by Frances Harper already in 1866, in a major public speech, of a vision of intersectional political responsibility is remarkable and singular. She clearly represented for attendees these very ideas of a conjoined, collective argument for rights for Black people and women in her own person, and was aware of the discursive arguments required to bring this political awareness to her audience. Invoking Harriet Tubman as a figurative Moses for the nation in her speech merged the two competing ideas of freedom and slavery in the form of a Black woman working on behalf of an idea of rights for everyone in the nation. Very shortly after this speech, the idea of a unity of purpose between White women and Black people would collapse in the face of the development of the Black codes and Jim Crow. With this went also the acceptance of a more capacious vision of racial and gender equality, for which Frances Harper was the foremost advocate in print in the decades after the War.

In 1869, Frances Harper published the book of poems *Moses: A Story of the Nile*, and she serialized her first novel,

Minnie's Sacrifice, in the *Christian Recorder*. She had been traveling across the Northeast and in the South, teaching and lecturing in the years since the end of the War, and her health was failing because of the rigors of the schedule she set herself (Still, 1872). It must have been a very physically demanding and precarious social experience to travel in the war-torn South at the time. Both published works engage directly with the theme of how to develop gender and racial equality in the society, and reflect Harper's commitment to the idea of rights and obligations for Black people in this new society.

As a consequence, in part, of this physical debilitation, in 1871, at the age of 46, Frances Harper was back in Philadelphia, where she settled, buying a house for herself and Mary. There she worked as Assistant Superintendent of the YMCA, and continued to write essays, fiction, and poetry. At this time, she also began working for the Temperance Movement.

Like many of her contemporary poets, Harper reissued published works with amendments and new material. In her lifetime, there were at least 20 editions of *Poems on Miscellaneous Subjects*, and 10 other extant volumes of poetry, her 4 novels, numerous essays, speeches, and letters were published. Harper was a poet and writer who, at 46, had already accomplished as much as most in their entire careers. She was a public figure, someone who was immersed in the work of national organizations.

Frances Harper belonged to a small set of women who regularly wrote and spoke in public, but was the only Black woman among them to brave the public organizational arena in addition to writing. Because Harper was an activist writer and poet, much of her written work involved experiences that occurred as a result of those movements and organizations of which she was a part. For her, the concerns of her art always existed alongside her concern for the place of the writer and poet in defining the political ideas that determine how people should live together.

In 1871, Harper published *Poems*, and then, in 1872, she published what many consider her most important volume of poetry, *Sketches of Southern Life* (Fisher, 2008, p. 57; Graham, 1988, p. xliv). Taken together, *Moses* and *Sketches* represent an important contribution to the African American poetry canon, a detailed and excellent analysis of which was produced by Melba Joyce Boyd (1994) in her book *Discarded Legacies* (Graham, 1988, p. xli). Frances Harper continued to publish poetry in the decades that followed, particularly – but not exclusively – addressing the themes of individual morality, gender, race, and temperance. She wrote the newspaper column "Fancy Sketches" from 1873 to 1874, which could be considered a short second novel, and serialized the novel *Sowing and Reaping* in the *Christian Recorder* from 1876 to 1877.

The gaps between the novels are filled with organizational activity, essays, and speeches, but the work that Frances Harper was engaged in after the Civil War was largely obscured by the social transformation wrought by the reconsolidation of White authority and new laws requiring Black subordination. The concepts of political rights and equality for Black people that Frances Harper had championed for two decades before the War had, by the 1870s, proven ephemeral and elusive. Her writing and poems represented a literary call to a collective counter-authority to resist the rise of a new restrictive White South after the War, which was taken up in the 1890s by a new generation of Black writers and poets who could depend on the publishing traditions and literary networks that she and others had developed in the decades after the War (Gordon, 1997, p. 54).

After 1871, Frances Harper's activism was defined by

combining the disparate strands of African American educational and social development, the Suffragist Movement, and the Temperance Movement into a theme of racial uplift for Black people (Terborg-Penn, 1998, p. 67). This was a more complicated field to survey for her and her audience than Abolitionism, and while her popularity never waned during her lifetime, the biographer William Still stopped his discussion of her life after the early 1870s.

In this period, Harper authored 3 novels, at least 40 poems, and numerous essays and letters. But she was also central to the development of the Temperance and Suffrage movements, participating in local, state, and national organizational efforts. In 1872, it would still be 20 years before *Iola Leroy* was published, which was one of the most popular novels of the latter part of the nineteenth century. What occurred during that time to dampen our interest today in that period of her life?

The 1870s and 1880s, like the more recent 1980s and 1990s, were periods of political reconsolidation and conflict, after major shifts in the social institutions that described racial difference. The 13th, 14th, and 15th Amendments to the Constitution, in a similar way to the Voting Rights Act and the Civil Rights Acts of 1965, transformed how people could bring their interest in racial inequality to bear on their social activity. Prohibiting slavery, making all Black people citizens, and granting all men 21 years and older the right to vote transformed the organizations that had formed around these issues before and during the Civil War (Dudden, 2011, pp. 162–3).

It seems too easy to make the stark claim that Black men did not fulfill their promise to Black women when, after being granted the vote, they refused to advocate vociferously for the rights of women. And yet, when we read Frances Harper's novels and poetry of the period after 1869, there is a missing element throughout – the widespread organization of Black men on behalf of women's rights. Even though many Black men, such as Frederick Douglass, did argue in conferences and in meetings about the importance of Black women to their cause of democracy in the society, the failure of the immediate post-War movement to secure the voting rights of Black women has to be seen as an intersectional compromise of race and gender, damaging to the effective development of the rights of the Black community in the decades that followed (Terborg-Penn, 1998, pp. 62, 81).

However, the truth is more complicated than a description of the capacity of a unidimensional gender politics to divide the nascent and fragile commitment to a collective Black community politics by Black men and women after the War. In fact, the major political contestation that occurred publicly within the national organizations was that between White and Black women, and the capacity of racial politics to split the women's Temperance and Suffragist national organizational effort along racial lines (Foster, 1990; McDaneld, 2015, pp. 395–402; Painter, 1996; Parker, 2010, pp. 129–36; Rosenthal, 1997, p. 159). The institutional expansion of a Whiteness that, after the War, would realize new possibilities for social advancement was too effective a political force and overcame the desires of both White and Black women to remain in coalition on the issue of racial equality. This wasn't the case of interpersonal politics overwhelming an opportunity, even though this is the focus of much research by historians – but a problem of how racial difference is reproduced within institutions.

As social imperative, through violence, and then as a political reality, the collapse of the institutions that supported the enslavement of African Americans required new institutional structures and processes. The auction system, the slave catchers, the transportation of slaves to market,

the banking and loan system, insurance agents, the plantation owners, and small farms that owned one or two slaves,
along with slave labor that engaged in everything from farm
work, household cleaning, nursing children, artisanship,
to prostitution on behalf of their owners, were replaced in
the years immediately after the War with a new description of racial inequality. While the women's rights national
organizations, as well as the activists within the Abolitionist
Movement, were important to this development, the defining elements were a series of decisions made by the US
government after 1865. Rather than ascribe racial politics to
a deterministic process, one in which a particular event or
material condition is primarily responsible for the perpetuation of racial inequality, it is better to be more realistic and
think of the many different things that would have contributed to the rise of a new Southern White authority after the
War.

Already at the War's end, Black codes were used to maintain the legal subordination of Black people in the South,
and the organization of the Ku Klux Klan and other mili-
tia groups threatened violence toward anyone with public
aspirations toward more equal social relationships. Lynching
began to occur as an institutional outgrowth of these
processes of consolidating Whiteness around violent suppression of the idea of equality. The Freedmen's Bureau and
Union Army were also important factors in this description of what was possible. But, also, Black people migrated
west and north, and had fought and provided care for the
Union Army, promoting in their activism the potential for a
longer journey to live elsewhere in the country. The effects
of the War on the population and the land were obvious.
Millions can't be killed, slave labor replaced wholesale with
wage labor, and the countryside burned, without there being
difficulties with maintaining economic processes that could

sustain stable living conditions for most in the South. The North was also deeply affected.

In this context, how effective would local initiatives have been, if they had existed, in addressing the idea of racial social equality after the War? How effective are the ideas of implicit bias and diversity training today, without a better understanding than we have of how race difference is described within institutions, in our lives? This is not to ignore the political and social consequences of the failure in the period after the War to unite White and Black women in the cause of racial equality, but it would be almost 60 years after the War when White women could first vote in large numbers in the US, and almost a century after the War before Black women could similarly vote.

It was not a failure of will or factionalism between women and Black people that resulted in these partial and imperfect democratic political processes in the US after the Civil War. We shouldn't blame the victims of the processes of racial and gender inequality for inaction and ineffectiveness, but instead look to the problem of the successful reconsolidation of authority in supporting the ideas of racial and gender hierarchy. By the 1880s, the possibility of Black men voting was likewise fading in practice, as a racial and gendered politics of inequality became a description of social relations throughout the South and North.

Frances Harper in the 1880s, 1890s, and 1900s

From the time of the ratification of the 15th Amendment in 1870, Frances Harper was involved in the Association for the Advancement of Women, the Women's Christian Temperance Union, the Universal Peace Union, the American Women Suffrage Association, the International

Council of Women, the National Council of Women, and the Women's Congress. She was also a founding member of the National Association of Colored Women (NACW) (Gordon, 1997, p. 49; Parker, 2010, pp. 128–38; Terborg-Penn, 1998, pp. 47, 85). With the exception of the NACW, the other associations were dominated and almost exclusively controlled by White women, and Frances Harper was usually the only Black woman in a position of leadership (Jones, 2007, p. 171; Painter, 1996, p. 231; Parker, 2010, p. 137).

Bettye Collier-Thomas points out that the only other African American leader in the nineteenth century, besides Frances Harper, who was able to work extensively with White Americans within a major national organization, was Frederick Douglass, in his work with William Lloyd Garrison in the American Anti-Slavery Society prior to the Civil War (Gordon, 1997, p. 56; Jones, 2007, p. 198) After the War, Frances Harper was the main Black national organizational figure within the Suffragist and Temperance movements. She was able to define a personal social equality with the major White women figures of her day, in terms of participation, presentations, and organizational skills. She was one of the most successful essayists, poets, and novelists of her generation, and the White women had to respect both her acumen and her public presence, if not her person. But her participation also required that White women had to address the issue of racial equality within these women's organizations and conferences (Parker, 2010, p. 128; Terborg-Penn, 1998, p. 109). From 1883 to 1900, Frances Harper was in the executive leadership of the Women's Christian Temperance Union (Gordon, 1997, p. 57; Jones, 2007, p. 201), which was the most powerful and far-reaching women's organization in the country (Tetrault, 2014, p. 87). By the 1890s, it had become more apparent to African American women that these national associations and organizations led predominantly by White women were not effective vehicles for advocating for the rights of African Americans. This is not to ignore the very significant work that Frances Harper achieved by working within these organizations, but she was fighting a losing battle because of the deterioration in the rights of Blacks in what is rightly called the nadir of the free African American experience in this country (Bruce, 1989, p. 3; Collier-Thomas, 1997, pp. 49–65, 86; Parker, 2010, pp. 133–8; Terborg-Penn, 1998).

Lynchings had become an almost daily occurrence throughout the US by the 1890s, and Blacks had no rights that Whites needed to respect. A lynching should be thought of as an extra-legal killing to establish a local description of racial authority. It is a consolidation of the idea of Whiteness as the possibility of a violence that is exceptional and necessary to preserve or secure advantages over the possibility of there being rights held by others, against the claims of those who were defined as White. According to Harper, that the local state governments had gradually capitulated to this authority, and were unable to successfully resist the usurpation of their institutional processes by this idea of racial difference after the potential was created for more expansive democratic reforms by the effects of the War, is the great national tragedy (Foster, 1990, pp. 217–19).

This collective acceptance of violence as required against those who sought to define Black equality was different from the authority that had defined the violence of enslavement. The codes and laws of Jim Crow that established legal punishments to enforce Black inequality were not slavery by another name. These laws were enacted on a free people, for a generation born after 1865 that had never known slavery as a condition. It is important to call the terrible conditions that lynching and Jim Crow laws created for Black people by their name, rather than reduce the struggle for equality that occurred to that which had ended two decades before. It was impossible to impose slavery again on Black people after the Civil War. This fact continues to be important as a description of racial politics, and the idea of racial inequality after Emancipation should not be reduced to a claim about slavery. Rather, what happened – and Frances Harper was at the forefront of this fight in the 1880s until her death – was that Black inequality was defined through the use of punitive and comprehensive social controls. Even if for a time Black men did vote, run for office, and establish businesses that catered to both Black and White customers, by the end of the century the political rights promised by the Amendments were gradually made largely symbolic.

In this political situation, the new generation of Black women leaders, and increasingly Frances Harper as well, did not see the utility of working within these larger White associations, instead forming their own organizations such as the NACW (Parker, 2010, p. 130; Terborg-Penn, 1998, p. 79). By the 1890s, Frances Harper had to contend with a new politics within the Black community. This new position argued that accumulating wealth while accepting the terms given by the continuing racial segregation, codified for example in *Plessy* v. *Ferguson*, would lead to a form of social equality in the absence of political equality. Harper's poetry and essays from the last two decades of her life reflect her criticism of these narrow aims for Black community development (Gordon, 1997, p. 60; Parker, 2010, pp. 133–4).

We come now to an understanding of the reason for the historical erasure of Frances Harper from her place, as one of its most important citizens, in the annals of American society. The need to minimize the importance of Black women in the major women's rights organizations, starting from the 1880s, led to the removal or marginalization of the record of the contributions of Frances Harper from organizational history (Terborg-Penn, 1998, pp. 33–5; Tetrault, 2014, pp. 133–5). At the same time, by the 1890s, Jim Crow politics meant that examples of Black artists, writers, and poets who were exceptional, and particularly those who argued in their work for equality between Blacks and Whites, had to be obscured or forgotten.

The very factors that defined the life of Frances Harper – education, charismatic and powerful speaking, successful activism, her many volumes of poetry about the consequences of racism and misogyny in the society, the four novels about social conditions and the ambition of independent talented women, and her essays about the politics of race and gender – all these accomplishments had to be reduced for future generations to the short story "The Two Offers" published in 1859, and the one major novel, *Iola Leroy*, published in 1892, if she was mentioned at all. Shorn of the context for an understanding of the sophistication of the politics that informed both pieces – though, again, but a small portion of her oeuvre – Frances Harper was described by academics and literary communities in the decades after her death as merely an early Black writer and sentimental poet of little consequence to the society. Generations would pass before her poetry and novels would be published again as significant artifacts of American literary and African American political history. Without the ability of African Americans to enter the academy as professors in increased numbers in the 1960s, it would never have happened. In a very real sense, our understanding of the life of this poet and activist, and of the development of our democratic polity in the last half of the nineteenth century, would not be possible without the continued work of Black academics today, a testament to the importance of Black lives to the understanding of how the United States continues to develop as a democratic society.

Frances Harper did not fit the model of the pathetic Black person in need of succor and charity from White benefactors, and she had not been a slave who escaped or was set free, aided by White people. She refused to countenance the social and legal walls being built around the idea of a distinction between the races that could be used to establish inequality for Black people. That some could succeed as exceptions to the expectation of a seemingly proven and innate Black inferiority to White people was, for Frances Harper, unacceptable. What we see in the novel *Iola Leroy* is an attempt to address this failure of conviction among Black people about their own right to political equality. Harper describes a vision of community development through the activity of her protagonist Iola Leroy, from the Civil War to the 1890s, that is an alternative to what has actually occurred. This is an offering, again, to her readers of a capacious vision of a racial equality to come – one that never arrived. Frances Harper was not just an incredible person, she was always also an incredible Black woman, and the possibility that she would symbolize and represent the Black community as its ideal for decades after her death in 1911 was, for many, an unacceptable concession to the idea of gender and racial equality.

We literally can't trace the influence of Harper's ideas in Black political culture and American organizational history, because these had to be repudiated and assigned for their origin to others. Problems of political vision that were not hers were readily attributed to her cause. In the same sense of a necessary rejection, her poetry and novels were denigrated as simply low culture, in contrast to the work published in high-culture magazines of the period, and described as too protest poetry – as a vernacular, common voice sophistication. Others have disagreed, for genera-possibility that racial and gender injustice, on of Black life that her poetry and writing, her activism, represented, were topics worth exploring in their own right, instead of as a description of White largesse and sympathy (Peterson, 1995, p. 333).

The work of Frances Harper was also too radical – too convinced of the need to ask both Black and White, men and women, to answer the call of a mutual implication in the racial and gendered description of injustice in the society. Her work was simply too intersectional, too invasive of social norms that have prevailed in the society to this day, and that still require racial equality to be defined by gender inequality. The one covers the other, and around again, like a shell game where the idea is that there is nothing really there to begin with – no difference, no purpose beyond the perpetuation of the inequality itself.

It should be remembered, some 50 years after the first African American Studies program was established at a traditionally White university, that not just Frances Harper, but generations of writers, poets, and thinkers have had to be rediscovered for their importance to just this American democratic polity that we as Black people desire to create. But it really is the change in ambition for all of us with regard to race and gender equality that allows for the work of recovery that has occurred now across several generations of contemporary scholars. As Frances Harper's poetry and fiction writing, lectures and essays are brought forward to our literary and political conscience, not only are we reminded of what has been lost by generations of a determined, brutal and inexorable racism, but also we begin to see the genius of a savant, a Black woman who gave her life to our cause. We begin to understand the call to conscience that she devoted her life's work to discovering.

It has taken us so long to understand our contribution to the world in the midst of all that was endured in the long song of Black suffering after the Civil War – the lynchin the chain gangs, the segregation to demean and reduce the ambitions of a community, the poverty and violence experienced as a people, the divisiveness and want that have been fostered to contain and exploit us all – everything that is still being done to Black people. The research made possible by the social organizations that established programs of study in African American Studies should be understood to be still doing the work that we need done, allowing us to consider the importance of those writers and poets, thinkers and public servants, who, together, might provide us with another country – another vision of how we can live together. Through her words, Frances Harper has offered us "a fairer hope, a brighter morn" (Graham, 1988, p. 199). We need to come to an understanding of what her poetry and writing are for us today, so that it can lead us to another shore, a different nation – one that Frances Harper envisioned in her work for racial and gender equality.

2

Iola Leroy: Social Equality

In William Still's introduction to *Iola Leroy, Or Shadows Uplifted*, we see the politics of gender and race with which Frances Harper had to contend in her lifetime (Harper, 1892, pp. 1–3). The novel, published in 1892, was for many the penultimate work by someone who had devoted her life to public service in a time when women could not vote and Black people had to address the challenge of what freedom was to mean in the United States. For Still, it seems, there was a need and a perceived right to assess the merits of a work by someone who had relied on his generosity and kindness when younger, but also to praise this person who had now become a household name for many.

William Still had been an important participant in the Abolitionist Movement as a leader in the Underground Railroad, and in 1892 when the book was published, it had almost been three decades since the end of the Civil War. For the African American public, it was significant that William Still wrote the preface. Therein, Still acknowledges his place in the life of Frances Harper, as her biographer and advocate within the Movement, but also seeks to elevate her standing as a major contributor to political thought in the latter half of the nineteenth century (Still, 1872). Both Still and Harper were concerned throughout their professional lives with the role of African Americans in the society. *Iola Leroy* was supposed to convince readers to attend to the problems that African Americans faced in the 1890s, which is what makes Still's introductory words so valuable. It is as though he is telling the reader at the time not to doubt the veracity and integrity of the author, but to trust the commitment and knowledge that Frances Harper brings to the problem of what is required for African Americans to achieve the promise of Emancipation.

Iola Leroy offers a direction and focus to the desire for some hope in the midst of the lynchings, the collapse of the rights regime for Black people throughout the South, and the calcifying of restrictions on Black equality in the North and across the nation. Still writes:

> I know of no other woman, white or colored, anywhere, who has come so intimately in contact with the colored people in the South as Mrs. Harper. Since emancipation she has labored in every Southern State in the Union, save two, Arkansas and Texas; in the colleges, schools, churches, and the cabins not excepted, she has found a vast field and open doors to teach and speak on the themes of education, temperance, and good home building, industry, morality, and the like, and never lacked for evidences of hearty appreciation and gratitude.
>
> (Harper, 1892, pp. 1–2)

We should consider this testimonial as evidence today of why Frances Harper's writings are an important attempt by a Black political thinker to develop the national conversation about how race should allow for equality and rights for all. In *Iola Leroy*, Frances Harper provides not only a refutation of the dominant public narratives about Black people that were used to justify racial segregation and inequality, but also a description of how individuals could develop the personal perspective and social capacity necessary to define racial equality. The main protagonist in the story, Iola, literally demonstrates through her journey the choices needed for an individual to become effective in addressing the collapse of public support for racial equality and rights-based racial progress. The politics of collective resistance that Frances Harper describes was explicitly developed in the novel through the person of Iola as an answer to the terrible conditions that were being implemented to eliminate the right for Black men to vote, and to otherwise curtail the community's political ambitions (Field, 2015, p. 121).

It is also interesting that, in the introduction, William Still mentions the books of poetry by Frances Harper and not her previously serialized novels. He describes having found confidence in the developing work through it being read to him, just as Frances Harper's poetry was read by her to an audience at a gathering. In doing so, he references what she was known for by the national public, suggesting that this same audience, 30 years after the War, would find her novel enlightening and important to their understanding of the conditions in which Black people had lived. He tells the reader that the work of *Iola Leroy* as a book follows naturally from the work of the most important Black poet, and one of the most widely read poets, of her generation. This is also a warning for us today in our interpretation of the novel. Still expected the reader of the novel to recognize the many allusive references to current events, political figures, other writers and novels, Harper's own poems, and the political controversies of the time. We don't have any easy way to reference these ideas completely, even though many can be puzzled out (Carby, 1989; Ernest, 1995; Foster, 1990; Peterson, 1995; Rutkowski, 2008; Stewart, 2018). What Still provides is more an admonition that we should respect the novel as a powerful intervention in the national conversation about how support for the rights of Black people determines the nation's democratic character.

Iola Leroy is both a novel of its time and one that offers us insights into how we think of ourselves and the place that race continues to have in our daily lives. It was one of the most successful novels of the latter part of the nineteenth century, not merely because it was a fictional record of how Black people lived immediately before and after the Civil War, but because Frances Harper developed the characters and the plot of the novel around themes that were, and continue to be, of enduring concern in the society. She used popular portrayals of slave resistance, Secessionists, events in the historical period, references to known popular figures in activist and literary circles – such as Frederick Douglass, Nat Turner, Martin Delany, George and Lewis Latimer, Ida B. Wells, and others – and repeated phrases and themes from her previously published poetry to make her readers understand the novel was a product of a common understanding of the War and its consequences (Ernest, 1995, pp. 198–204; Foreman, 2009, pp. 90, 102–12). In providing these intertextual referents, Frances Harper signaled to her readers the relationship they were to have with the text. Even the name Iola in the title was understood popularly as the name given for Ida B. Wells, who published her major work on lynching, *Southern Horrors: Lynch Law in All Its Phases*, in that same year of 1892 (Foreman, 2009, pp. 76, 90–2; Wells, 2016).

In encountering a woman protagonist named Iola, readers at the time would have understood that the book they were about to read was in a tradition of political and social activism by Black women, represented by both Frances Harper and Ida B. Wells (Foreman, 2009, p. 96). They would have expected to read about the journey of a young Black woman from relative innocence and vulnerability to becoming a confident and generous political intellectual with solutions for just their generation. This was, as Still points out, the book by which to make sense of the political quandary the nation was in, decades after the Civil War. It was the book everyone was waiting for, and thus its references throughout were designed to appeal to the many perspectives and disparate ambitions of a divided nation.

Because of Frances Harper's lifetime of political engagement, this discussion of *Iola Leroy* depends on the relationship that we accept between writing and events taking place in the society around the production of texts. Poetry and fiction are often written to illustrate or define a political moment for the writer, such as the novel *Meridian* by Alice Walker or the poetry of Maya Angelou for the Civil Rights Movement in the 1960s (Angelou, 2015; Walker, 2003). Through the character and actions of Iola Leroy, Frances Harper describes the effects of the Civil War and its aftermath on Black people in the society.

This novel reflects the experience of the author decades before, as first developed in her collections of poetry published after the War. It seeks to make sense for her audience at the time of what should be done about the circumstances they find themselves in, post-War. What should African Americans do, certainly – but also how should Black life define the ambitions of a democracy such as the United States? For Harper, Black lives were indelibly linked to the destiny of the nation, and her readers understood this. In this sense of mapping out what was possible for the reader, we can see *Iola Leroy* as a novel offering up for us today a glimpse of the road not yet taken, toward racial equality in the United States.

The idea that the political is something distant and removed from everyday life – a perspective that we often experience today in the constant appeals by the two major political parties to fund candidates for election, and the inundation of messaging from social media and television – distracts us from the value of creative work that attempts to reflect the importance of values that we as readers should share. *Iola Leroy* offers a description of a shared community of political interests that was diametrically opposed to the increasingly fraught description of racial segregation, physical violence, and legal disenfranchizement of Black people in the society of the 1890s. It was in the years just before the novel's publication in 1892 that the first literacy tests were used to disenfranchize Black men, and there was a concerted effort to organize the society around the idea of a Whiteness that must be protected and rigidly enforced against the possibility of not just a social but a political equality.

In her works, Frances Harper, like Jane Austen and Charles Dickens, provides everyday descriptions of social issues in ways that may seemed forced if attempted today. The sheer volume of writing we are exposed to now in our daily lives is dramatically different from that available to readers in Harper's lifetime, and so I argue that, in addition to the changes in our material circumstances from those that existed in the United States in 1892, the role of writing allows for a distinction between poetry, fiction, and what we think of as daily political events. It is not that we don't have a similar urgency to our lives with regard to puzzling out our experiences that relate to race and gender, but that today we think of these ideas as the stuff of professional academics, in a sense that was not available to these earlier authors. We also have professional occupations that purport to address the issues of race and gender, for example, as their explicit object of research. We have the researcher, the public intellectual, and the pundit as occupations, and so are much more likely to judge a work of poetry or fiction as being too close to its political object as a result.

Iola Leroy directly considers the problems of race and gender, in the period just before the Civil War and in the years immediately following. The major part of the book takes place after the War and concerns how Black people attempted to bring their families back together, after having been sold away from one another as slaves. It considers how those who had been enslaved thought of their own future as a people for whom America now held a new description of promise and possibility. It does not continue in the tradition of the slave narrative, for after the War what was a slave but the newly free, supposedly suddenly arriving on the scene where before they had lived invisibly as less than human in the shadow of bondage? The novel does not focus on the violence and the attempt by others to curtail the ambitions of a people recently thought of as property. Instead, Harper explores the questions that she believes members of the freed community itself must ask if they are to thrive with one another. This isn't an oversight, but an offering to the reader in her time – and for us as well – of how the society should address the impossible demand for Black inferiority, by some, whatever the cost to the nation. The question of who is a member of the Black community is addressed throughout the novel, describing how Robert Johnson chooses to remain Black, because he has been a slave and Black all his life, though he can pass as White. Iola Leroy refuses her mother's solution of passing as White and instead aligns herself politically and socially with her grandmother, who was always Black, defining in her actions, thus, the value for the Black community not of phenotype but of the inheritance of a condition of solidarity, the refusal of the description of a Black inferiority and gender inequality (Field, 2015, p. 120; Foreman, 2009).

In the face of racism, Iola Leroy's personal choice to identify as Black is an act of freedom that, for the readers after the War and today, would more than symbolize the refutation of the blandishments of a racial difference that was imposed as a supposed badge of inferiority. Her choice to be Black when she is described by White people she meets as able to choose, is an acknowledgment for the reader of how important the act of refusal is. Frances Harper knew the fundamental importance of refusing to accept the definition of race as something real and indelible. None of the Black people in the novel questions Iola Leroy's choice. How arbitrary and capricious is the assignment of a difference, then, that shouldn't make any difference. The popularity of the novel in its time, as well as its resonance today, lies in this simultaneous acknowledgment by the characters and the readers of what must be done together to create equality, the personal choices necessary to address injustice, and, at the same time, the requirement that the reader refuse the description of race as an invidious distinction between persons.

That Iola Leroy is able to pass phenotypically is not considered a problem for other Black people in the novel, once she makes her decision. No Black person questions her loyalty to the cause of racial justice, or the source of her commitments to a particular freedom to come. In other words, Frances Harper provides for us a moment to reflect on a problem we have today of internalizing as a community the idea of a difference between those who are lighter-skinned and those who are not. For Harper, being able to pass is not something enviable, desirable, or something to foster resentment between Black people. Instead, it represents a social and political fault line along which the community experiences loss. This possibility requires the acceptance of the meaning of race as always debilitating and pernicious, a wound that defines a limit to the community, symbolized in the failure of some to join the struggle against racial injustice and inequality. To be a descendent of Black and White people as Iola Leroy was, for Frances Harper, is not a curse or blessing, but a consequence of the very humanity that we all have, the equality that we actually represent to one another. To act otherwise – to reject the children, to refuse important social relationships – is, of course, to accept the language of a difference that shouldn't exist; it is to refuse a future together.

The importance of this claim to future generations, of looking to the future of the country in her writing of the novel, is provided for the reader in the first few pages of the book, long before we encounter Iola Leroy. Uncle Daniel, when discussing why he won't leave with the other slaves to join the Northern Army encamped nearby and thus gain his freedom as contraband of war, describes how he must stay to protect the children, to honor his commitment to a future with the former Master's family, as well as to his fellow slaves. He describes how he had taken care of his Master since he was a toddler, and then was given responsibility for the future of his Master's children and wife when the Master went off to fight the Northerners. Even in the moment of admitting a desire to win the War and keep him enslaved, the Master asks the slave for, and is given, a promise to protect his family. Now Uncle Daniel has to explain to those slaves who, when given the chance to self-emancipate, crossed over to the Northern Army forces, why he stays, implicitly challenging the perception that slaves accepted their condition, that they were happy as slaves, and, when the book was published, in 1892, were miserable in the uncertainty of their own mastery of person (Harper, 1892, pp. 24–8).

Uncle Daniel actually represents the freedom to choose – what the other slaves are seeking in their escape – in his refusal to leave. The decision to honor his commitments, even if made under the duress of enslavement, is in fact a sign of his own freedom – a volition that refutes claims, made in the decades that follow the Civil War, that the slaves regretted their Emancipation, that Black people needed paternal guidance to fulfill their destiny in the country (Harper, 1892, pp. 28–9). Another slave present for the conversation in the novel, Ben Tunnel, also announces that he must stay on the plantation because of his mother, whom he must look after. Thus, for the reader, the principle of choice and family for the slave supersedes that of obedience to a Master and a personal desire for freedom.

If we juxtapose the promise of family protection by Uncle Daniel, whom we meet before we encounter Iola Leroy in the novel, with the idea of a woman able to resist accepting her availability to sexual predation by the Master as a condition of her person, we can see the limit to slavery's inscription on Black life for Frances Harper and her readers. What could not be acquired in owning another human as property was their capacity to choose what was important in their relationships with other persons. No amount of abasement or degradation could expunge this capacity, the definition of the human as able to place their desires and affections as they might choose.

Robert Johnson doesn't hesitate to abandon his owner when the chance arises, in spite of an intimacy that he could not have refused. As he says:

> "My ole Miss knows I can read the papers, an' she never
> tries to scare me with big whoppers 'bout the Yankees. She
> knows she can't catch ole birds with chaff, so she is just as

sweet as a peach to her Bobby. But as soon as I get a chance
I will play her a trick the devil never did."
"What's that?"
"I'll leave her. I ain't forgot how she sold my mother from
me. Many a night I have cried myself to sleep, thinking
about her, and when I get free I mean to hunt her up."

(Harper, 1892, p. 34)

And, of course, he does find Iola's grandmother – his mother
in the story – and she is the measure by which moral success
is assured.

For those who had experienced slavery – as property, as
owners, and alongside slaves as free Blacks – the volition of
the enslaved was never in doubt. Slavery was a legal condition, not a racial ascription of human difference. What
freedom meant for the slave, as the novel *Iola Leroy* reminds
its readers, wasn't a capacity for choices, but the ability to
travel, own property, testify in court on one's own behalf,
provide for one's own welfare, but also freely engage in the
creation of a community with others. That Uncle Daniel
would escape once his Master died, or returned, was explicitly stated. He would then have fulfilled his own sense of
obligation to a future that he imagines.

In *Iola Leroy*, Frances Harper argued that, once free,
the slave was no more a symbol of Black life than White.
Instead, Black people in much of the South and North were
poor, lacked access to education, and desired opportunities
for social advancement. That former enslavement had left
many without any means to acquire a living meant that, since
the government had an obligation to secure the life, liberty
and happiness for all in the society, there was an obligation
to this population that it refused to meet. The conditions
arose from slavery, but it was not as slaves that the government refused to answer the call to a democratic future of

racial equality for Black people. This refusal was obvious to everyone in the society through the lynchings and the suppression of the Black vote, the use of laws to incarcerate Black people and sell their labor as prisoners, the elimination of due process, and the violent enforcement of racial segregation statutes and social norms when the novel was published. The government was complicit in the oppression of Black people, as a population, and for their part those Black people who had been formerly enslaved often represented those most vulnerable to the consequences of this view of a necessary material and social Black inequality.

The reader at the time the book was published would most likely have known that Frances Harper was never a slave and that the text, therefore, was not a statement of atonement or testimony. Instead, it was a contribution to political thought by a Black person who epitomizes the truth of innate racial equality, someone with whom readers – both Black and White – share a common humanity without the attribution of slavery. In the introduction, William Still reminds us of the experience and scholarship that Frances Harper has, which merit our respect for the novel and its importance as a document of intellectual thought. He writes:

> Before the war she was engaged as a speaker by anti-slavery associations; since then, by appointment of the Women's Christian Temperance Union, she has held the office of "Superintendent of Colored Work" for years. She has also held the office of one of the Directors of the Women's Congress of the United States. Under the auspices of these influential, earnest, and intelligent associations, she has been seen often on their platforms with the leading lady orators of the nation. Hence, being widely known not only amongst her own race but likewise by the reformers, laboring for the salvation of the intemperate and others equally unfortunate,

there is little room to doubt that the book will be in great demand and will meet with warm congratulations from a goodly number outside of the author's social connections.

(Harper, 1892, p. 3)

To appeal to ideas of a common humanity, a shared cause in the development of the nation, an equal social partnership in the context of this widespread refusal to acquiesce to the possibility that Black and White people differed only as individuals, required a story, a fable, the idea of Iola Leroy – the woman in the novel, who, with her decisions and foresight, was for Frances Harper designed to represent the future of the Black community for the nation.

Frances Harper is, in this act of writing, therefore, creating the political audience, the community that she wants to address as culpable in this time. In practical terms, this means that the popularity of *Iola Leroy* was also due to the curiosity and concern that White Americans had for the effects of the Civil War and the description of the struggle Black people had in the years following the dreadful conflict. What was it like to suddenly be freed, and how did these former slaves find their purpose so that there was something they had together beyond the fact of having been enslaved? Their goal must have been to join together with those who had always been free, to erase the stigma of former enslavement in the promise of education and social progress represented by people such as Frances Harper. My claim is that the ambition of Frances Harper in writing *Iola Leroy* was to establish a history that allowed both Black and White people, men and women, to build a future, all bound up, together.

Iola Leroy was published 27 years after the end of the Civil War, not a mere few years after the end of the conflict – a fact that should not be ignored by the contemporary reader. Frances Harper wrote this book for those who, a generation later, were thinking about how they found a way through incredible adversity to the place they were currently in, as an explanation for how things had come to be just the way they were in 1892. In taking this perspective on the novel, I am not eschewing the characterization that Claudia Tate (1992) makes in her writing about the 1890s as a unique decade for novels written by Black women – nor am I ignoring the circumstances whereby, at the end of the century, a new group of writers and poets were finally ushering in a period of renewed interest among the general public in the conditions of Black life (Mossell, 2010 [1894]).

Instead, I am claiming that the novel is Harper's own answer to the challenge she makes in the blank-verse long poem from 1869, *Moses: A Story of the Nile*, of the need to wait a generation or more for the maturation of the social progress necessary to achieve racial equality. That Frances Harper sees the young activism of Ida B. Wells, "Iola," as the voice of the new generation isn't surprising (Mossell, 2010 [1894], pp. 46, 76). *Iola Leroy* was Frances Harper's last novel, the first to directly consider the effects of the War and its aftermath. If anything, we could see this novel as an example of the mature work by Harper, even though she would continue to publish poetry collections until the early twentieth century. As such, instead of seeing her as similar to other new Black women writers of the 1890s, we must remember that, in 1892, Frances Harper was, in fact, an important author and famous poet, at 67 years of age – an author on whose work the younger generation could model their own writing and literary production.

By 1892, Harper had been publishing writing for more than four decades. In 1896, she would go on to co-found the National Association of Colored Women, one of the most important organizations for African Americans historically. This was largely in response to the conflicts that had continued to take place within the Women's Christian Temperance Union, where she was for many years part of the organizational leadership, over the place of Black people in the Association's work (Collier-Thomas, 1997, pp. 55–60; McDaneld, 2015, pp. 396–402; Parker, 2010, pp. 128–35). In 1866, she had helped to found the American Equal Rights Association, a national organization advocating the voting rights for Black men and all women in the society (Field, 2015, p. 115). When *Iola Leroy* was published, therefore, she was not beginning a career, but had been working for decades alongside the most important of the public proponents for the rights of Black people and White women.

This is a novel that is not just a place-holder for the thoughts of the generation that reaped the consequences of the road to racial equality not taken after the Civil War. It is also a model for how to account for the social divisions that arise when building organizational resistance within the Black community to the constant attrition caused by the arguments for racial inferiority that continue, some 50 years after the most active struggles of the Civil Rights Movement. It is in some sense a detailed psychological study of how human beings cope together with adversity and recovery from horrific events in their lives. The novel allows its readers to work through the idea of what freedom meant for Americans after the end of slavery, and as the credo of "separate but unequal" rose to define everyday life for Blacks in the society. The novel's popularity and importance at the time of its publication are not surprising. I think we, in our time, would do well to respect the wisdom found in its pages.

The plot

The novel begins with the two slaves Tom Anderson and Robert Johnson trading greetings, using coded language about food for sale in the marketplace to signal how the Civil War was proceeding. Harper offers up a description of how these codes were used, and suggests that slaves without access to newspapers, or unable to read, watched their owners for the effects of the news about the War. The implication that slaves were not only intelligent but eager for news about the outcome of the War, understanding that in this lay their destiny as well, provides an opportunity for some humor on Frances Harper's part at the supposed ignorance of the owners, rather than being something that needed to be proven to the readers of the novel. The novel has many humorous elements in it, and is also one of the earliest attempts at using African American dialect in literature. Throughout the novel, the different educational levels of the Black characters are evident in the language that they use with one another, and in these beginning pages Tom and other slaves employ dialect differently than does Robert Johnson, who, as we learn, was a special favorite and had been taught to read by his Mistress.

As the novel proceeds, the slaves discuss holding Sunday prayer meetings in the woods near their plantations, where they would regularly discuss the progress of the War and trade information as a community. This is an important point for Harper to emphasize, as it allows the reader to consider the Black slave population as less defined by their living and working at respective plantations and, instead, recognizing a common goal, having a political community, already prior to the end of the War. At the meeting that is then held in the novel, the slaves discuss the proximity of the Union Army and their individual desires to flee there. A discussion is held about what the terms for loyalty to slave owners should be – under what conditions should a slave leave and when should they stay? As a result of Uncle Daniel's refusal to leave his Master's family, there is then a discussion of the difference between the Christianity of the slave owners and that of the slaves, as moral systems. Shortly after this, Tom Anderson and Robert Johnson leave their plantations to escape to the Union Army encampment, and then we meet Iola Leroy.

It is useful to provide this brief summary of the first chapters to give some sense of how Frances Harper sought to immediately build a common history for readers of the novel. For many readers, so long after the War, this was a reminder or new information about how the slaves perceived the end of the War and their relationship to their owners. A brief outline of the rest of the plot follows.

A wealthy White Southern planter, Eugene Leroy, marries his Black nurse Marie, who is manumitted, and they have three children – Harry, Iola, and Grace. Due to racial prejudice, though Marie passes as White to her children, the neighbors know she is a former slave and Black, and as a result the family has few visitors to the plantation and the children grow up oblivious to their heritage as African Americans. To further insulate the children from the effects of a racial discrimination by neighbors that will reveal their status, Harry and Iola are sent North to boarding schools. Later, on the journey to visit Iola at her school commencement, her father dies. The father's cousin, Alfred Lorraine, inherits the plantation and its goods, and promptly has the marriage between Iola's father and mother dissolved. Remanded to slavery, the mother collapses with shock, and her youngest child, Grace, dies of sorrow.

The cousin, Lorraine, finds a letter the mother wrote to Iola Leroy saying that the father had died and, now knowing her location in the North, sends a solicitor to retrieve what he feels is his property. Iola is tricked into journeying South to visit her sick father – who has already died – and upon arriving is likewise remanded into slavery. It is in this act that she is, for the first time, made aware of her heritage as an African American. Her brother, Harry Leroy, is informed of his status as an African American, but is not discovered by Lorraine and so remains in the North at school. The Civil War begins and Harry wants to volunteer, given his new self-awareness, to fight for Black freedom. Because he looks White, he is given a choice whether to join the White or a Black regiment. He wants to find his lost sister and mother, and so ostensibly uses this excuse to join the Black regiment; thus, he refuses to pass as White. His ability to search in the Black soldier camps in the segregated Army for his family emphasizes the impact of racial segregation on their lives. However, it becomes clear other concerns weigh in this choice, and Frances Harper signals by Harry's decision the problem of passing and individual adherence to an ideal of community not merely of circumstance, but of principle.

It is in this same context of defining this developing Black free community that we first meet Iola Leroy. She has joined the nursing corps and she finds herself befriended by many Black soldiers, one of whom she later discovers is her long-lost uncle – the same Robert Johnson whom we have met at the beginning of the novel. It is while writing of Iola's experiences as a nurse that Frances Harper returns to the idea of interracial relationships, first described between Iola's parents. Paralleling the story of the White patient and a Black nurse falling in love through an ethic of care, as occurred with her parents, the young White Doctor Gresham falls in love with Iola. Watching her attend to the plight of her patients, as well as the time they must spend together caring for the sick, kindles strong emotions. Gresham proposes but

Iola refuses, not because she cannot care for him, but because the condition for their love is that she must refuse her status as a Black person. Unlike her mother, she refuses to do this. She chooses to remain Black rather than return to the status of a Whiteness that requires the oppression of others. This demand Gresham makes clear when he says that he will not be able to tell his mother of her Black ancestry, but that she can live without fear as a White woman.

Unlike her mother, Marie, who lived in the South and kept slaves as servants on the plantation, Iola refuses to cast off the mantle of racial difference and the prejudice it occasions from Whites, including Gresham's family in the North. She decides to allow her dedication to the cause of racial uplift to guide her personal intimate relationship choices as well. This thematic question of what is required of individuals in the midst of a constant and serious redefinition of racial difference in society is developed further in the novel, when, years later, Gresham encounters Iola soon after her family is finally reunited in the aftermath of the War. Iola again rejects Gresham's suit, and he understands that the problem of racial categorization is his to bear, not hers. He is unable to see past his own desire for a Whiteness that refuses to accept racial equality – even though he is willing to love Iola, he cannot do so if she is a Black woman.

Rather than provide the reader with the personal stories of Iola's brother Harry Leroy, or of her uncle or mother, Frances Harper stays with Iola as the protagonist, allowing those around her to provide a contrast and serve as foils for Iola's development and choices. A serious, religious, and forthright individual, Iola is focused on her life's object, the betterment of the condition for African Americans. Often the dialogue explicitly portrays Iola as a Black woman desiring to go to intellectual gatherings where those in attendance discuss subjects such as the progress of the race, rather than to dances and other social gatherings. For example, she attends a gathering where each attendee has submitted a paper to discuss. The novel describes the intellectual arguments between the individuals, and Iola at one point contributes by saying "We did not . . . place the bounds of our habitation. And I believe we are to be fixtures in this country. But beyond the shadows I see the coruscation of a brighter day: and we can usher it in, not by answering hate with hate, or giving scorn for scorn, but by striving to be more generous, noble, and just" (Harper, 1892, p. 249). When it is Iola Leroy's turn to discuss her own paper contribution to the gathering, the topic is a speech that Frances Harper gave in public herself, on the "Education of Mothers" (Harper, 1990h).

After the War, the desire to recover from the dislocations wrought by their family's history with slavery is described through the urgency felt by both Iola and Robert Johnson to reunite the family. Quickly discovering that, in fact, they are niece and uncle, the two set out and find Iola's grandmother, Robert's mother. This event provides for the possibility of finding both Iola's brother and her mother, Robert's sister. The search for relatives, long-lost children, parents, and loved ones, for those who had been enslaved was a fraught and difficult emotional burden for those recently freed from bondage. The conditions of their enslavement, where often the choice of developing family relationships, friendships, and partners was a decision that involved their owners, meant that having social volition, the freedom to be in a relationship with whomever they chose, was an important right. Frances Harper acknowledges this consequence of freedom – the centrality to those formerly enslaved of the right to choose one's social relationships, for the sake of their own self-perception – as also necessary for Black people to form the community required for social progress in the future. It is only after this process of social recovery for individuals, as a symbol in the novel for the many concerns someone freed might have, that it becomes possible to consider what freedom should mean as a collective politics for the society. Literally, the former slave had to decide their relationships to other persons without the intercession of an owner and with a new legal status of equality with those people they encountered.

Frances Harper provides a description of what this change in status meant for individuals at the time in the description of the migration of people throughout the South, and in a scene where Robert and Iola return to the site of the Plantation and its environs, where they first were in the military camp. She had herself traveled throughout most of the former slave states repeatedly after the War, and so was familiar with the anxiety and concerns of those who had been freed. The choice to emphasize the reunification of family as the theme for not only finding the terms of this idea of freedom, but, in doing so, discovering a new community, is for Frances Harper a gesture to the absence of conviction as to the rights of Black people in the 1890s in the larger society.

In their search for their family, Iola and Robert are invited to come to a gathering in the woods. This time, however, there is no fear of slave patrols, and the discussion between the freed people concerns what has happened since the War, as a few years have gone by, and questions arise about the whereabouts of those they once knew as slaves, as well as their owners. The community concern with knowing the fate of others provides the impetus for a larger community, one that must develop for the description of what is possible after the War to become available. This plot invention of a time when Black people are able to gather, in the woods where once they had to pretend to be having prayer meetings for fear of violence from their owners, offers the reader the opportunity to imagine a common social space developing around the idea of progress and care after the War. That this is conceived for Frances Harper as a community in prayer, following Christian teachings that address the difficulty in each person's life, isn't surprising.

Eventually, the family is reunited, and Iola tries to find work in the North, and the novel provides a frank assessment of the difficulties of finding employment and the problem of racial exclusionary mechanisms. Iola's plight allows the reader to follow the journey made by freed Blacks in their search for freedom across the South and North – the struggle to find a living in the workplace and within the newly formed communities.

Iola eventually finds a partner, Dr. Frank Latimer, who tends to the health of Black patients with the same care as Iola demonstrated as a nurse during the War. Latimer, like Iola, is someone who can pass for White but does not do so, refusing thereby the easy racial categorization sought by the politics of racial segregation and the oppression of Blacks at the time. *Plessy* v. *Ferguson*, the landmark case arguing for separate but equal public services based on race, would be decided in 1896, arising from the arrest of Homer Plessy on a train in 1892 (*Plessy* v. *Ferguson*, 163 US 537 [1896]). They marry, and, after some last messages centered around the family and the idea of inheritance that witness to what their union means for the good society, the novel ends.

Racial healing

The theme that runs throughout the novel – and, I suggest, a major reason for its widespread popularity when it was published – is that of identifying a path toward healing some of the national trauma of the preceding decades. Frances Harper develops a remarkable set of principles and strategies for addressing the effects on individuals of having been enslaved or of having owned slaves. She charts a path between North and South that is ripe with requirements for Whites, for want of a better word, to describe the consolidation of a social ideal that defined itself as holding common norms. The novel considers what is required of this new-found freedom for slave and Master alike, to build a nation together in spite of this legacy. Iola Leroy wants to find work once her family is united, and finds it difficult because of the color line, as employers will not hire a Black person. Eventually, she finds a job caring for an ill young woman, and successfully nurses her back to health. As a reward, the girl's father hires her at his store, telling his employees beforehand that Iola is Black, and if they don't like it, they can resign their positions. None leaves the job, and she starts working without further incident (Harper, 1892, p. 211).

Frances Harper defines a Black American community through her characters, allowing the reader to imagine a united community responding to the new challenges not only of being poor and undereducated, but also of the effects of violence and resistance by Whites who resent the scope of a newfound Black collective identity. For example, at one point, Iola Leroy's mother, Marie, is so worried about her son Harry, who is organizing Black people in the South, that she falls ill. She says, "I am so worried about Harry . . . he is so fearless and outspoken. I do wish the attention of the whole nation could be turned to the cruel barbarisms which are a national disgrace" (Harper, 1892, p. 241). One of the characters, Dr. Gresham, for example, says, "The problem of the nation . . . is not what men will do with the negro, but what will they do with the reckless, lawless white men who murder, lynch, and burn their fellow citizens" (Harper, 1892, p. 217).

This was one of the first books written in the United States that delineates the social life of Black people absent the requirement that its description be expressed through a relationship to White desire. In fact, Iola Leroy's rejection of Gresham is important for just this reason, as, unlike her mother, Marie, the desires of the White man do not require her concession to his terms. She is free to make a choice, and not as a slave. Harper was no doubt aware that, in her description of the desires of Eugene Leroy for his nurse, the interests of Marie would have been weighed by her against the condition of slavery. Readers are left to wonder at the relationship begun between owner and slave, such that Marie would be able to decline his proposal.

Once free, the aspirations of the novel's characters are defined without significant references to constraints of racial inequality. Frances Harper describes a national ideal through a depiction of the lives of Black people, providing a description of their ambitions, the goals they have for their lives in building a better world for one another. Iola Leroy is surrounded by African Americans with different ambitions and concerns. The story about Iola is one of trying to define what it would mean for a woman to be both slave and free, and the choices she must make as a calling or purpose after the Civil War. From this perspective, Frances Harper explicitly criticized the Cult of True Womanhood that was the popular description of gender politics in 1892 (Carby, 1989 p. 74; Cutter, 1999).

Iola Leroy, as a character, is similar to the author Frances Harper in their common ambition of dedicating a life to racial uplift. And, at one point in the novel, Frances Harper even suggests that Iola Leroy might write a novel for Black readers to use to come to an understanding of their own condition in the society (Harper, 1892, p. 263). *Iola Leroy* is a novel about how Black people might imagine their struggle for a life free from the constraints placed upon them by the racial standards in the nation. The questions that it asks are those we ask ourselves today, if we dare to think of a world where the description of racial inequality is not paramount to our choices.

Frances Harper provides a script for a Black life in the relationships between the characters, the adversity and challenges that they face, their success and sense of optimism at the end of the novel, and in the descriptions provided of what slaves and then newly freed people did to make sense of their place now in the nation. This book provides an opportunity for healing, instead of revisiting the trauma of loss; it allows for readers to consider what it would be like to understand their fellow Black people as equals in mind and body. The journey itself isn't easy or lighthearted, but Frances Harper spares us from pathos and the suffering that must have been the lot of the slave. Instead of being a story to stir the sympathy of the guilty heart, the novel requires that the reader think about what is being asked of those who have survived this terrible trauma, as a personal and national mandate.

This process communicated through the actions of Iola Leroy, of discovering a new definition of racial equality recently thought impossible, resonates with the reader today. More than 50 years after Jim Crow was challenged by the new legislation and government policies, today we experience a situation similar to that which Frances Harper writes about in the novel, where the effects of racial inequality are so severe as to make it difficult to imagine a national ethos and social fabric together. The question of how to define the ideals of a Black life, determined in relation to the assumptions of White people in a larger segregated society, or developed through self-reflection and principles that represent the nation as an ideal, are at the forefront of our public conversation. What should be done by Black people about the extent to which we as a society fall short of the goal of racial equality? It is not as simple as describing how the policies we have today define a politics of the Black exception, in which some, as DuBois would suggest some two decades after the novel *Iola Leroy*, could point out a talented few to lift up the welfare of those who remain at the bottom of society. This model of exceptions to the rule of Black incarceration, underemployment, poverty, and homelessness has failed to realize the conditions for racial equality in our contemporary society. Frances Harper in *Iola Leroy* is not suggesting that some few lead the way, but that certain tasks must be accomplished, certain areas of the development of the nation must be addressed, through a collective effort.

In the years after the War, Iola Leroy was clear that her duty was to become a teacher, for a new country – one not yet realizable given the conditions within which Black people had to live. The violence of a resentful and angry White population (not just those living in the South), the social description of racial inequality, and lack of material opportunities for those who sought to improve their own personal situation made this a challenge, one that the novel develops our awareness of through the description of the characters that interact with Iola Leroy. At one point, she starts teaching at a school, and, as Harper describes it:

> The school was beginning to lift up the home, because Iola was not content to teach her children only the rudiments of knowledge. She had tried to lay the foundation of good character. But the elements of evil burst upon her loved and cherished work. One night the heavens were lighted with lurid flames, and Iola beheld the school, the pride and joy of her pupils and their parents, a smoldering ruin.
>
> (Harper, 1892, p. 147)

Her uncle, Robert Johnson, is the new owner of a hardware store, after having been enslaved his entire life. Dr. Frank

Latimer, whom Iola marries, is a Black person trained in the North, who decided to come South to dedicate his career to healing the effects of racial inequality on the Black population. The other Black people with whom Iola interacts are similarly positioned as able to provide some example of industry and thrift, ambition, and an important role in the community, including, for example, those former slaves who have managed to buy the plantation of their old Master and turn it into a successful cooperative enterprise. The pastors who minister to their impoverished and anxious congregations are, in the novel, able to engage in public debates with the ideas of Black inferiority held by Whites, and represent the community as principled advocates for social probity. While it is not necessary to the understanding of the novel, it should be remembered that not only had Frances Harper spent years in the South after the Civil War doing exactly the type of work that she describes for Iola Leroy, but also she was very familiar with the types of leadership required for successful improvement of the local living conditions for the Black community.

Frances Harper equates the requirements for racial uplift in a flawed society to that of a doctor making a diagnosis and treating an ill patient. It is a medical doctor that is twice described as a fit partner for Iola's social, and therefore personal, interests. Iola's mother defeats the prejudices of her patient and Master through caring for his health as a nurse. As a result of this treatment, he literally frees her, as she has saved his life, and by intimation the life of the nation. Upon being liberated from bondage, Iola works as a nurse in the nearby military encampment, and this is where she faces her most obvious ethical challenges and the major part of the story first develops. It is as a nurse that she meets her first relative, her uncle, who was thought lost to slavery forever. It is as a nurse that she provides for the distinctions between the men in her life and the ambitions she should set for the future.

Frances Harper doesn't make the church and religious congregation the focus of organizational work by Iola Leroy and the other major characters in the novel. This may be surprising, given the heavy religious themes of Harper's poetry and the connections between Christianity and her service organizations. While pastors do make an appearance in public gatherings in the novel, no mention is made of the main characters going to church. Harper does not discuss the church as important to the cohesion of the Black community, but instead focuses on the personal moral principles derived from Christianity. The question that must be raised in this context is how Iola Leroy believed that people were to acquire their moral values? What was to form the basis for a community of knowledge and principle?

In 1853, at age 28, Frances Harper first published the essay "Christianity," which was subsequently included in the book *Poems on Miscellaneous Subjects*, published in 1857. This essay first brought her prose writing – in contrast to her poetry – to the attention of a wider readership. It established a religious context for the majority of her writing and political activism to come. In the essay, she describes how individual genius, art, philosophy, and science all concede their place, and contribute, to the wonder of the Christian faith (Harper, 1990b, p. 97). Describing it as systematic, uniform, and pure, Harper writes of Christianity as providing the courage, foresight, and joy required for human flourishing. Without equivocation, she subordinates the works of humankind to the truth of Christianity as she asserts that "Philosophy searches earth; Religion opens heaven. Philosophy doubts and trembles at the portals of eternity; Religion lifts the veil, and shows us golden streets, lit by the Redeemer's countenance, and irradiated by his smile. Philosophy strives to reconcile us to death, Religion triumphs over it" (Harper, 1990b, p. 98). For Harper, the Bible offered a moral guide through the trials of a life. But this description of faith is distinct from the church itself.

The idea of caring for others, of a dedication to the welfare of other persons, that is developed in the life of Iola Leroy arises from her understanding of the trauma and conflict that she had experienced. Prior to her enslavement, Iola, while a generous person socially with her equals, is contemptuous and dismissive of the lives of slaves, describing them as servants. By not acknowledging the place of slavery in her own life, and not understanding what slavery was to those who were enslaved, Iola is set up by Harper for a fall that transforms her into the avatar for social change that is necessary for the coming community. A key aspect of the experience of slavery that Harper offers up, which must be resolved to heal the community, is the sexual assault of Black women slaves by their owners (Harper, 1892, p. 115).

Intimacy

In the initial pages of the novel, the intimate relationship between Robert and his Mistress is referenced, but when we first encounter Iola Leroy it becomes apparent for the reader that Frances Harper is willing to address the matter of race, intimacy, and community head on. She views the choices people make when choosing intimate partners as parallel to that of defining racial difference, asking what difference is supposed to make a difference for someone who maintains that race matters? But Harper does more than merely describe interracial desire – throughout the novel, she returns to this idea of intimacy and choices as a model for how the Black community should approach the problem of a White racism, anchored in segregation, that seeks to make personal relationships its fulcrum. Harper provides an important description of the sort of political activism required to resist and eventually overcome a definition of racial difference based on social segregation.

It is after Iola, acting as a nurse and friend of the patient, kisses the forehead of the Black man, Tom Anderson, upon his death, that Dr. Gresham reacts. He thinks Iola is White, and explains to the Army officer, Captain Sybil, who is a Quaker, that "I can eat with colored people, walk, talk, and fight with them, but kissing them is something I don't hanker after" (Harper, 1892, p. 57). Iola's ability to supposedly reach across the racial divide to provide the care that Tom needs in that moment is too much for Dr. Gresham. That Iola was herself sexually assaulted by her White Masters – her phenotypical markers of fair skin, long hair, and blue eyes notwithstanding – is something the reader already understands. The doctor's response therefore doubles down on the social distance required to maintain racial categories. Since she is Black, as a slave she could be assaulted with relative impunity by a Master, and then her kissing Tom is acceptable. If she is White, her sorrowful mien and purpose for being a nurse in the Army camp require explanation, just as does the kiss. Dr. Gresham thinks he is owed an explanation for how she could kiss a Black person, as he says he could not himself. That the two men discuss this together, and Captain Sybil feels compelled to offer an explanation, provides insight into how White confirmation of a difference from Black people is produced today.

The easy assumption that the two could discuss the racial proclivities of someone else, that they would in fact be in the habit of monitoring and disciplining socially the behaviors of those also considered White, is ominous when thought of this way. They are referencing not Iola's appearance – blue eyes, long hair, and fair skin – but her family. As the saying goes, "You can't help who your parents are," and they resort to this common theme of racial difference to allow Captain Sybil to inadvertently warn off Dr. Gresham.

Captain Sybil expresses that he doesn't see why Iola being Black should dampen the ardor of Dr. Gresham, demonstrating how Whiteness could exist alongside the political activism being developed through Iola Leroy. Later in the novel, Harper does attend to the problem of how Whiteness as a social idea is developed between persons, through claims of common ancestry and family ties, social behaviors, appearance, and language use – things that depend on social segregation for their delineation. But in the moment between the men, the reader can see the racial differentiation that allowed for Iola's original enslavement reproduced in the gazes of the two White men in the Army camp.

The idea of race is still a problem for Gresham, who initially balks at continuing his love interest but then, in time, capitulates. He does this because of what Iola represents for the reader: the idea of a future racial equality developed through social proximity and attention to the needs of the Black community. It is not only her care for others, as a symbol of how to resolve the animosity and contempt that racial difference requires, that weakens Gresham's convictions. After all, the idea of care that allowed for her mother to marry her father depended on Marie, and therefore Iola, becoming White. This ethic of care was defined by the refusal of racial equality, requiring that slavery define the difference between racial categories, and that everyone define Whiteness as a necessary precondition for freedom.

What weakens Gresham's resolve to reject Iola is that he begins to see the arbitrary designation of racial difference in her person, and finds support for this in his social attachment to her. If he finds her desirable, how can she be Black? Since he must remain White, so should she become White, as her mother chose to (Harper, 1892, pp. 58–9). She refuses, and he is unable to leave aside his own social investment in a Whiteness that now reveals itself as ethically bankrupt. Why can't she lie to his mother, and to their eventual children, as she was lied to? We should be careful, however, in attributing to Frances Harper the idea that social proximity is enough to assuage the descriptions of racial difference. This is why Iola's availability to sexual assault as a slave is hinted at, and the language used by Whites to describe Black people they are socializing with throughout the novel does not necessarily reflect the idea of equality.

In *Iola Leroy*, Frances Harper provides a vision of racial equality predicated on an idea of Black self-sufficiency and moral rectitude, rather than the provision of assistance and resources by White Northerners or Southerners. The well-meaning and charitable White person that is a fixture of Black stories of advancement today is missing in the novel. In part, this is because of how we define social equality today, as companionship and interaction across racial lines, as though merely interacting is a sign of progress after the decades of Jim Crow segregation. In the novel, Black characters do not rely on the support of Whites or the idea that White approval is required for them to thrive against racism and inequality, a position that sets Frances Harper apart from other writers at the time.

The text argues that, if left alone and facing no great obstacle, Black people will quickly become equal partners in the national political and economic landscape. Iola's husband the doctor, and her uncle, the owner of a successful hardware store, are examples of the rewards of thrift and industry in the period after the Civil War. The reprisals and violence by Whites given in other accounts of the period aren't missing from the novel, but they occur as background conditions rather than as something Iola and her family must contend with directly. These events just aren't central to the story or to her ambition.

It is hard to shake the feeling that the perfection of Iola and her family is described as an antidote to the anxieties of a readership that otherwise is concerned about the contributions of Black people to their society. It is simply not enough that the Black characters in the novel are smart, thrifty, and Christian; they also must be without any criticism of the existing democratic institutions in the society. In the novel, there are no radical positions, but instead those of conformity and democratic association. Public platforms, elections, and private conversations all affirm the value for African Americans of contributing to the ambitions of the nation to heal from the effects of a devastating war, and to make a home equal to those of White Americans.

Frances Harper develops a principled politics of intervention, ministering to the ills of society, portraying enslavement as immoral, a recoverable lapse in the health of the national body. This perspective is one that is global, something applicable by the government, in the form of the Northern Army and its struggle and victory over the Southern rebellion. But there is also a repetition of the theme of individual debauchery and sin, moral decay, related to the fact that slavery allowed for depravity and acts of shame by Masters and Mistresses. This portrayal was a rebuke to the prevailing narrative among those who increasingly sought to deny Black people opportunities and rights, on the grounds of their supposed debasement and immorality (Carby, 1989, pp. 92–3; Painter, 1996, pp. 230–3; Parker, 2010, pp. 130–1).

Ways of being

The recipe for a future of social harmony and racial equality described throughout the novel isn't material success or activist organizations, but finding something in common

with one's oppressors, so that they understand the consequences of injustice as also negatively impacting their own
lives. The defeat of the Southern planter class in the Civil
War was, for the reader in 1892, still a palpable social stigma
that represented real material loss from which recovery had
been difficult. Their former property was now demanding
evidence of a political equality that could only be denied
through violence and extra-legal local initiatives to deny
due process, the vote, and other protections available otherwise to Blacks in the law. To this overturning of the social
order was added the idea of Black social equality to Whites,
a loss of the social distance from Black people afforded to
Whiteness as a socially re-enforced and reproduced idea.

Frances Harper was no stranger in the 1890s to the
attempts by Whites to enforce social norms of exclusion
and hierarchy in the aftermath of the War, and she was a
central participant in the organizational struggles to ensure
rights for Black people in the decades that followed. In 1892,
when *Iola Leroy* was published, race science was in its heyday
throughout the academy in the US. Experiments supposedly
proving the differences between Whites and Blacks were
important to the argument for a new social order and the
denial of political rights for Black people. Martin Delany,
whom Frances Harper knew well, having published her
short story "The Two Offers" already in 1859 in the first
issue of the *Anglo African Magazine*, alongside his serialized
novel *Blake; or, the Huts of America*, was the leading African
American scientist attempting to refute the campaign to use
scientific methods to prove racial differences (Delany, 2017).
Frances Harper includes Delany's argument against this "science" in the novel, in an evening gathering of Iola and her
friends.

In spite of this intervention in the novel to make sure the
reader is exposed to the rebuttal to these popular arguments

for an innate Black inequality, in order to make a claim against racial difference, Frances Harper is aware that she has to reach outside of the scientific argument. She can't explain the problem of racial inequality through a description of the material difference in access to resources, markets, and education. There was no argument for social prejudice, just as today, that doesn't merely beg the question of how a person came to consider race as a useful surrogate for disparities of condition. Harper has to demonstrate the equality of those who are defined as Black, and to show how Black life matters to Whites in ways that commit everyone to a politics of racial equality.

Harper also cannot put forward this argument by appealing to the political rights of Black men. In 1892, the dominant discourse outside of the claims of the Suffragist Movement relegated women to the status of dependents on men in their families. There was also an increasingly acrimonious division between White women and Black women organizers at the national level, as a consequence of the reluctance of the major Temperance and Suffragist associations to fight against the collapse of the promise of rights for Black people in the decades since the War. In a speech in 1891 to the National Council on Women, titled "Duty to Dependent Races," Frances Harper describes how no claim of success by individual Black men can obviate the counter-claim of racial inferiority (Field, 2015, p. 119; Stancliff, 2011, pp. 131–2). Instead, some form of universal claim to a common humanity must be offered, in which men and women are considered equals, as are Black and White people. Those who say that men are superior to women, and then say that Whites are superior to Black people, must be confronted not by accepting the terms of difference but by claiming that something establishes a prior equality. The alternative is to view a hierarchy of racial and gendered difference that doesn't depend on the actions of any one person, and is immutable.

For Frances Harper, this idea of human equality was premised on the relationship all humans had to a Christian God. If all humans were equal in his eyes, this established an equality that could bind all of humanity together. The response to racism and sexism for Frances Harper, therefore, lies in demonstrating this common equality of condition to those who would argue otherwise. Of what did this equality consist for Harper? In the figure of Iola Leroy, we see how Harper imagines an egalitarianism based on a common capacity for true intimacy and companionship. Rather than concede the value of racial difference or gender difference, Iola refuses the offer to love where this equality is not found. She is independent of purpose from the ambitions of the men in her life and does not define her own worth to others based on the men in her family. Instead, Iola seeks out relationships on her own terms. Dr. Gresham is capable of loving her because of this very capacity for equality that Iola represents for him, in spite of the fact that she is Black. She refuses the offer to truncate her own fundamental sense of equality for marriage, signaling to the reader the terms for negotiating the conditions necessary for a radical egalitarianism.

Corrine Field suggests that this egalitarianism in the work of Frances Harper was described in terms of assisting the least advantaged (Field, 2015, pp. 117–21). She observes that the argument Harper would make in her speeches and in her writing was based on an appeal, to those who viewed racial difference as important, to consider instead a Christian charity toward those less fortunate. I disagree. The reader of *Iola Leroy* is immediately struck by the relationships of equality that Iola desires to create with those around her, in terms of purpose and the capacity for ideas and actions of importance to her. When confronted by racism, for example in her

workplace in the North after the War, Iola does not appeal
to the idea of being unemployed or needing money, but
argues only in terms of the injustice of the claims of a racial
inequality that would prohibit her from being as valuable in
the workplace. Iola also does not define herself by her charitable works for the least advantaged, but by her own capacity
to be generous to everyone she encounters. Some she helps;
others she does not need to.

While Frances Harper had to make an appeal to a non-
hierarchical egalitarianism against the claims of racial and
gender differences being used in the society, this was not
merely directed toward erasing material and social differences. Harper's position pushed listeners and readers
to acknowledge the mistake they were making by defining the human condition in racial and gender terms at all.
Galvanizing an audience to care about the plight of those
without the vote and few rights, those without the welfare to
survive or in desperate need of assistance, could be done only
within a community of persons with common values, within
the circles of race and gender equality already developed in
the associations and organizations which she was a member
of and spoke to.

In the novel *Iola Leroy*, Frances Harper has to show how
human equality is the precondition for all that follows, and
the two choices that Iola makes – to be Black, and a woman
equal to men – are made not because others attempt to limit
her capacity for action, but because she understands that
there is nothing innate to these hierarchies of value that she
need obey. In other words, the story of Iola Leroy is that
of a woman who thinks at first that she must define herself
through the men in her life, and the death of her father disa-
buses her of that notion. Then she learns that being Black
isn't a matter of appearance, but a struggle against the definition of racial inferiority, when she is enslaved. After this

crucible of experiences, Iola is able to understand that her own value does not depend on the desires of men or those of White people, but instead on how she meets others and develops relationships to those around her. The actions of Iola in the novel are disarming in their commitment to egalitarian action. This is, of course, exactly what Frances Harper is hoping to convey.

Instead of a Christian charity, Iola represents in her actions toward Tom Anderson, and others throughout the novel who need her assistance, an equality of status that for the reader represents the racial and gender equality that Frances Harper is trying to develop in them. This is not the Christianity of good works and charity toward those least advantaged, as though some are of different status and to be pitied, but an acknowledgment of having to model the equality of all humans in the relationships that we develop with others. In this context, Frances Foster is correct when she describes Frances Harper's conceptualization of Christianity as a civil religion (Foster, 1990). How effective was this appeal when the book was published? We know the novel sold very well, and we do read it today, now that it becomes possible again to entertain a more expansive idea of racial and gender equality than was possible between the 1890s and 1950s. *Iola Leroy* is an example of the political road not taken in the nation.

The argument that Frances Harper develops against race, explicitly based on Christian values, is similar to that found in the speeches much earlier, in 1830, by Maria Stewart (Richardson, 1987), and follows a tradition of thinking about race and Christianity that included Sojourner Truth and many others in the generation before Frances Harper (Painter, 1996). The source of moral surety is biblical, and the conviction is assumed as something held in common with readers. Those seeking to up-end the hierarchies of race and

gender had to appeal to a text that was held in common with
their opponents, to establish a moral or ethical imperative
against the types of ideas that would allow for slavery and
the refusal of the vote for women. Today, this explicit reference to a common Christianity may seem too parochial
or misplaced, but we should in turn answer the question
ourselves of what forms the basis today of our criticism of
racial injustice, our own actions with reference to moral
problems? What do we claim in common with those who
see us as also always available to ill treatment, based on an
inequality of difference we are told to accept? Throughout
Iola Leroy, Frances Harper explicitly asks us in her modeling
of relationships between characters to consider the difference between a condescension that reifies and hardens our
distinctions of race and gender, even as it ministers to the
material and social needs of those we assist, and an equality
that we must allow to come forth as the basis of who we are,
in spite of the differences of station between persons.

In "Enlightened Motherhood," Harper outlines the duties
of mothers and repeats the messages from *Iola Leroy* regarding the artistry she feels is required of motherhood – the
need to provide guidance for children through love, to give
the innocent the knowledge they need to resist temptation,
and to guide their steps into adulthood. She adds the caution against marrying a man of poor moral character, writing
that a woman when building a home "should be careful not
to build it above the reeling brain of the drunkard or the
weakened fibre of a debauchee" (Farrar, 2015, p. 67; Harper,
1990c, p. 287). For Harper, a home requires that a woman
be able to determine men of character, self-respect, and
self-control.

Harper is clear that women, and particularly Black women
in this situation after the Civil War, must do the work to
redeem the family as an idea, and thereby also the home as

the basis for the nation. This larger project of which she speaks is more than simply a concern with the sins of a single person or the needs of a local community, as she places the responsibility for how the health and wellbeing, the character, of the nation develop in the future in the hands of women. Invoking the figure of Mary establishes the concept of heredity and culpability that she wishes her audience to embrace as their own, and it also sets the scale of moral supervision that she demands of them. This is where her own Christian faith in the importance of individual works is explicit. To change the society, for Harper, is to work on the sanctity of one person at a time, to work as a mother and woman to teach the children and the men, and to build first a righteous home, and then from this a just and true society.

But what is the content that is to be communicated to the world by Black women, in a way that this is both accessible to those without significant literary training and available as a measure or value that can be assessed by others? To determine the credibility of a moral system in the breach isn't the same as confirming its values through successful compliance by its adherents. Frances Harper also sees her own contribution to those around her – the legacy of what at this point was more than 40 years of writing, public speaking, and organizational commitments – as occurring within this Christian ideal.

In the novel, Frances Harper writes approvingly of how Iola's mother Marie redeems the fallen status of the slave Master Eugene by nursing him back to health after the years of dissolution had taken a terrible toll on him, mentally and physically (Harper, 1892, p. 71). Though this assistance is provided to him from her position as a slave, her ministering of care and attention allows him to recover, fall in love, and become both an advocate for racial equality and an upright individual henceforth. The contrast that this relationship sets up between a racial political equality that depends on racial social equality and that of a description of a necessary social hierarchy is made explicit by Frances Harper through a conversation between Eugene and his cousin Lorraine, as Eugene explains why he will not be content to keep Marie as his slave now that she has provided him with the moral perspective necessary for his survival (p. 68). Again, we can see how Frances Harper perceives racism as a deadly illness for the nation. Lorraine objects vehemently to the idea of Eugene marrying someone Black, no matter her appearance, and refuses any possibility of racial social equality:

> Lorraine says, "But has not society the right to guard the purity of the blood by the rigid exclusion of an alien race?"
> Eugene asks, "Excluding it? How?"
> "By debarring it from social intercourse."
> "Perhaps it has," continued Eugene, "but should not society have a greater ban for those who, by consorting with an alien race, rob their offspring of a right to their names and to an inheritance in their property, and who fix their social status among an enslaved and outcast race?"
>
> (pp. 66–7)

Lorraine continues to explain how one drop of Black blood taints all of the favorable characteristics of the person to make them inferior and unsuitable for social equality. For Eugene, this social norm is defeated by a new understanding of the virtues of an equality represented by the Black slave. That someone might be enslaved despite being virtuous and pure of heart, human as much as himself, seems now reprehensible to a person who is a Christian in the way that Eugene describes himself. The renewed faith fostered by Marie provides no alternative for Eugene but manumission and marriage, to make right the relationship between them. To up-end the hierarchy of values described by racism requires for Eugene a recognizable moral acknowledgment of the intimacy that he shares with Marie as his wife. Frances Harper's message of the duty of morality as requiring the political equality of persons is unequivocal. Eugene is unmoved by the disgust and contempt of Lorraine at his newly discovered moral commitment.

The same intervention occurs later in the novel between Iola and her brother Harry's uncle, Robert Johnson, when the older man is said to be an important guide to the younger man through the perils of youthful temptation in society. And, of course, it is through Iola's nursing of soldiers at the military encampment that Dr. Gresham first is infatuated, and then tries to reject racial differences as unimportant to falling in love with her. Iola's devotion, later, to tending to the educational needs of the newly free slaves then becomes a form of call to action for every reader, just as it is the most important purpose for her. This isn't personal, but representative of a collective ambition, one that defines a national purpose or goal in racial equality, in contrast to the efforts of those who would at the time create slavery by another name and otherwise ensure the conditions for Black inequality.

It was only through addressing the collective needs of a population with equal political rights in the society that the United States could resolve the democratic crisis of social inequality that existed in the 1890s in the society. Today, as a result of the successes of the Civil Rights Movement in the 1950s and 1960s, in the US we have formal political rights that are eroded by the reproduction and reinforcement of a stultifying racial and gender social inequality. In the novel, Frances Harper uses the position of social equality to challenge the argument against political equality. She presents an ethic of care in which individuals assist other persons, a sacrifice not of worldly cares, of a decent standard of living and material success, but of bringing the skills and training of an individual to uplift the moral condition and political ambitions of the nation.

Harper describes a life of equal service among persons, but the novel makes clear that, for Iola Leroy and this generation born after the War, the concerns are first the needs of Black people and women. Iola does remark on the poor education and living conditions of fellow Black people as the reason for her calling, but does so with an acknowledgment of their inherent equality to Whites, just as she does in her relationships with men throughout the novel. She and her family represent in this way not only a social equality but a political one, an assumption of equal rights in the new description of the nation. The novel is thereby the first such articulation of the rights of Black people as citizens of the United States after the end of slavery. It provides a recipe for how Black people and women can assist in achieving this goal as individuals.

Iola Leroy should also be thought of as a response to the rise of legal codes and strictures described in the 14th Amendment, which limited the social extension of the racial political equality. In fact, Frances Harper has an example in the novel of an incident in a railway car similar to that experienced by Homer Plessy, in which Harry Leroy is asked to move from the car reserved for Black people because he looks White, as he is sitting there and talking with his darker-skinned companion Lucille Delany. Eventually his status as a Black person is acknowledged and he is allowed to remain, but the similarity to the arrest of Plessy that led to the case *Plessy* v. *Ferguson* is notable for what it implies about the egalitarian politics that Frances Harper wants the reader to accept (Harper, 1892, p. 245). Unlike in the case of Homer Plessy, Harry insists he is Black, and that he therefore can sit in the section reserved for Black people. He doesn't want to sit with Whites on the train, just as Iola refuses to marry Dr. Gresham if this means having to pretend she is White. To be White is not more advantageous than to be Black when measured against the moral authority of equality between persons.

The call to action

In her description of the heroine Iola Leroy, Frances Harper created a character who doesn't care about educating Whites about how Black people have the same humanity and innate talents as they do, but, rather, focuses on improving the lot of those she feels have been mistreated and reviled. Iola Leroy provides a model of political activism as a calling, which is the first description in widely read literature by a Black author of what today is a common role for an individual in the Black community and larger population: that of the social activist and educator. Frances Harper was herself similar to Iola Leroy in her professional ambition and personal life, and it is not a coincidence that she took the popular pseudonym for Ida B. Wells, "Iola," as the name of her protagonist and the book's title. In her activism against lynching, Ida B. Wells modeled the type of fearless equality of result sought by Frances Harper herself. They knew each other well, and Frances Harper likely perceived Wells as representing in her person the next generation of Black woman activists.

If we do not attend to this call to equality that defines the plot of the novel, the financial wealth and material comfort of Iola and her family place the story in a strange historical vacuum. The choices the characters make are not based on scarcity or the absence of special skills that are in high demand. The narrative follows the generation after those newly freed, whose plight is no longer immediate or pressing. Instead of taking on a problem of recovery in the South and healing of the nation, Harper makes a claim against the background of what hasn't worked, a story of how things came to be as they were. To ask the reader to recall the chaos and urgency of needs immediately after the War is to create a narrative about what they were doing, how they survived, and the choices that they made that led to the rise of a concerted White collective action campaign to circumvent the progress made in granting Black people rights in the decades since the War. For Iola to choose a Black struggle is therefore to argue that this is one thing that defines the nation – the problem of racial inequality and injustice.

The novel remakes a story about the War and its aftermath in this second-generational context, which makes the assumption of the family wealth itself an appeal to how Black people now are to live – a provocative presentation of normalcy and social expectation. In 1892, the retrenchment of White control was in full swing throughout the South, and the North was allowing for a corresponding limitation of the rights of Blacks. A romantic view of Black progress, social struggle, and financial success in the novel was important as a measure of how much had changed and where problems still existed in the country with regard to race. It was a call to action, even as the distance for the reader from the real events depicted in the novel make the realism of the situation – in terms of the abject poverty, uncertainty, and anxiety of the former slaves at that time – less important. The depiction of the largesse of the newly prosperous cooperative farm that was a former slave plantation toward the bereft and now-poor former Mistress, for example, speaks to this idea of how the reader should remember what happened, and how the future might look if Black people were given the rights that they should have.

White equality

Instead of describing Whiteness as a comprehensive condition whereby it is impossible to perceive the equality of Black people, Frances Harper describes, through the characters in the novel, a choice that individuals have concerning how White people accept Black equality. That this is a choice available to all persons who are White, in both the North and the South, is explicit. Similarly, Frances Harper makes it obvious that the realization of Black equality by White people does not thereby make Black people indebted or obligated to these individuals, who can then work alongside them as equals for this greater good. In fact, Iola Leroy turns away from the prospect of marrying Dr. Gresham not because he is White, but because he is unable to fulfill the promise of an equality that would force his family to accept his choice of a Black partner. He is unable to join Iola in her life's call to lift up Black people. He is willing to let race be a fact of his social life, rather than require an equality that she demands, and he is unable to share in the goals of a gender equality of purpose, to agree to her decisions about how they should live their life. He fails both choices provided to him by his relationship with Iola.

Interestingly, the novel does not provide an example of a White person who acts with equality toward Black people, leaving the burden of this decision up to the reader. In this perspective, the entire novel can be viewed as a call to conscience for those who continue to argue for a racial inequality that, for Iola, and Frances Harper and Ida B. Wells, is nonsensical. Even Captain Sybil, in his question as to why

Robert Johnson doesn't pretend he is Black, assumes that Whiteness is something better – different in quality than being Black. Even though Sybil does this by referencing how much easier Robert's life would be, the implication is that, in fact, Whiteness is the better choice for anyone who can become White, so to speak.

The novel develops two examples of people who, because they are White, act in ways that are reprehensible and immoral. The first is Lorraine, the cousin of Iola Leroy's father Eugene, who is not only a wastrel but furious with Eugene for freeing and marrying Marie. Once Eugene dies, Lorraine inherits the estate and promptly proceeds to nullify the freedom and marriage papers. He then tricks Iola into coming south so she can be remanded into slavery as well. We are told through the words of his agent that "Lorraine knows her market value too well, and is too shrewd to let so much property pass out of his hands without making an effort to retain it" (Harper, 1892, p. 102). His role in the novel is limited to these actions, since we are not given insight into how he sold Iola or the events around his treatment of her mother. Iola speaks only in vague terms of violation and brutish treatment meted out upon her because of her status as a slave.

The second example is that of Iola herself, when, at school in the North and still oblivious to her racial status, she speaks of Black slaves as poor specimens of humanity in need of assistance to achieve the social status of those who are White. She says, for example, "My father says that slaves would be very well contented if no one put wrong notions in their heads" (Harper, 1892, p. 98). Once she realizes that she is herself Black and is remanded into slavery through deceit, Iola admits to having been venal and uninformed. She regrets her callousness, but remarks on it as a problem of how Whites in her situation would talk together about race and Black people. The casual neglect of the cost, to

Masters and Mistresses and the slaves, of the brutal practices of enslavement in these conversations comes back to haunt Iola, as she recalls thinking, as a young woman at school in the North, that the servants on her plantation were both content and well taken care of.

The assumption of Whiteness by the person innocent of their own status – in this case, Iola – allows for their description of Black inferiority. The implication of this assumption is that, absent some form of not merely empathy but a counter-politics of equality, a person is vulnerable to ideas of prejudice. As Harper has young Iola say in defense of slavery to her friend who is critical of slavery, while at boarding school, "our slaves do not want their freedom. They would not take it if we gave it to them" (Harper, 1892, pp. 97–8).

Iola's early misunderstanding of her own circumstances reveals how ideas of race are more enduring than any one individual, providing for a topography, a blanketing field of social meanings that define the concepts used by persons to make sense of their world. This interpretation of how race is available as an idea for individuals coincides with how Frances Harper describes the differences between the North and the South. In the North, Harper has Dr. Gresham say that most Whites don't like slavery and don't like the African American. The description of racial difference as defined by enforced social distance and limited – if any – political rights for Black people in the North was perceived as superior to the institutional processes that reproduced enslavement. That both regions had slaves and free Black people prior to the Civil War is an important fact to remember, as often today we think of the South as the only place slaves were present in the United States. For example, Sojourner Truth was a slave in the North, not the South, and Frances Harper would have lived with slaves in her vicinity both in Ohio and in New York.

The presence of slaves would be a constant reminder for Frances Harper of the conditions that also defined her own life as a Black person prior to the Civil War. The South as a region was thought of as the source of the processes of enslavement because of the structure of its economy. *Iola Leroy*, and Frances Harper's other texts that consider Black life prior to the Civil War, are unique in that they consider the perceptions of free Blacks and those who are passing without knowing they are Black, and are not a study of how Black slaves experienced the lives of free Blacks or Whites around them.

The focus of the novels on the problem of being free and Black amidst slaves, and of those who were the children of White Masters by slaves, who were then sent North to be allowed to pass as White, reveals a concern felt by Frances Harper for the conditions of Black freedom during slavery, and provides a topography of racial social consequences. For example, in her earlier novel *Minnie's Sacrifice*, Frances Harper provides a real-world example of a Black slave who arrives at a safe house on the Underground Railroad, only to die from exhaustion due to the trauma of his escape. That the slave dies on the very threshold of his freedom, having reached his destination, in the house of succor owned by White abolitionists, is for Harper an example of how fraught the distinction between slave and free was, how difficult the journey across the conceptual landscape, rather than being a simple statement of a difference in status. That the arrival of the escapee heralds the transformation of the heroine in *Minnie's Sacrifice* from White to Black isn't a coincidence, but provides important context to explain the tragedy of the experience of race. The young woman, Minnie, exclaims at one point how terrible it would be to be Black and experience the prejudice of others – only to soon discover she is in fact Black, as well.

The events from *Minnie's Sacrifice* are repeated in *Iola Leroy* published more than 24 years later, when Iola finds out that she is Black only in the moment of being enslaved. Her White characteristics are not enough to spare her when a particular description of racial difference is suddenly enforced. The cousin, Lorraine, employs slave catchers to journey north for her, but these two men have a conversation when they arrive where Iola Leroy is studying, about the moral bankruptcy associated with what they are about to do. These characters provide a contrast for the reader with the principal of the school, who has known Iola's racial heritage and who suspects something when they ask to see her. Their confrontation makes a point about the capacity for someone White to determine how to apply the social consequences of being Black. The principal has known all along and never had issue with Iola being Black or with her ignorance of this fact. Frances Harper addresses this idea of partial enforcement through events in both novels, revealing the perfidy of race as an idea through the differential application of its meanings. The very arbitrariness of the assignment of a prohibition on social equality is used by Harper to demonstrate the claim that race is both immoral and a condition not of nature but of human decision.

Through the many juxtapositions in the stories within the novels, Frances Harper clearly conveys that race is a concept used to arbitrarily decide how to treat people differently, usually with very tragic consequences. Within this conceptualization of race, it is possible both that someone who is White could seek intimate relations with their slave and sell their own children, and that someone White could fall in love and free the slave, hiding from their children the fact of their racial heritage. How does race work as a social idea in a way that sometimes it matters as a prohibition and sometimes it doesn't? Why is it observed most often in the breach of rules of difference with regard to intimate and personal relationships? In the novels, race is used as a way to manipulate others, to control the actions of persons according to immoral desires between men and women, within families.

One of the most important aspects of the novels of Frances Harper is her use of the tropes of family, sexual intimacy, and love to display the contradictions in racial assignments. For contemporary readers, the novels seem a flurry of relationships and personal choices that are easily overlooked as superficial and hard to puzzle out, just because today we experience race behind a similarly rigid prohibition of intimate relationships between races. We react with betrayal when someone reveals they are passing as White, or when someone claims to be Black when they are White. There are still very few interracial relationships between Blacks and Whites, as this is one of the defining aspects of race – the prohibition of intimacy itself. Thus, the novels in which White men and women have forced intimate relations with their Black slaves seem doubly foreign today, in terms of both the authority permitted to one person because of racial status, and the idea of socially being permitted to admit and fulfill the desire by someone White to be intimate with someone Black. In the absence of enforcement mechanisms in the law to control the relationships between race, how is race defined today? It is through very explicit social norms and standards, rules of behavior, and sanctions.

We often prefer to view the definition of race as a problem today only in terms of employment discrimination, policing, and material resource inequality, because laws currently exist against these types of racial discrimination. In the 1960s, the importance of the law as a determinant of interracial social relationships – for example, against what was called miscegenation – was gradually eliminated across the country. In its place are laws against social actions that are defined as racially discriminatory, without thereby changing the social stigma and prejudice that arise from the material and social description of racial differences in the society. In other words, we currently have no mechanisms that directly encourage racial social equality, but rather laws that prohibit the social expression of racial prejudice. This distinction between encouragement and prohibition today makes it seem as though race is an expression of circumstance, where someone grew up, the jobs they have, their education, their wealth, and who they socialize with – a matter of culture, rather than condition. This acknowledgment of race by individuals therefore depends on the personal social policing of the description of racial differences – the ideas, for example, of having different social interests, of differences of perspective – rather than formal, legal prohibitions. The way that we think of racial difference today matters for how we read the descriptions of race in *Iola Leroy*.

For Frances Harper, race was, of course, a huge factor in her own living conditions, as a teacher, as a dairy farmer, and as a poet, defining the choices she was able to make as to career and the opportunities available for employment. However, Whites were expected to police the social description of Black inferiority, both in public and in their private relationships. The response by Dr. Gresham upon discovering that Iola Leroy is Black reflects that of Eugene's cousin Lorraine; there is a difference that is supposed to make an indelible difference, then, in social status, such that intimate personal relationships are not to be those between equals. Relationships between owner and slave are stigmatized but acceptable. This was the fate that Iola escaped when she was freed, and which her mother Marie partially finessed by being manumitted, but their equality with Eugene and those who were White in their environment was never fully accepted.

This requirement of inequality between Black and White people is perfectly demonstrated by how Frances Harper describes the actions of the cousin after Eugene Leroy dies. Lorraine, having filed suit with a local judge for ownership of his cousin Eugene's property, surprises Marie with the fact that he is now her owner and that she has been remanded into slavery in a terrible scene of social subordination. After telling her about these circumstances, Lorraine describes the situation thus, "Judge Starkins has decided that your manumission is unlawful; your marriage a bad precedent and inimical to the welfare of society; and that you and your children are remanded to slavery" (Harper, 1892, p. 96). Gresham, on the other hand, after thinking about it for some time, finds that personally he can set aside his social prejudice, he can love Iola as an equal, so long as he doesn't have to address the social stigma that Eugene and Marie experienced, and Iola agrees to pass as White. When it comes to racial inequality, public opinion, which is where social relationships are formed, is too great a thing to manage for Gresham.

In *Iola Leroy*, Harper largely – but not completely – elides what today would be considered a traditional approach to the study of the justice of racial difference, in favor of the study of how race is defined within the most personal and intimate of relationships. This is a powerful decision, and challenges the reader of today to consider how we also use race socially to decide how we live with others, and the price that we are willing to pay for allowing race to exist as a social idea. The seeming innocence of youthful teasing and mocking, and the claims of inferiority and pity expressed by Iola Leroy – when she perceives herself as also White – in conversation with her peers, becomes something much more sinister, a debilitating self-abnegation, once she finds out that she is Black. Harper provides this social description of racial difference by Iola

Leroy as a form of self-mockery to the reader, as we know that she is in fact Black. Harper describes race in the novel as something internally inconsistent, as something that, if the purveyor of the social concept could understand their own situation, would embarrass them. What is Whiteness after all but hubris? What differences are worth holding on to in the context of a description of a commonality with other humans that always must be true?

Late in the novel, Frances Harper has Iola and Dr. Latimer discuss what can be considered *Iola Leroy's* express purpose for the reader. Dr. Latimer says,

> "Miss Leroy, out of the race must come its own thinkers and writers. Authors belonging to the white race have written good racial books, for which I am deeply grateful, but it seems to be almost impossible for a white man to put himself completely in our place. No man can feel the iron that enters another man's soul." "Well, Doctor, when I write a book I shall take you for the hero of the story."
>
> (Harper, 1892, p. 263)

Iola goes on to explain that this is because he refused his grandmother's offer to bequeath him her wealth if he would only pass as White. He turned down the promise of material comfort and ease, social equality with White people, and the absence of racial social prejudice to work on behalf of the Black community of which he is a part. Explaining that he was merely doing what he felt was his duty, Iola responds, "But ... when others are trying to slip out from the race and pass into the white basis, I cannot help admiring one who acts as if he felt that the weaker the race is the closer he would cling to it" (Harper, 1892, p. 263).

The novel is, therefore, not about the problem of passing – of how someone knowing they are Black pretends to be

White – as this perspective, according to Iola and Harper, derives from the attempt to define racial difference as a social prohibition, which is shared by Blacks and Whites. Nor is the novel about the plight of light-skinned Black people, in contrast to those who are darker. The issue of color was not the subject of Frances Harper's novels, and became only gradually a means for enforcing racial meaning by Blacks as well as Whites – as it is today – in the absence of regular intimate relations during Jim Crow. Dr. Latimer, in the conversation quoted above, states this explicitly: "My mother . . . faithful and true, belongs to that race. Where else should I be?" (Harper, 1892, p. 263). He then goes on to point out to Iola that she in fact could also have passed but instead sought out her lost relations, in effect seeking her connections to Black people in doing so. When she was bereft and alone, she refused the offer to pass into material comfort and security, in a parallel to Dr. Latimer.

The novel *Iola Leroy* is clear that someone who can pass shouldn't, because they lay aside their moral claims of equality in doing so, accepting that to be Black is also something to be hidden or concealed out of shame. Eugene Leroy admits this implicitly when he decides with Marie that the fact that the children are Black should be kept from them. After an incident in which a girl is discovered to be Black at Iola's boarding school in the North, and the mother of two other children attending the school objects to the girl's presence, Eugene describes how, "it is more than a figment of my imagination that has made me so loth to have our children know the paralyzing power of caste" (Harper, 1892, p. 91).

After she refuses the marriage proposal of Dr. Gresham, Iola Leroy is again confronted directly with the possibility of passing, with her employment in the North. Iola is fired from her position after she is discovered to be Black, because of where she goes to church (Harper, 1892, p. 207).

Following this event, Iola realizes that her moral integrity requires that she tell employers that she is Black, and she is refused employment because of this decision. She is also refused living arrangements in a house run by Christian women because she informs them that she is Black. One of the matrons physically recoils from her when she learns this information (p. 209). The social segregation of race extends throughout Iola's life, from church to employment, but she doesn't waiver in her determination to challenge the effort to exclude Black people from the equal life that they require. Harper demonstrates a commitment to this collective justice by demonstrating to the reader Iola's resolve not to pass, and the injustice of each refusal Iola experiences. The double refusal – by her to pass, and then by Whites to accept her social equality – is designed by Harper to expose the reader to an understanding of what is required by someone Black, and what is required by someone White, to resolve the problem of racial injustice.

Iola eventually finds an employer who doesn't accept this description of racial difference and who states that all those who are currently employed who refuse to accept working alongside someone Black may leave his employment. Through these events, Harper is arguing that the problem of passing and color is created as a consequence of the idea of racial hierarchy, and therefore must be rejected as a correct moral decision by Iola, Harry, and Robert Johnson. This treatment of Iola should be considered as an indictment of White descriptions of racial social difference, and not as the basis for pity.

In a lengthy discussion of Whiteness in the novel, Robert Johnson describes how ownership and mastery did not provide one common definition of Whiteness. Just as Captain Sybil is a believer in racial political equality and yet is constrained by social norms to support racial social inequality,

Johnson describes how in the same way the owners of slaves could find ways to lessen the burdens of slavery or to make of slavery an opportunity for terrible violence and depredations upon their fellow humans. Johnson's owner taught him to read and count, and yet, when the Mistress' cousin was visiting the plantation and was told about how he had been taught, she said that, if she owned Johnson instead, she would immediately cut off his thumbs to stop this.

The response by the husband of his owner to this suggestion by the cousin reveals the perspective of White ownership that Harper wants to convey, in spite of the generosity and kindness of that particular authority. He says, "Oh, then he couldn't pick cotton." Johnson describes how in that moment it didn't seem to occur to any of the White slaver owners what Johnson would feel about losing his thumbs (Harper, 1892, p. 46). Johnson then recounts the story of how the sale of a woman's child from her, as an example of cruelty, led to her becoming a devout Christian. He contrasts this faith with that of the Masters and Mistresses, and his interlocutor Captain Sybil agrees, saying in turn that Christianity has been a "golden thread woven amid the somber tissue of their lives" (Harper, 1892, p. 48). Here, Frances Harper provides for the reader a moral compass by which to assess the actions of both Whites and Blacks during slavery, and suggests that race does not define faith and constancy, but, rather, human actions speak for themselves.

This argument about whether racial difference is natural or social, and therefore conditional on the desires of humans, is taken up in *Iola Leroy* in another example of the immorality described through a particular claim to Whiteness. Dr. Gresham coincidentally meets Iola Leroy years after she rejected his proposal. Now she has reunited her family and is, according to one of the arguments she made for rejecting his proposal, able to make a new decision as to the merits of their relationship. Iola rejects Dr. Gresham a second time because he still refuses to acknowledge racial difference as socially defined, relying instead on the idea of racial equality as defined biologically. This second rejection reaffirms the refusal by Frances Harper to accept passing into Whiteness as a position of social integrity. Instead, this possibility is described in the words of Iola Leroy as a betrayal of the conditions for racial equality.

While in town, Dr. Gresham stays at a hotel with another White gentleman, Dr. Latrobe, a Southerner who is adamant in his rejection of the idea of racial social equality. As in Lorraine's reaction, years earlier in the chronology of the story, at the announcement that Eugene Leroy will not only free Marie, the woman who has cared for him, but also marry her, Dr. Latrobe is vehement in this conviction of the social inferiority of Black people. Frances Harper sets up a scene where Dr. Gresham and another young man – the supposedly White doctor, Dr. Latimer – also staying at the hotel, have a dinner conversation with Dr. Latrobe and several Black guests. That even Dr. Latrobe must admire the force of the arguments by the Black guest Pastor Carmicle sets the stage for the final reveal, as Dr. Latrobe holds forth on his ability to identify the racial composition of his interlocuter – to be able to detect the taint of Black natural differences (Harper, 1892, pp. 238–9). Dr. Latimer reveals that he is, in fact, Black, and Dr. Latrobe angrily leaves the company, feeling tricked and lied to.

The book is a direct attack on the romantic perception, after the end of the Civil War almost 30 years earlier, that the social relationships of slavery, and thus the material relationships upon which they depended, were legitimate and moral. This scene between the doctors was also a direct refutation of the claims of race science developed by Herbert Spencer and others at the time, and Dr. Latimer echoes the claims of Martin Delany when he says that there are no biological determinants of racial difference that can be discovered as important to the description of human equality (Foreman, 2009, p. 104). That these material descriptions of racial inequality are not attributed to a social description of racial difference is tragic as it obscures the moral responsibility that should attach to these conditions for everyone.

Frances Harper provides a scene after the departure of Dr. Latrobe, where Dr. Gresham and Dr. Latimer share a laugh at having demonstrated the inconsistency, and therefore false pretentions, of those who claim that being White is a natural difference that must be acknowledged socially to preserve something important to the nation, individual integrity, and morality. At the end of the encounter, the reader, as with Dr. Latrobe, is unable to find a reason to persist in making a claim that racial difference is discoverable, and the rejection of race as something important to retain as an idea is explicit in the shared camaraderie of the White man Dr. Gresham and the Black man Dr. Latimer as they continue to eat breakfast together at the hotel. As Dr. Latimer remarks elsewhere in the novel, "This idea of social equality is only a bugbear which frightens well-meaning people from dealing justly with the negro" (Harper, 1892, p. 228).

Conclusion

In *Iola Leroy*, Frances Harper defends an idea of racial equality that today would be rejected by many readers as too radical. It requires that we accept racial differences as socially immoral, not as merely immaterial and an unnatural distinction of difference between humans. We readily accept today that someone Black or White has what we define as cultural, learned differences that are important to preserve as collective – not merely individual – differences. That these designations are applied then with difficulty to legal and informal descriptions of equality is taken as a part of how we develop the society – an inadequate and partial definition of racial equality at best, but at its worst a description of racial injustice that would immediately be recognizable to Frances Harper and her readers in 1892, as simultaneously abusive and damaging to persons. For example, when Dr. Latimer says that "The negro is not plotting in beer-saloons against the peace and order of society," this is Harper's attempt to refute the description of Black people as lascivious and immoral by White temperance activists (Harper, 1892, p. 223; Stewart, 2018, pp. 190, 195). Such a description of Black people as alcoholics and misanthropes persists as part of our racial politics today, as well. Harper's position of radical egalitarianism as a politics between persons is repudiated even to this day.

The most important claim in *Iola Leroy* is, therefore, given in the rejection of the suit of Dr. Gresham for the second time by Iola. When she claims that her calling to heal the wounds of slavery, experienced by Black people still years after the War, forces her to reject his proposal, this is done not out of a lack of sympathy or mutual admiration, but simply because her commitments to the needs of Black people, as representing the blight of inequality in the nation, matter to her more. That Dr. Gresham understands that he doesn't share this ambition personally does not mean that, as a White person, he couldn't become someone who, in the terms of the novel, began to care for the wounds of Black people caused by the effects of racial prejudice, but simply that injustice isn't important enough for his person. For Iola, the acceptance of White support is qualified by the requirement that they commit to securing Black community development and the healing of the wounds of racism. This presents a standard for acting with equality that Gresham, for all of his generosity toward Black people, cannot accept. That Iola subsequently falls in love and marries Dr. Latimer, who is introduced to her through Dr. Gresham, plays with the idea that, because he is Black, and has experience of racial prejudice, this collective designation, writ small and individual, provides just enough of the missing ingredient that then explains his dedication to the need for racial equality for the nation to progress.

For the contemporary reader, the language of hierarchy and difference seem confused in *Iola Leroy*. Racial inequality is described as existing within the framework of middle-class equality, and racial prejudice as existing divorced from material conditions, in contrast to the argument often made today that racial equality is defined by the possibility of class equality – the contemporary exceptional Black individual that achieves material parity with their White counterpart. Race is often in this way, today, falsely connected to a difference in material conditions. The definition is linked with the relationship that a person has to the means of production, rather than acknowledging, as does Frances Harper, that there is a difference between the claims of economic racial uplift and social inequality. Iola Leroy evinces no optimism about the capacity of economic progress to foster political equality, but suggests instead that it is the other way around. The Southern gentleman Dr. Latrobe has a similar class status to Dr. Latimer and Iola Leroy, but would never be social with them or admit to desiring social interaction with them as equals in care and intimacy, because they are Black.

Today, access to the argument against the perpetuation of racial social inequality is purposely obscured by this same definition of race. This is defined as the problem of individual attitudes and beliefs without reference to the processes by which someone comes to understand racial differences.

More than 120 years after the publication of *Iola Leroy*, the problem of race in our lives is just as prevalent. The economic effects of social exclusion and collective segregation have persisted, rather than been mitigated, over time. The answer provided by the politics of racial uplift that defines the life of Iola Leroy and Dr. Latimer is to appeal to a radical egalitarianism, in spite of the active constraints of the social definition of race revealed in the attitudes of Dr. Latrobe and Lorraine. If we consider that it was 60 years after the publication of *Iola Leroy* before there were effective social movement challenges – beginning with the Montgomery Bus Boycott – to the consolidation of economic resources through social differentiation, we can see that the strategy of not addressing the collective description of racial social inequality suggested by the indifference to the attitudes of Dr. Latrobe in the novel did not work. The capacity to monopolize political resources, as a racial difference for Whites in a representative democracy – through the extra-legal violence of lynching, economic expropriation, incarceration, and no legal recourse for Blacks – was effective at limiting the accumulation of resources for the latter. But this was not the problem of racial difference, the issue of equality as *Iola Leroy* develops, but rather the means by which to emphasize and reinforce the idea of a difference that – if not natural – was social, material, and permanent.

In *Iola Leroy*, Frances Harper appeals to her readers to build the type of community that is capable of embracing an idea of Blackness that isn't exclusionary. Her vision is one that is multiracial and political, discussing electoral representation and advocating the education of a middle class able to address the problem of Black political inequality. What Harper was providing is explicitly defined by the characters in the novel, and that is the idea of the creation of a new political community able to control the economic and social resources available to everyone, through a collective-action ethos based on individual equality. This explains the popularity of the novel in 1892. It offered hope for a free Black people one generation after slavery had ended, and held out a promise to everyone of something new and rewarding – the possibility of racial equality.

3

Trial and Triumph:
The Public Demand for Equality

Responsibility and judgment

The politics of equality that Frances Harper presented in *Iola Leroy* assumed a Black community that was united and striving together. Harper sought to provide a national purpose, a clear vision with which to rally against the deterioration of political rights for Black people. And she rightly saw this as an issue of gender as well as race. How might social equality develop to support and define the scope of hard-won political rights, if not in the mind and will of an ambitious and generous Black woman? It was through Iola Leroy's actions in the novel that the reader could envision a future democratic America, a place of writers and enlightened public conversation with a capacious description of equal citizenship. It is important to have provided this perspective so as to understand the ambition of its author – how, after a long life of activism, creative work, and public speaking, Frances

Harper brought together the threads of decades of public memory into a collective journey of human achievement.

Now we turn to a consideration of how Harper imagined gender and race as descriptions of the former slave and free Black community. What was the basis for equality within the relationships that could be described for those who had sloughed off their bonds and joined their fellow Black denizens in the aftermath of the Civil War? In *Trial and Triumph*, a serialized novel in the *Christian Recorder*, a newspaper read primarily by African Americans, Frances Harper provides us with a portrait of how difficult it was to find an equality of purpose among members of the Black community after the War. The community she describes is not accepting of others, judges moral failures harshly, and struggles to find a common term by which to measure the equality between its members. While *Iola Leroy* offers a vision for our own future today, *Trial and Triumph* forces us to look at how we allow race and gender inequality to, in turn, determine social inequalities. For Frances Harper, the solution was to discover the importance, for individuals, of education. The novel provides a study in how people come to understand the value of becoming a supportive and generous community.

Situating a young girl's journey to adulthood at the center of a novel about Black community building is extremely important. For readers, it allows the problem of misogyny to be addressed as one of the core assumptions about what is required for a just Black community. It also normalized her experience as the measure of how we form our relationships and what the society means by racial equality, because there were so few novels available at the time that discussed intimate Black life.

"Oh, that child! She is the very torment of my life. I have been the mother of six children, and all of them put together, never gave me as much trouble as that girl. I don't know what ever will become of her," Mrs. Harcourt exclaims about her granddaughter Annette (Harper, 1994, p. 179). In the novel *Trial and Triumph*, Harper tells a moral tale of individual duty and constancy. Framed as a story of the consequences, across generations, of the choices that women make for themselves, it is also an allegory of the requirements for sustaining a community able to improve its collective condition.

In the novel, the moral character of a people is definitive. Even though she considers everything from constraints on housing and employment to how Black people allocate their resources toward their community in the face of concerted racial opposition, Frances Harper suggests that the most important aspect of community-building is how individuals define the idea of cooperation with one another. The limits that they encounter together are a part of the description of the community, but this idea is also formed in a shared set of mores and rules for behavior. It was not the case that, upon freedom, all slaves were at the same starting point in life. Age, skills, the experience of slavery, the situation of the family, friends, and the opportunities each experienced made a difference. What was the same was each individual's potential to work with others to build a community as a nation of moral equals.

In *Trial and Triumph*, we meet our characters several years after the end of the Civil War, when the residential neighborhoods and resources available to Black families are no longer in a great deal of flux. There is still plenty of migration, as leaving a town is the same as disappearing from the lives of people there in the 1860s. An interesting feature of the novel is that we can't tell, as readers, who was recently a slave, and who was born and lived as a free Black person prior to the War. In the novel, all Black people are equal in status, and, therefore, all share a concern for the progress of this subset of the larger society. We don't read about how

White people form their own sense of community in relation to that of the Black people living in the town. And we don't read about whether some Black people are worse-off because of having been slaves. It is as though this burden, a blight on the life of the person, once lifted, is ignored or set aside for equality alongside all those who experience the constraints of being Black in the society. This portrayal lends credence to my own assertion earlier that a focus on slavery as the necessary definition of a Black life in the US provides only a partial explanation for the difficulty with resolving racial inequality in the society as the society developed after the Civil War.

Harper wants the reader to consider what Black people should do among themselves, recognizing the existence of racism, yet not making that the measure of the success of those in the community. When Harper is publishing this serial novel in the 1870s, some aspects of a former slave's experience must remain, artifacts of terror, obedience, and desire. What, for the novel's audience at the time of publication, is the former slave? This status of having been enslaved would tell or be held against those who had always been free, if in fact slavery was such a caul on the life of an individual. Rather, in *Trial and Triumph*, as in *Iola Leroy*, the reality of this potential divide in the Black community is set aside by Frances Harper for an aspirational collective, one where, in the novel, those without resources are looked down upon, but industry and thrift are described as providing for dramatic improvements in a personal situation.

The community as a people is already given for Harper and her audience in the 1860s, an aspirational claim to a common Black experience that is founded in the conflagration of the War. That Harper herself, as a free Black person, no longer could reference a slave owner and a slave, meant that something was lost after the War – a divisive wound, but also a pernicious distinction. What then was the free Black person, if the fortunes of every Black person were in play without reference to someone White? Did those who formerly carried papers announcing their free status toss them away after the War's end, or hide them for safe keeping, anticipating the return of the owners? What we get as readers in answer is a novel about pettiness and small-minded behavior, as well as a message about what must be done to achieve some semblance of loyalty to a larger ideal beyond pecuniary self-interest. Harper, therefore, provides a mirror in which readers are able to ask themselves what they do to foster a sense of shared community. The novel makes plain that this collective responsibility is crucial to the survival of the population, in the face of a concerted effort by others in the society to limit the opportunities available for Black people.

The plot

While *Trial and Triumph* addresses the trials of Black people due to racism, the plot revolves around how Black people address the differences among them within the social community of the town. Annette is the illegitimate child of Mrs. Harcourt's daughter Lucy. Not long after Annette's birth, Lucy essentially dies of grief and loneliness after being ostracized by her five siblings and her friends as a consequence of her being abandoned by the young man who fathered the child, Frank Miller. Annette is raised by her grandmother and lives in the shadow of the sins of her parents – as the neighbors and community treat her as responsible for the supposed tragedy of her own existence. The implication is that, if not for her birth, not only might the mother still be alive, but the couple might be together still, and the moral failures of all those associated with her existence might be expunged from the conscience of the community.

The story opens with Annette as a supposed willful child having acted out against someone who was contemptuous of her, and the neighbor whose steps have been covered with cooking oil complaining that Annette should be beaten to discipline her. Her grandmother disagrees, suggesting in the quote above that Annette is really ungovernable, and explicitly not controllable through violence. That this reflection is committed in the context of a slavery where violence was the prerogative of a Master, distinguishes what should be passed down across the generations as a measure of discipline from the idea of a refusal to capitulate to injustice on the part of a young child. While the grandmother is gentle and kind, she isn't loving and generous in ways that the young child needs. Annette doesn't find acceptance for her ambitions, only tolerance and forbearance.

With this grudging acceptance, Harper points to the presence of a moral problem within the community. We have inherited a life with the freedom to err, and so there must be a reckoning. In *Trial and Triumph*, Harper attempts to persuade the reader of the importance of constraining behaviors and ambitions, of forming a table of values that isn't the same as that which surrounds the community. It is not a coincidence that the major force for corruption comes from outside, by way of a returning son, so to speak. This force is represented by Frank Miller, the father of Annette, who signals the inability to escape the responsibility that accrues from our actions. He must atone or be punished.

The disengaged attitude of the grandmother, creating a measurable social distance from Annette that defines something indelible and vulnerable in the girl due to the circumstances of her birth, is repeated in the larger Black social community of the novel, with one exception. Parallel to the experiences of Annette, Harper portrays the problem of social alienation, and the hubris this implies, as an internalized problem for this new fragile Black community after the War. How the community treats Annette mirrors – if without the explicit violence – how Whites treat Black people socially. The task, then, for Harper, as well as for Black people with regard to the White society that constrains and defines Black racial status as inferior and contemptible, is to resolve the problem of how Annette feels, to find purpose and direction in life, and to discover self-respect and the capacity to love and befriend others. These ends are accomplished through the relationships that form around Annette in her life. She finds herself maligned and scorned as a child, thought to be aggressive and irrational, prone to bitterness and moods. But, throughout the novel, no specific behavior is registered as a slight or action Annette commits against others to merit being shunned. Instead, she receives the contempt of others simply because of her lowly social standing.

Annette's one champion is Mrs. Anna Lasette, who, we find out, was the close friend of Annette's mother, Lucy, before her social scandal. Anna does not feel that accidents of birth should reflect upon the child, and she mourns her lost friend. Anna regrets the fact that, when Lucy was deemed immoral by others, she was forbidden to continue as her friend. Guilt, and also a sense of right, guide Anna to offer Annette books and conversation as she is growing up. A memorable encounter occurs a few years after Frank Miller abandoned Lucy, when he returns to the town and turns his attention to Anna.

Lucy is dead and the child Annette remains unclaimed by her father. Frank Miller has come into money while away, earning a fortune selling liquor on the West Coast. He returns to town and builds a saloon that is very popular with the social elite. Instead of being shunned, as Lucy was – and because of which she eventually perished – Frank is fêted and remains socially acceptable, because, as Harper makes plain, he is a man and he is wealthy. He is popular with the young women, as though what happened to Lucy is forgiven by everyone in the community, except for Anna. In a telling scene, at a dance, Frank Miller grabs Anna's hand and she not only withdraws it but, in front of the audience at the party, demonstrably throws the glove from that hand into the fireplace, to burn with the intensity of her righteous anger.

Anna's action clearly invokes the symbolism of Miller's immoral desire for women leading to him being cast into the flames for his sins, and it also captures the attention and interest of the man who would eventually be her husband. Her refusal to absolve Frank Miller at the expense of other women, or because he can buy his way into the affections of others, allows for Anna to become available to a higher, morally fulfilling relationship. Looking on at the party, as she casts the glove in the fire, and sharing her contempt for this reprobate, Mr. Lasette is drawn by her principled and righteous act of moral condemnation. Soon after, they are married.

In a similar fashion, Annette is at a graduation party for Anna Lasette's daughter Lucy when she meets the man she falls in love with. Across the generations, the same theme is played out, but this time with Annette being ostracized as unwilling to wear gaudy expensive clothes and gossip with the other girls. She is simply too serious and standoffish, prim and proper, because of the burden of proving that her inheritance isn't that of immorality. Frances Harper doesn't allow the reader to feel contempt for this social requirement, but instead portrays this social rejection as a necessary stance by Annette.

The shadow of sin cast over Annette by her mother's actions is too much to allow for carelessness, and the eventual death of her grandmother and the reluctance of her uncles and aunts to have her come to live with them further marginalizes Annette socially. She is not the image of her mother, but rather of a person who refuses to be won over by insincere blandishments and false promises. The glitter of material riches and the witty banter of the other young girls don't amuse her, and when Clarence arrives at the party, he finds her being ignored. In counterpoint to Anna Lasette's rejection of Annette's biological father, Frank Miller, Clarence sits next to Annette and engages her in animated and serious conversation. As events proceed in the novel, eventually the two fall in love and Clarence proposes marriage. The couple is sitting together in the local park, and, just before Annette responds to his proposal, in front of them appears Clarence's long-lost wife. Clarence thought his wife had died after she had left him years earlier, and he had not mentioned his previous marriage to Annette as a result. But a mistaken identity, and her having run away from their home in New Orleans years ago, led to the error in his judgment.

While the relationship between Clarence and his estranged wife is now defunct, Annette says that she will refuse to marry him if he gets divorced. Since this was a marriage sanctified by God, Annette declares, it must be upheld and not dissolved for personal convenience or desire. To do otherwise is to repeat her mother's mistake, this time through the tearing asunder of a marriage instead of becoming pregnant without marrying. Annette resigns herself to do her selfless duty and devotes herself to being a teacher within the community. The years then go by and finally Clarence is single and unable to forget the love with Annette that he was forced to give up. He seeks her out and finds her at a schoolhouse in another town, surrounded by mothers and children, teaching and being revered as the center of knowledge and moral guidance. The two rekindle their relationship and the book ends with the anticipation that they will finally have a life together.

Race and public opinion

In the late 1860s, after the War, any writer describing the Black community would have to attend to how the idea of Blackness persisted after slavery. Frances Harper provides a description of several everyday techniques that both consolidated White economic and social interests and provided real limits to the capacity of Black people to generate sufficient resources to be independent. The idea expressed by Harper is that, while it was necessary to exclude Black people from social equality with Whites, it was also necessary to rely on Black labor, trade, and consumers for White economic success. To describe this balance between social exclusion and economic inclusion, as a means of defining racial difference after the War, Harper shows how Whiteness was defined by social acceptance after the end of slavery. She describes the prejudicial actions of a White store owner after the War: "I think there never was a slave more cowed under the whip of his master than he is under public opinion. The Negro was not the only one whom slavery subdued to the pliancy of submission" (Harper, 1994, p. 214).

While she doesn't truly equate the two conditions, Harper considers what was required for someone to be White, recognizing that the enforcement of the terms for racial difference was largely dependent on a White individual performance – a gaze, a gesture, a promise of retribution – and social activity. The White person would be expected to conform to the social strictures of other Whites or risk ostracism, possible violence, and other forms of social punishment.

Disobedience was met with the harshest of responses by a public defined by this idea of White racial difference. During slavery, this was certainly true. For example, as was discussed earlier, in *Iola Leroy*, written long after *Trial and Triumph*, it is accepted as a commonplace that, upon Eugene Leroy's death, the cousin Lorraine would find some way to annul the marriage agreement and remand Eugene's wife Marie into slavery. Lorraine's pursuit of the children, Iola and Harry, who lived in the North as Whites, demonstrates that there was no limit to the acceptable lengths someone White could go to enforce the idea of a Whiteness both superior and authoritative. But was this still the case for Whiteness after the collapse of the system of slavery?

The idea of racial difference has always been tied to this idea of destruction – a threat that brings with it complete annihilation for both the White betrayer and the Black transgressor. This is evident today in the claims against a Black President of the United States that he can't be accepted as a citizen. The public pursuit of a birth certificate to verify his citizenship is a statement of a difference that must be maintained, between those who are White and those who are not. What would have happened if Obama had, in fact, not been a citizen? Joe Biden would have become President, and the racial progress signaled by Obama's election would have been proven deceptive.

This public attempt to label successful achievements of racial equality as fake, the truth subject to confirmation by Whites, is an important statement of racial difference in itself. Harper shows us how several specific things were done in her lifetime to normalize this idea of a seemingly necessary social superiority after the War, even as the Black population was also considered important, and politically defined as equal to those who were White. This social definition of an immutable difference would be enshrined in the law again soon after the publication of the novel *Trial and Triumph*, constraining the actions of both White and Black people who sought to transgress or challenge the idea of racial inequality.

Harper describes this condition of a double implication – a dependency between White and Black communities that results from a necessary adherence to a description of racial inequality on the one hand, and the acquiescence to a necessary racial injustice on the other hand – when she states, "It has been said that everything has two handles, and if you take it by the wrong handle it will be too hard to hold. I should like to know which is the right handle to this prejudice against color" (Harper, 1994, p. 213).

Harper's answer is important for how we also think of racial inequality today. Remembering that the society has just emerged from two centuries of the legal enslavement of Black people, she writes in *Trial and Triumph*: "I do not think there is color prejudice in this country." The young man who hears this statement exclaims in disbelief, as he has just been fired as a clerk when the store owner realized that he was Black. Harper uses this example to show how the new regulation of racial difference occurs after the War: Charles Cooper is the son of a Black woman who works as a teacher at a school with a White superintendent. The superintendent has seen Charles with his mother at the school, and so asks the store owner whether he had ever "employed a nigger as a cashier?" The owner says no, but the response from the superintendent is: "'Well,' he said, 'you have one now'" (Harper, 1994, p. 210). Charles is fired that afternoon, so it is understandable if he thinks of the problem of race as one of color prejudice.

Harper argues instead, through the person talking with Charles, Mr. Thomas, that the problem of racial social injustice is really that of associating persons with the idea of a historical and indelible collective inferiority. It is his assignment as Black that is at issue, not the color of his skin. To make the point, Mr. Thomas goes on to discourage Charles from leaving his mother, who needs him, and to forgo passing as White because he is light-skinned, somewhere else in the country. Arguing instead that there are White people who don't agree with this idea of racial inequality, Mr. Thomas seeks out Mr. Hastings, a wealthy White businessman of his acquaintance, and, in what is one of the most powerful conversations about race and the new description of racial injustice in the novel, convinces the businessman to hire Charles as a utility worker in his store (Harper, 1994, p. 225). Mr. Thomas challenges Hastings, who also owns a store, to stand by his beliefs as a White person who sees the collective assignment of inequality as wrong, and to make good on his values regarding race and justice.

In these events, Harper draws parallels between Charles' struggle and the quandary that Annette experienced in being made to represent the face of a sin she didn't commit. Why hold an individual responsible for the actions of others, and what better argument is there for innocence than that of a child? Through these narratives, Harper demonstrates that this same idea of collective responsibility, of a stereotype or prejudgment of individual character based on race, prohibits the opportunity for anyone Black to find acceptable and industrious employment with White people. The reader learns that Mr. Thomas had a similar experience as a young man, of being turned away for employment because he was Black, only to eventually find a White benefactor, someone who was willing to refuse the requirements of racial public opinion. This is a political legacy passed down from one generation to the next in the novel – this capacity or willingness to ask that someone White risk their own reputation and livelihood for the cause of racial equality. The reader of the novel can infer from this example that what is being critiqued is the idea of racial social segregation, asking the question of what someone has done to deserve the treatment meted out on others. What are the ties that bind someone so that race is enough to exclude and prohibit employment, social standing, and equality? What is inherited and what is earned (or learned) that should determine a person's fate?

At the same time, by introducing a character such as Charles Cooper briefly into the story, Harper suggests that those who were children and grandchildren of former Masters, those who had been sold away or kept close by, and were able to pass, or those who were simply very pale but still had Black ancestry, were Black because of the ongoing legacy of the distinction made between racial communities. To pass was to lose all ties to family and friends, to give up not only on the possibility of racial equality as an ideal, but on the pursuit of racial justice in their lifetime. In this Charles Cooper scene, Harper provides not just a description of how race is defined socially in terms of employment – via public opinion before the creation of the Jim Crow laws used later to reinforce the prohibition on racial transgression – but also a recipe for resistance through the refusal to accept the terms for Black inferiority and the creation of a Black intransigent subject position. This is a politics of refusal, rather than acquiescence to the idea of racial hierarchy through the Black person's attempt to pass as White.

Individuals who are capable of passing experience pressure to be White in a society where Black people are described as inferior. As was pointed out in the discussion of *Iola Leroy*, for Frances Harper these individuals challenged the idea of color prejudice which was also a public, visible politics of discrimination. To succumb to the force of public opinion, instead of rejecting what Harper describes as an immoral description of human differences, is to be venal and thoughtless in the same way that those who are Black oppress Annette. As Harper has Mr. Thomas say: "Men fettered the slave and cramped their own souls, denied him knowledge and darkened their own spiritual insight, and the Negro, poor and despised as he was, laid his hands on American civilization and has helped to mold its character" (Harper, 1994, pp. 214–15). For all their desperation because of their plight, the experience of the slave defines the American experience just as much as that of the wealthy landowner living in the plantations that depended on the labor of the slaves. What person would choose to create the slave to which they would be forever bound? That is the America that Harper introduces us to as readers, a place where the now free and the Masters must both again find a way to distinguish between themselves. They do this in the context of a segregated neighborhood by living under the new rules for social differentiation that are created immediately upon Emancipation.

We can imagine a scene similar to that described in the beginning of the novel *Iola Leroy*, where the slaves simply leave without letting the owner know, going to the military encampment nearby. Once there, they are effectively freed. Iola is liberated, in the sense that the soldiers went and retrieved her directly from her owner. Tom Anderson, who was directing the soldiers toward their object, Iola, was present during her liberation, and he says that the owner was mad enough to bite his head off. Robert Johnson's remark that it would be too big for him to do so is a way of suggesting that Tom shouldn't take too much credit for her freedom. It is what is right to do at this point – not brave or something to be proud of, simply accomplished. To be free is now, for the three of them, a fact of the act of physical removal from the owner to the camp.

For other slaves, freedom might not have been so obvious an option – or even possible – until the actual end of the War. Then the leave-taking must have been literally a life-changing event, but also something fraught – a collapse of authority over the slave for the owner that gave the War a unique and important meaning in the future for America, a caesura or sundering of the right to own other persons in the society. The absence of a journey or separation, a break such as that described in running away from captivity, must have been a profound expression of the law – a process of over-whelming, almost impossible to imagine, human potential. It not only was possible but actually happened, just as the decades of slow erosion of Jim Crow political segregation led to a remarkable aspirational politics – one that led to the election of a Black President of the United States. For the community of Black people described in the novel *Trial and Triumph*, this aspirational ambition was the foundation for coming to terms with Annette and what she must become to allow the community to achieve its goals.

From this moment of radical freedom something beyond a repetition of the social experience of racial difference that already described the lives of free Blacks had to become the goal for this new community. Those who would main-tain today that the Civil War wasn't about slavery don't understand what happened as its result; they don't fully com-prehend what the sudden incapacity to own another meant for owner and slave in that moment of the South losing the War. But it is also logical that how the slave lived afterwards, either alongside the owner or leaving, would determine the relationship, and would have as its basis both the former relationship and something uncanny and new. The idea of equality would be fraught and difficult to define through the interactions between a former slave and a former Master or Mistress, and so Frances Harper offers the reader a model for what racial equality requires of everyone in this new Black community.

In *Trial and Triumph*, what we read occurs several years after the War's end, and the pattern of life reflects the incomplete equilibrium or resolution developed for how a good enough racial equality is described for the former owners, and what it means to be White. This will change by the time of the publication of *Iola Leroy*, but points to the capacity for rapid change in the social description of racial constraints on equality that can be mobilized through White collective action over two decades. For former slaves, there was often little to no encouragement or material support available. For Annette's grandmother, Mrs. Harcourt, Frances Harper describes this relationship with freedom as leaving her with few resources, with her social refinement being determined not by formal education or biblical training but by emulating well-bred people for the definition of self-respect and self-reliance (Harper, 1994, p. 188). She moves north with her husband because of the racial injustice they experience, and upon his death she learns to care for herself and her family. She manages to raise her children, and only Lucy gets in trouble. Harper is explicit that the problem for Lucy was public opinion, in the same way that racial prejudice works to require White conformity to a specific description of racial inequality.

The fact that Frank Miller wasn't punished for his indiscretion is immortalized by Harper in a short poem: "But where was he who sullied / Her once unsullied name; Who lured her from life's brightness / To agony and shame" (Harper, 1994, p. 191). In other words, if Whites conform to public opinion in acting with this prejudice toward Black people, where is the judgment on their behavior? Why are only Black people assessed and not White people, and isn't this unidirectional assessment of behavior by gender with regard to Lucy and Frank the same as that by race? Lucy dies from the prejudice she experiences, and Annette spends much of the novel trying to respond to the misogyny defined by her supposed implication in her mother's behavior.

It is important to make this comparison between gender social stigma and racial social prejudice because the former slaves have to acquire the education and resources to substantiate a claim to social equality. How are they to do this? If the relationship between White and Black people reflects this difference in condition without reflection on how they have been enslaved, the very same people that caused the inequality are now blaming Black people for it, instead of their own prejudices as White people; this is similar to the lack of responsibility assigned to public opinion for Lucy's demise and Annette's shame. The reader can use the description of gender and Annette's struggle with social injustice in the novel to work through the problem of how Black and White people wrestle with the idea of racial inequality across the so-called color line.

After slavery

Without slavery as an immediate social referent, the description of a Black inferiority that was still required by Whites had to be defined in material or social terms. In *Trial and Triumph*, Frances Harper provides an important intervention for us today. Without some referent to an inequality that matters between persons, the social definition of racial prejudice collapses. Creating or maintaining the unequal distribution of resources is how racial differences are described as a result of incapacities on the part of a specific population. Frances Harper provides examples of how individual decisions about racial difference are reinforced by processes that provide substandard or inferior material goods and opportunities for Black people. The idea of human industry after the destruction wrought by the Civil War and the remaking of the nation afterwards, the desire among freed Blacks for employment and work, are also defined in the novel with regard to housing. In the narrative descriptions of *Trial and Triumph*, Harper has provided an anthropological description of the institutional processes that were developed to produce the social construction of racial inequality for individuals after the end of slavery. The very fidelity to a politics, writing for the needs of a specific reader that the serial novel represents for Harper, serves us well almost a century and a half later as a description of how Black people negotiated the developing definition of their material inequality in relation to the definition of a desire for White superiority.

The Black people in *Trial and Triumph* find it difficult to buy houses in areas that are not run down or of substandard housing stock, and in the novel the fortunes of the neighborhood are described in terms of the quality of the dwellings in which people live. The problem that Black people had in reinforcing ownership and property claims, as a description of racial subordination, is addressed, both in terms of homesteading but also as a condition of where it was possible to live. This was the period when the racial neighborhood segregation of freed Blacks from Whites was substantiated by rental and purchase agreements. Today, we would see the racial segregation in neighborhoods, services, and housing stock as a deliberate means, developed over generations, to substantiate racial difference. Housing segregation is a stark and comprehensive, existing legacy of this initial response to deprive Black people of resources required to claim equality after Emancipation. That, so soon after the War's end the novel is written with a clear description of a segregation that we recognize today, should be shocking to us. This is when the conditions for a permanent post-slavery Black inequality were developed, both materially and socially, throughout the nation.

The area of racial differentiation in *Trial and Triumph* that is most interesting, however, is Harper's description of the integrated schools and the way in which race was developed in the classroom as a consequence of social interaction. Well over 100 years after its publication, the description of racial social segregation it provides could have been written today. One day, Annette says to Mrs. Lasette, "I never want to go to that school again" (Harper, 1994, p. 215). Annette is rude to an Irish girl, Mary Joseph, in the seat next to her in the classroom. Annette explains that, in response to the girl squirming in her seat next to her, "I asked if anything was biting her, because if there was I didn't want it to get on me" (p. 215). Suggesting that, because she was Irish, Mary Joseph would have lice, is a rather direct aspersion, one that is laced with racial connotations about the variegated conditions of Whiteness and the capacity of Black people to criticize its value.

The Irish girl is considered not Black, but White, and as Annette's grandmother says, when describing the seating arrangements made by the teacher, "Ireland and Africa, and they were not ready for annexation." The conflict between the girls escalates after that, coming closer to the real issue at stake, of the description of racial difference and inequality, as Annette describes the girls at lunchtime later that day at the school:

> but that isn't all, when I went to eat my lunch, she said she wasn't used to eating with niggers. Then I asked her if her mother didn't eat with pigs in the old country, and she said that she would rather eat with them than to eat with me, and then she called me a nigger, and I called her a poor White mick.
>
> (Harper, 1994, p. 216)

When the school day is over, Mary Joseph's father threatens Annette with a thrashing, and, in describing the situation to Mrs. Lasette, Annette demonstrates in further conversation a prejudice toward the Irish, and an assumption of equivalence between Black people and the Irish that reveals a great deal about how racial difference worked in the absence of slavery (Harper, 1994, p. 217). She says, "Grandmother says that an Irishman is only a Negro turned wrong side out." Annette goes on to complain about being called anything with racial meaning, even Black, by Mary Joseph.

In the conversation between the two women that follows, Mrs. Lasette explains to Annette that, while there are no physical differences that matter between someone White and someone Black, race isn't a problem of that difference between persons, but of the historical use of the physical differences – of color, as Harper puts it – to maintain a portion of the population in "slavery, poverty, and ignorance." Mrs. Lasette goes on to offer this maxim: "You cannot change your color, but you can try and change the association connected with our complexions" (Harper, 1994, pp. 219–20). This phrase seems strange to us as an idea because we are taught today that race is an attitude, and not derived from material differences developed over time to define racial inequality. We have forgotten that Black and White are always derived by the material and social differences attributed to them. That is what makes someone being seen as Black or White, without specific attributes and material conditions, as experiences so provocative for the reader, both then and today, and worthy therefore of inclusion as a character in the novel from the perspective of Frances Harper.

This description of race in *Trial and Triumph* gives the contemporary reader permission to consider the social implications that underlie our own perspective on race. If it is, as Harper suggests, a wound that hasn't healed (Harper, 1994, p. 219), how do we account for our sensitivities about racial assignments today? What happened in the intervening period between today and when the novel was written for a racial slur to remain possible? And what of the fact that the same words produce the same social result, an attack that presages the totalizing end of a life? Because, of course, the result of racism was no longer slavery – that is the entire point of the novel's argument about racial difference: it is warning of the increasing lynching violence that had begun already during the post-War period. Witness the ease with which the father threatens to thrash Annette without expectation of reprisal or censure. The prospect of White people thinking that violence is necessary to teach Black people what is impossible for them socially was present to Annette, and to the readers.

The use of the slur wasn't for Annette a call to enslavement but an assignment of inferiority that allowed the children to reproduce a refusal to eat together, and that was understood by both adult and child as a possible social position, something that the society would permit. The public opinion – the idea that at school this type of exchange of racial slurs between children was acceptable – is echoed by Annette's response in the conversation with Mrs. Lasette about how the teacher handled the situation. Annette suggests that the teacher believes that Black people are inferior and would not take her side, no matter what the slight.

Frances Harper is willing to use various elements of social experience to show how Whites undermine the struggle that Black people engage in to claim racial equality. Asked where the teacher was during the entire scene between Annette and Mary Joseph, Annette explains, "she was out of the room part of the time, but I don't think she likes colored people, because last week when Joe Smith was cutting up in school,

she made him get up and sit alongside of me to punish me."
Mrs. Lasette describes how this puts Annette at risk and
was inappropriate. Annette describes how Joe said, as he
sat there, "that the teacher didn't spite him; that he would
have sit by me as any girl at school, and that he liked girls."
Mrs. Lasette's response, "A little scamp," perfectly captures
the problem of maintaining a commitment to racial justice
even as those in authority attempt to mobilize against you
(Harper, 1994, pp. 216–17).

For Mary Joseph's father to approach the child of 14,
Annette, grabbing her arm and saying that he will beat
her, is for Harper a warning to the reader of the fragility
of the compromises that have allowed Blacks and Whites
to exist side by side not just in school, but anywhere, given
the requirement of a necessary Black inferiority. Both Mrs.
Lasette and Annette know this, and the threat of a violence
without surcease that Annette's initial aggression has caused.
What resources exist as a recourse for someone who is Black
that is attacked? None. Both Annette and Mrs. Lasette
understand this stark reality as the child describes the situation. Mrs. Lasette has to come up with a way for the child
to survive when facing a fight she cannot win – but that,
instead, may seriously harm her.

Mrs. Lasette suggests that Annette focus on healing the
associations, fixing the sources of stigma – studying, writing, reading, and becoming better – as though there are
things about being Black that can't be remedied except by
changing social description of the community itself. Annette
should therefore try to represent the best of the community
and its potential, rather than confirm her own vulnerability by acknowledging the fact of her condition – that to be
Black is also to be associated with slavery, poverty, and ignorance. Rather than accept the conflict at hand, she must rise
above it.

Anger won't protect her, and retaliation won't resolve the conditions of difference described between the races. For Harper, the idea is not that racial difference is a function of real differences between the communities, even though she is referring to this fact in both of the conversations about how young people experience racism. She argues instead that the Black person must address the capacity of Whites to act with racial difference by simply living as they should, not reacting to the contempt and scorn of Whites. There is no other option available, because the conflict based on reproducing unequal material conditions cannot be won. This isn't about strength or intelligence, or proving equality, at all – but inferiority. Mrs. Lasette and Annette know that they are equal to anyone White as persons. This use of the slur is something else entirely, a warning of what will happen if Annette acts as though she is superior.

To find a solution to this problem of the unequal reservation of resources, the novel centers the narrative around the relationship Annette has with the community, exploring how she can find solace from their comprehensive contempt. It is only when speaking with Mrs. Lasette that she is made to feel whole and capable, complete in herself. That Annette is a descendent of shame and contempt makes her own situation reminiscent of how Blackness is defined through poverty and ignorance. How can she work through the problem of a difference that is realized personally and yet is also an inheritance, something for which she was not responsible? That this social stigma is itself a wound, an attempt to limit the progress that Annette makes socially, and that White people are doing things to limit the ability of Black people as a population to succeed in their lives, is something Harper addresses obliquely, as a problem of moral character.

What else can Annette do? To persist in spite of the social odds is all to the good, literally, but this doesn't confront the problem of an implacable resistance by Whites to Black social progress. When Mrs. Lasette compares Mary Joseph and Annette in terms of sensitivity to being called White and Black respectively, this is different from an exchange of racial slurs. Why does Mary Joseph not have to take offense at being called White or rosy? Because, in Harper's time, as is true in most instances today, there was no stigma in being thought White, as a member of a community that had enslaved and mistreated Black people. The author offers up the wealthy White man's disparagement of the reasons why the storekeeper fired Charles Cooper, and this does make him feel guilty at the treatment his fellow White people meted out upon Blacks. But Mr. Hastings doesn't thereby take offense at being called White himself. This is because, for Harper, White people are not assessed for the quality of their life, no matter the condition, just as no one in the community questions the morality of Frank Miller as he opens a saloon after Lucy dies. This is the equivalence that Frances Harper believes will stir the reader to a conscience, because clearly Frank Miller is guilty and should be made to atone or account responsibly for his actions, to Annette as his child if nothing else.

The contemporary reaction of anger at being called White is similarly not based on a description of a community that is responsible for injustice, but instead a reaction to the idea that someone Black has the authority to make associations. The claim of anger is made not as was done in the novel by the Irish and Black child against one another as mutually vulnerable populations, but in the context of a refusal to accept the authority of someone to make an association of White people as a community and something pernicious or immoral. To speak of Whiteness in this sense is today fraught for the interlocutor, perceived as authorizing a narrative similar to that brought against Mr. Hastings, in which

Whites in the South and North after the War are described
as purposefully constraining Black community progress, and
thereby continuing the unjust claims against Black people
begun during the period of slavery.

Harper does something brave as she provides a public criticism of the way that White people converge on an idea of
racial difference that would provide for new techniques or
instruments for Black social control and subordination. To
suggest such a thing today is perceived as similarly problematic, as both personal and a matter of public opinion, just as
Harper points out Frank Miller can't be accused publicly of
causing Lucy's death. If this claim today was possible, what
would it do for someone who was in fact White to argue
that, in being a member of the community, they were also
personally complicit in the racial injustice in the society?
This is what Harper describes as the situation for Annette
in the words of Mrs. Lasette: that she lacks the capacity to
make a larger claim against the very consolidation of social
interest – represented by the other girl's father, for example
– that continues to define her own person as Black and inferior. Her only option is to ignore the slurs as best she can
– just as Annette ignores the presence of her father, Frank
Miller, in the town.

But this concession also means that Mrs. Lasette and
Annette understand that there is little they can do against the
importunities and encroachment brought by a White community that is determined to stifle progress and remove the
rights of Black people. It is discouraging to have to accept
that, within the Black community, this sense of entitlement
and avarice is also implacable, set against and in opposition
to the social ambition of Annette. Annette's story of failed
love and thwarted ambition reflect this. The solution of emi-
gration that is briefly mentioned in the novel, of finding a
place where there isn't the too easy association of a problem

with racial difference, doesn't exist for the community and society as a whole.

For Annette, on the other hand, it is enough to merely remove herself to somewhere that the story of her mother's tragedy doesn't define her person. She becomes the source of love and morality for this new local community at the end of the novel. And, unlike in the threat provided by Charles Cooper when he says he will leave and pass into Whiteness, Annette does not. Frances Harper knows, in her critical comparison of both North and the South for Black people after the War, it is not easy for Black people in the society to find a place of refuge from persecution.

The theme of personally seeking refuge within the community instead of leaving proves a fiction impossible for Annette, because there is no source or avenue available to her for redemption. How could Annette absolve herself of her mother's deeds, and why does her father experience little moral disapproval? The idea of Frank Miller coming back to the place of his perfidy without blame is a problem for the society, and Harper reveals this in the description that Mrs. Lasette gives concerning the shame of Lucy and her death, as an appeal to the Black reader. There is, similarly, no solution provided by Harper in the novel to the predations of a consolidating White community, except to appeal to the moral character of those who are also White.

In both cases, this is an appeal to the idea of the principles of the society in which Black and White people live, not the conception of racial difference being described. Harper provides principles of morality that are external, not implicit, as a limit on the consolidation of racial difference. The community reflects internally the social conditions of racial inequality that determine its existence externally, through the definition of Blackness. Just as Frank Miller can return after a long sojourn, bringing whatever he has acquired into the community, so can Annette leave to search for a better place for her ambition outside. This idea is important to the resolution of the problem of racial inequality in the society, both in the 1870s and today.

Turning race inside out

In *Trial and Triumph*, Lucy, Annette's mother, is bereft and ostracized once she has been abandoned by Frank Miller. The relationships that she valued were suddenly prohibited by those who once could admit they loved and needed her in their lives. Her having a child without a male partner served as a constant reminder to others of the cost that Lucy should be made to pay for her independence. As she grows up, Annette demonstrates an independence from the social expectations of others; she will not be allowed to forget who she is for them, and so she rebels against the idea of being wrong in her person. It is only when Lucy lies on her deathbed that her siblings and her mother exclaim at their impending loss.

In Mrs. Lasette's recounting of the deathbed scene, it is clear that the family members don't recognize their implication in the despair that devours Lucy's life. And the idea that Frank Miller should be made responsible for the death of their sister clearly isn't even a consideration. Lucy was made fully responsible for the possibility of sin, loss, and shame even as she died, and then, upon her death, in the life of the child Annette. This transfer of the problem to Annette is important, as it defines the daughter's entire life and is the central dilemma of the novel. What would be required to make Frank Miller and the community responsible for alleviating the privations of, first, Lucy, and then his daughter, Annette? What would be required to make everyone equally culpable and responsible in finding a solution to racial injustice? Why is Christianity enough for Harper as a ground, a means of absorbing the anguish and uncertainty of the conditions that Black people experience and yet can't fully encompass? It creates justifications, rather than solutions, for the effects of racial difference in the lives of people. In other words, are moral principles waived rather than integral to the process by which racial difference is constructed? The associative principles of difference contain no necessary limit; anything is possible, and must be, when deciding to connect the treatment of a person or community to something external. Phenotypal difference is not distinct in this regard.

What terms are socially necessary to define the conditions for a differentiation between humans that allows for racial inequality to persist and be reproduced? It must also be possible to substitute phenotypal differences – hair, skin, and physical features – once set as factual categories for groups, for something else, to use racial physical determinations via the gaze – or bloodline, as Harper's protagonists phrase it – but not reference these aspects of the human being directly in social interactions. This is in the same way that it is possible for material resource differences between persons to be subsumed in a discussion of individual choices, merit, and desert, rather than an understanding of the processes that occur, of which an individual is merely a part.

For example, the associations of specific social and economic conditions, behaviors, norms, and standards to racial groups could be referenced without using terms such as Black or White. This is what Annette and Mary Joseph experience – the availability of racial slurs for social use isn't what is interesting or shocking for anyone involved, including the teacher. What is provocative, for Mrs. Lasette and the father of Mary Joseph, is that Annette sought to test out the problem of substitution itself, calling out the idea of racial difference directly between the two girls. The conditions of inequality were present before she did so, but it was her bringing this fact up that was considered a problem.

Why did Harper describe a scene in which the child refuses to accept the terms for Black inferiority, even as Annette at first seems to be testing the possibility of reframing the social description of the Irish as inferior to Black people? The answer is, of course, just the impossibility of using the social conditions of the one designation for the other – Black inferiority is required; this is the position that can't be elided, regardless of the description of the social conditions for Whiteness. The entire structure of social relationships is based on this idea – what should therefore be thought of as a politics, a description of the consolidation of a specific interest or demand by a collective. In the context where a newly freed population is trying to describe the limits of their freedom, Frances Harper is explicitly opposing the two arguments for a democratic polity based on racial inferiority and ethnic difference, using the social interactions of the two girls in an integrated public school.

The site of the location of the conflict is, of course, not a coincidence, but a recognition by the author and readers that it is the definition of the public, of the place where they are to share resources, that is the source of anxiety for both the formerly enslaved and those who wish to define a continued set of social exclusions based on being "White." There is no more public social space – in the sense of a politically contested place – than the public school. The political exclusion of Jim Crow laws and Black Codes has not yet become possible in the town being described in *Trial and Triumph*. But this is, for both author and reader at the time, the impending threat to which the Black community is forming its own social resistance in the framing of the conflict between the girls. To claim, as Annette does, that someone Irish can be both White and inferior to Black people is to riff on the idea that was being developed in the society at the time about how important it is that Whiteness include the Irish and new immigrants from Europe to create a united front against the Black population. This scene in the novel provides insight into the ways in which the social development of race was explicitly contested during Harper's time.

On the surface of our reasoning here, this scene developed by Harper would suggest that acceptance and accommodation to racial difference should be learned in school. The message of the conflict is that racial differences should be defined as given and not mutable, reconciled through their social attachments to historical forces that must be accepted. This is exactly how Mrs. Lasette decribes the solution to Annette, encouraging her to rise above the historical description of racial difference, not as an exception, but to actively fight socially against the predeterminism desired by those who wish for a Black inferiority. That this assignment of a necessary difference should occur all the way down into the history by which a person arrives in the world is exactly why the novel develops through the struggle for Annette to escape the consequences of her mother's shame. Annette is expected to live, uncontested, with the effects of her mother's shame, while Frank Miller, as the father who impregnated her mother and fled rather than owning a responsibility to the life of the mother and the child, is allowed to shed any responsibility for their plight. In the same way as there is no recourse in the society by which to hold accountable the former Masters and the community of people described as White for their responsibility for the conditions of Black people. Annette's rude gesture is a form – obvious to the reader at the time – of opposition to the claim of innocence by White people.

The fact that the Irish are new to the society is exactly why Frances Harper uses the children to explain to the reader that the continuing social description of racial difference between persons, and not a historical condition or circumstance of which the new Irish immigrant is innocent, is responsible for making the legacy of racial inequality a feature of the society after the War. These two antipodal social positions are described as fixed, given by the very terms of gender inequality, and mirror the development given by the racial difference described between Annette and Mary Joseph. Gender and race define one another, are coexistent in the children, the parents, and for the author and reader in such a way that specific problems are identifiable.

In the case of Annette and the classroom, Mrs. Lasette says to Annette that she must not accept these conditions of social inferiority, even as she must avoid challenging them directly with other persons since the consequences will be prohibitive. Annette should instead strive to overcome the associative conditions that describe racial difference themselves, to lift up the Black community through her labor and moral claims upon others.

Direct challenge, the idea of a rights claim against Black injustice or inequality, requires that some limit exist to the organizational capacity of those who defend the development of racial inequality, that there are tools available that provide a constraint on the actions of those who would defend existing relationships of racial difference. Mary Joseph's father pinched Annette's arm and said he would beat her if she persisted, which was a warning that Mrs. Lasette needed to communicate to Annette about the impossibility of imposing limits on the capacity for White people to defend their authority.

Without constraint, Annette's own life was at stake in confronting directly the social description by White people of Black inequality. The discovery of the terms for defining a constraint, its delimitation, was to be the goal of the Black community for the next century. The failure to do so was illuminated historically in the murder of Emmett Till and countless lynchings, the assassinations of Malcolm X and Martin Luther King, Jr., and the death of Black men and women today at the hands of the police, but was already a central concern among Black people with regard to the politics of race in the society after the end of the Civil War.

The problem is that merely repeating the litany of instances of racial injustice to an interlocutor is not enough to move the dial toward equality without some acknowledgment of a decision to correct the problem by both parties. This is literally what Harper has one of her characters, Mr. Thomas, say to the White shopkeeper Mr. Hastings, when he makes the appeal to Hastings to hire Charles Cooper, after Charles is fired for being Black. Mr. Thomas says, "But I might go on reciting such instances until you would be weary of hearing and I of relating them; but I appeal to you as a Patriot and a Christian, is it not fearfully unwise to keep alive in freedom the old animosities of slavery? To-day the Negro shares citizenship with you" (Harper, 1994, p. 224). In the description of Annette, rather than Cooper, Harper provides a way of considering this problem, instead, through the conditions set up for women within the Black community – how gender defines the potential for the community to find a way to not only survive racial injustice but also change the conditions of racial inequality.

Christianity

What is the definition of equality for the Black person, when the social description of difference is an enforced inequality with Whites? What should Mrs. Lasette and Annette depend upon to measure their own social progress relative to other persons? It is in this context of determining an equality with others that we can see the importance that Frances Harper places upon the role of Christianity as a description of morality in *Trial and Triumph*. It is here that we see the early articulation of the idea of a necessary equality between persons described in the novel *Iola Leroy* two decades later.

What is the definition of equality that is sought by Harper through her fiction, and what do the characters want of other persons? The answer to these questions, for Harper, is provided by the idea of a human equality in relationship to a God who is omnipotent and the architect of every relationship and purpose. No human being can know this design or have privileged access to the workings of this higher force, and so accepting the conditions for our lives on earth is both necessary and a call to action. The highest ambition for individuals is to realize this equality between persons through the work of social uplift and moral constancy.

Harper develops the meaning of this call to action in *Trial and Triumph* through describing the contrast between the lives of learning, art, and personal growth of Mrs. Lasette and Annette, and the particular corruption wrought within the community by the den of iniquity purchased and maintained for the young and ambitious by Annette's biological father Frank Miller. Harper describes how:

> young men who would have scorned to enter the lowest dens of vice, felt at home in his gilded palace of sin. Beautiful pictures adorned the walls, light streamed into the room through finely stained glass windows, women, not as God had made them, but as sin had debased them, came there to spend the evening in mazy dance, or to sit with partners in

sin and feast at the tables ... his place was a snare to their souls.

(Harper, 1994, pp. 192–3)

Harper is explicit about the Christian moral crisis that this place creates for the community, writing that such an establishment represents a violation of the teachings of the Bible, when, as she writes, "the head of the woman is the man, and the head of the man is Jesus Christ." In contrast to the threat to progress that Frank Miller offers, are other individuals, as Harper writes:

> a few thoughtful mothers old fashioned enough to believe that the law of purity is as binding upon the man as the woman, and who, under no conditions, would invite him to associate with their daughters. Women who tried to teach their sons to be worthy of the esteem and love of good women by being as chaste in their conversation and as pure in their lives as their young daughters who sat at their side in their pleasant and peaceful homes.

(Harper, 1994, p. 192)

Harper makes it clear for the reader in a conversation between Mr. Thomas and Mrs. Lasette that she thinks that what Christianity offers, and not the church itself, is central to the progress of the Black community and the society generally. It is in this conventional distinction between faith and church that we are able to consider the Christian moral framework of the characters in the novel as representative of an equality that challenges the social world in which individuals live together.

Mr. Thomas explains that he will not enter the ministry because he has failed to find another occupation – that Christianity is not to be the refuge for thoughts of the community, but the ambition, the rock upon which the society is to be built and sustained. Harper has Mr. Thomas say:

> I think one of the great wants of our people is more reverence for God who is above us, and respect for the man beside us, and I do hope that our next minister will be a good man, of active brain, warm heart and Christly sympathies, who will be among us a living, moral, and spiritual force, and who will be willing to teach us on the Bible plan of "line upon line, precept upon precept, here a little there a little."
>
> (Harper, 1994, p. 188)

That this moral life is defined in contrast to one defined by racial inequality leaves unaddressed the conditions by which racial difference becomes possible, except through association, the failure of a public as an opinion. But why would the misery and want of an individual require categories of difference? Why should race exist as the measure of a society, constraining the democratic aspirations of its people? Harper suggests that we don't have the possibility of questioning the demand itself, the necessity of racial difference, but that we can bring to bear moral values to create limits on what this difference allows for those in the society. Answering "What are the principles that we can live with, not live without?" is the conundrum that Harper tries to answer, and one repeatedly raised by the characters in her novels.

Harper poses this question in the context where Black people were being forced to accept a description of their lives after the end of slavery that required dependence on the favors and desires of White people, where Black people were associated with depredation and loss, want and need, and therefore must make what are impossible collective demands for reparative justice, because of the impact of slavery upon the society. In the collective memory, the Civil War was the complete destruction of the known world, and Black people and their claims to equality were associated with this in the lives of everyone. To have been a slave was less important in the aftermath of the conflict than it was to realize a Black community that could offer the wounded partial democracy a hard-working, reliable, generous, and forgiving mien. Christianity provided the bedrock for this message, even if it was unequal to the task of limiting the desire by many for continuing the description of a necessary Black subordination to White demands. It was the basis for a Black sensibility of equality, and that was sufficiently different from the Christianity described by Whites to warrant suspicion and contempt.

Harper addresses this problem of the role of the church in this situation of dire material need for the freed slaves explicitly in a discussion late in *Trial and Triumph*. Mrs. Lasette opens her house to provide for public conversations that buoy up the community, giving attendees access to knowledge that had been denied Black people for the last two centuries, and, while at a gathering, Mr. Thomas, who is a carpenter, talks to a Revd. Lomax about his church (Harper, 1994, p. 246). Mr. Thomas then goes on to describe in detail what a church should provide to meet the needs of this community that is both beleaguered from within and without. The sense the reader gets is that Black freed people are desperate and want for everything, particularly when White people define themselves collectively as those who must seek to refuse employment and improved resources to anyone Black. Unable to address the capacity of this social description of Whiteness to constrain the ambitions of Black people, Mr. Thomas seeks to provide what he can, as does Mrs. Lasette. To this aim, he suggests a safe house for homeless boys should be a permanent part of every church – a place where all are welcome and meals are served at a price below that offered for a drink at nearby saloons (Harper, 1994, p. 247). A room should also be set aside in the parish building for women such as Mrs. Lasette to hold mothers' meetings. For Mr. Thomas, the church must play an important role in defining a community where moral, spiritual, and intellectual life are the core principles. What is of concern, according to him, is the allure in this time of desperation of palliatives, "the influence of low grogshops, gambling dens, and houses of ill fame" (Harper, 1994, p. 248).

He suggests that women could go out from the church to visit homes across the neighborhood, providing the type of instruction necessary to inoculate the community against the possible perils that are associated with abject poverty, a lack of education, and daily humiliations. He then discusses the reason for their vulnerability as a problem of financial investment and employment practices by Black people in the community. Mr. Thomas criticizes Revd. Lomax not just for employing only a White contractor to build his church, but also for not requiring the contractor to use Black carpenters and workmen when these men are out of work because of the color line.

He suggests that the contractor could have been forced to hire Black people rather than attempting to reinforce a White color line, simply because to do otherwise was to lose a job worth some 30,000 dollars. These opportunities for challenging the description of a social authority based on the need to define Black inferiority should be taken when possible, and he provides an example of someone who, though skilled as a saddler, is unable to get work because he is Black. Mr. Thomas also asks why Black people are unable to be wholesalers and traders of cotton when so many of them pick it (Harper, 1994, p. 249). That the church could make financial investments in the welfare of the people, as a part of its mission, is important. The implication in this scene is that Revd. Lomax has not thought of these possible effects of the church's presence on the community. Harper is making a claim that the best way to communicate the tenets of Christianity is to provide examples in the good work of those who are in the congregation, and to allow the church to stand as a veritable source of material, as well as spiritual, resistance to the description of racial inequality being developed to shore up White superiority. It is in this way a fount of equality, and a source for the argument that must be made in material terms, for racial equality.

This argument for buying Black, from institutions that either depend on Black labor or provide a service to Black people as consumers, is important because it addresses something that the practices of separate but equal – which were being developed to discriminate against Black people through exclusion – were doing immediately after the War. While Whiteness could be defined through financial strategies as a coherent authority, it was not possible for Black people to do the same thing, to arrogate their resources as a definition of the community, of a shared purpose, simply because the politics did not demand it. There was no collective impetus on the part of Black people to be superior, but there also had been no definition of racial difference based on withholding or refusing investments and financial assistance by a population that was largely impoverished and cast adrift in the immediate aftermath of the Civil War. With this description, Harper is suggesting that the church could provide just such a vehicle for consolidating financial resources and building a community, but not as a description of racial superiority and difference. Instead, the church would define an equality between Black and White people through its investments. In other words, the equality being described by Frances Harper was not a reversal of positions, but the idea of breaking the relationship between Whiteness and resources in the society. This was an attempt to arrogate authority across the color line, not perform in turn a reversal of the fortunes of those who could be thought Black or White. How else to achieve equality, except by refusing to participate in the processes by which material and social inequality were reproduced?

Harper is aware of the problem with trying to build a financial base for a community that refuses the solidarity of racial assignment, and is instead defined as Black through exploitative distributive processes that recently included the ownership of their persons by others, as themselves commodities. This awareness is obvious in how Mr. Thomas couches the argument for Revd. Lomax. In other words, Black free persons were not making choices in a field of decisions about resource allocation where racial difference wasn't defined already. The world was for them saturated with the effects of a description of Whiteness that was not only socially coherent, but considered – after 200 years of development – natural and immutable. Where were the educational opportunity, the financial resources, and the professional network to facilitate the large-scale advancement of a Black community to come from? The call to action, for Frances Harper and her fellow activists, was obvious. But this idea was grounded in the equal capacity by all persons to succeed, and not racial difference.

What defines this capacity is the result of education – the development of the community through an education provided for everyone in the society. A public school, in truth. And this was the message of the novel – its purpose, so to speak, in its serialization in the *Christian Recorder*. The novel ends appropriately with Annette as a teacher of the community, surrounded by children and their parents, elders in the community, listening and learning to love books and knowledge as she does.

Conclusion

What seems obvious is that the new community that Frances Harper describes, with regard to Annette and Mrs. Harcourt, Mrs. Lasette and Mr. Thomas, develops through moral strictures that have to account for the requirements of gender equality, as well as account for the resource needs of a population that is both indigent and uneducated. This population cannot do this alone, not if also experiencing at the same time the full force of a White community mobilized to deny them the opportunities they would need to succeed. Harper, in *Trial and Triumph*, demonstrates the intersectional moral requirements necessary to cohere as a Black community that could provide the type of economic, social, and therefore political direction she felt was important to participate fully in the life of the nation. In the relationships that Annette has, Harper demonstrates the risks to this population if they do not find allies, and work to engage Whites constructively, even as they sought to define a life after slavery.

Some 20 years after the end of the War, what did the Black community look like? Harper describes a Black population whose desire for material wealth and social acceptance mirror those supposedly in White society. She claims that there is an alternate vision of the community that would not merely reflect White society, but in fact challenge the idea of racial inequality that is accepted by too many, two decades after the War's end.

At the same time, it is clear that Harper understands something readers at the time did as well, something that we have obscured almost a century and a half after this novel was published: that slavery set its mark on everyone, those in the North as well as those in the South, to the extent that, more than two decades after the end of the Civil War, she can still write about the Black population being uneducated, poor, and struggling to form a moral community. This is a full generation after the end of slavery, and now there are Black children of slaves that have never known the formal legal authority over their person that their parents experienced. So, what happened, if not the brutal suppression of the freed Black population through synchronized and monitored processes of exclusion and violence, developed as the definition of what it meant to be White? In the novel, Harper offers the reader the perspective that not everyone was willing to participate in this description of a consolidated oppressive Whiteness. She offers a hope that some people, Black or White, are trying to work together to build lives of a tentative, fragile equality across the color line.

4

Sowing and Reaping:
Personal Solutions and Conviction

Complicity

In *Sowing and Reaping*, Frances Harper attempts to find a different solution to the problem of racial injustice. The novel has similar themes of predation, exploitation, and morality to *Trial and Triumph*, but here the plot has the young woman reject, rather than accept, the love of a man because of his inappropriate behavior. In spite of the initial difficulty of this rejection socially, eventually the protagonist finds someone who matches her own moral strength of character. Instead of a concern with society or community, in this novel we have a story that provides an opportunity for the reader to consider what we need to accomplish as individuals – how we should negotiate our own presence within the communities being formed, to, on the one hand, engage in a politics to counter the formal description of Black inferiority in *Iola Leroy*, and, on the other hand, to create the educational processes that must be in place for the community to be able to define an equality that persists in *Trial and Triumph*. *Sowing and Reaping* provides the missing personal piece to a solution that, I argue, Frances Harper allows us to consider regarding the possibility of a future racial equality in the society.

While ostensibly a study of the importance of a woman's personal choices and moral fortitude as a definition of community, *Sowing and Reaping* sets out the problem of how morality can be used to claim a new community, to build a different society from that which is given for the individual. In fact, because race is not mentioned explicitly in the novel, in the context of her other novels we should think of *Sowing and Reaping* as the first attempt by an African American author to have gender describe the conditions for the resolution of the major problems of the Black community, without thereby erasing or effacing the problem of racial inequality. Instead of describing the idea of a personal choice between being White and Black as itself a flawed racist politics for the titular character, Iola Leroy, in that novel, in *Sowing and Reaping* the plot describes the lives of the women protagonists as requiring a gender politics.

The argument made by Harper through the character's choices in the novel is not to subordinate gender to race, as the quote from a speech by Harper suggests: "When the question of race I let the lesser question of sex go" (Dudden, 2011, pp. 161–88). In what should be seen as a rejection of a split between White feminists and Black feminists on the question of the rights of women and Black people in the society, Frances Harper provides a description, in this novel from 1876, of how women must negotiate the problem of moral certainty and social progress without extricating race from gender (Fulton, 2007, pp. 210–11; McDaneld, 2015, pp. 403, 411; Rosenthal, 1997, p. 159).

In 1876, when *Sowing and Reaping* was serialized, it

had been ten years since Frances Harper had given her famous speech at the Eleventh National Women's Rights Convention signaling her specific position as an interlocutor on the intersectionality of gender and race within the Women's Suffrage Movement. In her speech "We Are All Bound Up Together," given at the Convention immediately after the end of the War in 1866, Frances Harper no longer had to speak of slavery and freedom, but instead of a common condition for all Black people (Harper, 1990h, pp. 217–19). In this case, she was speaking at the major national feminist organizational conference alongside Susan B. Anthony, Lucretia Mott, Elizabeth Cady Stanton, and others famous for their organizational work on behalf of women's rights. Frances Harper was considered one of their number, and her speech was an important moment in establishing the cooperation of the White feminist organizations and Black political organizations after the War. In the context of the national conversation around voting rights, Harper was one of the few Black women able to work closely with those organizations that wanted women to have the right to vote but were reluctant to support the voting rights of Black men. Harper was an advocate for Black male suffrage because of her conviction that, without the vote, the freedom won through the War would be lost. But, as we saw in previous chapters in the discussion of her novels, she was also convinced that, without the vote, women would never achieve the necessary freedom to define the gender equality required for a democratic society.

Harper opens her speech by describing her own experience with gender injustice upon the loss of her farm after the death of her husband. She explains that, until that loss, she had not understood how gender was as central to her experience as race. Of course, it wasn't true that she had not experienced injustice because she was a woman. But, through this example, Harper provided a comparison between the two forms of injustice, and an explanation of how they intersected in her own life. Because of her husband's death, the bank repossessed her milking equipment and forced Harper to repay his debts. It was with her money from the sale of her poetry that they had originally bought the farm, but without the equipment to make butter for the market, Harper was forced to return fulltime to her occupation as lecturer and poet.

Harper observes here that "justice is not fulfilled so long as women are unequal before the law" (Harper, 1990h, p. 217). She relates that, in her absence from the farm, a neighbor to whom she had once lent money came and took possession of her featherbed, claiming that Harper no longer resided there. This she describes to demonstrate how not having rights as a woman made it impossible to keep the farm, and to emphasize that, had the situation been reversed, the bank would never have repossessed her husband's property or allowed his bed to be stolen by a neighbor. The assumption would have been that he would promptly remarry.

It is this last claim, of remarriage, that reminds the contemporary reader that, as a single woman and then as a widow, it must have been very difficult for Harper to garner respect in public as a lecturer (Boyd, 1994, pp. 42–5; Foster, 1990, p. 12). In both conditions, her relationship to men would define her public identity. She saw her four years of marriage elided through the assumption of her husband's debt, understanding that, as a property owner, he would have easily remarried and would never have faced the stigma or social constraints she faced, if she had died instead.

Harper continues with the observation that to oppress the weakest is to blight the soul of the society, and uses the language of "you" to implicate her audience both in slavery and in the recent Emancipation. She claims that the chains of slavery simultaneously deprived White men of free speech and freedom of the press, crippling the country, and penalizing White men who did not own slaves. The resentment and anger of poor White men today are a consequence, Harper quips, not of Emancipation, but of the effects of slavery on the development of the national character. Claiming that what is occurring after the War is a "grand and glorious revolution" that will not stop until the entire American Republic is color blind, Harper makes a distinction between the claim of rights for White women, and her own sense of wrongs and injustice as a Black woman. She states that the vote for women will not cure the society of ills, not when Harper cannot take a seat in a street car in Philadelphia without the conductor stopping the car, rather than let her ride as a Black person (Harper, 1990h, p. 218). She described being placed in the smoking car with the White men on a train ride from Washington DC to Baltimore, only to refuse the second time. She goes on to describe similar indignities and asks of her audience the question: "Have women nothing to do with this?" The claims against her presence in White sections of street cars and train cars are, she points out, due to her being a Black person, not because she is a woman. And yet the White women are also responsible for the racial segregation that she experiences.

In this speech, Frances Harper lays out some of the parameters of the struggle that will take place between the national Suffragist Movement and Black Women's organizations over the next 40 years of her life. That Harper felt that both gender and racial injustice were important, and worked for decades with White women organizing for women's rights, as well as Black women's organizations, gives her speech of 1866 importance as a precursor of the contemporary tradition of Black feminist criticism, where the intersection of race and gender provides for Harper's unique position. She is discriminated against because she is a woman with regard to property rights and social expectations, while also experiencing the problem of segregation in public transportation and the threat of White violence.

Harper provides this description of gender and race as a personal experience, without suggesting that one has priority. In her opinion, despite the acceptance of voting rights of Black men, to speak of Women's voting rights and not also address racial inequality is to misunderstand the political consequences of a focus on the one and not also the other. That Black men and White women could vote would not address the problems she experiences as a woman and as a Black person. As Harper puts it, while some would vote on principles, others would vote according to "prejudice or malice" (Harper, 1990h, p. 218), and some would vote with whichever side they believed was going to win. Harper is not saying that women's rights are less important than those supportive of racial equality. Instead, as she points out, "Today I am puzzled where to make my home" (Harper, 1990h, p. 218). For her, it is self-evident, as it should be for us today, that justice requires working together, as women and Black people, to find a solution to these problems.

Frances Harper in *Sowing and Reaping* demonstrates the political potential in continuing to address the moral uplift of the community using a formulation of an intersectional analysis, juxtaposing the material security of the newly freed community a decade after the War with their inability to similarly secure what she describes as cultural progress. Harper describes it thus: "while their wealth had advanced their culture stood still" (Gardner, 2012). She discusses this problem with the reader: of the values that individuals should cultivate alongside a concern with other values – specifically, economic and gender equality – to develop a complex description of a community that can continue to thrive in the post-War period. This makes *Sowing and Reaping* a crucial element in the oeuvre of Frances Harper, and a novel consistent with the ambition of her other works.

Harper's writing in the novel provides for an incisive and important statement of how the issues of race and gender are defined in US society. The novel was serialized in the *Christian Recorder*, an organ of the American Methodist Episcopal (AME) Black church, with a largely African American readership, and with the expectation that this audience would accept and understand the importance of the claims for a gender equality in the context of temperance rhetoric. Frances Harper had participated in the organizational split in the national Suffrage Movement over the political priorities of the organizations in the post-War period. But the argument made in the period immediately after the War, suggesting that a political trade-off between equal rights of race and gender was necessary at the time to achieve some form of legislative success in DC, should not be confused with the idea that gender and racial equality are not always imbricated with each other.

Harper is explicit in the novel that the argument for temperance is a way to claim some measure of gender equality in social relationships when women cannot vote and have few, if any, political rights not mediated through the men in their lives. At the time of its publication, Harper was directly involved in the national mobilization by women in the Temperance Movement. *Sowing and Reaping* can be thought in this context to offer the audience a clear statement as to the importance of political rights for women at the time.

When, in the novel, Harper provides dialogue that references conventional African American social tropes, the audience, then and now, is to understand that race is always also in the room, working in the social situations that involve the characters in the novel. In this sense, as Doveanna Fulton

points out, in *Sowing and Reaping* Harper creates "racial inde-
terminant characters as a strategic act" (2007, p. 211). Harper
provides for her African American readers the opportunity to
participate in a conversation about the importance of moral
constancy and gender equality for the development of their
society. At the same time, it is important to understand that
she would also have tried to appeal to multiple audiences,
beyond that of the largely African American readership of
the *Christian Recorder*, with a theme of temperance. Her own
experience as a temperance activist, and her immense popularity as a poet and public speaker, would at the time have
meant that there would have been a ready White audience
for her novel. In the novel, Joe Gough is a homonym for a
real-life White temperance activist John Gough (Foreman,
2009; Fulton, 2007, pp. 212–13), just as Mary Gough is the
name of the wife of the real-life John Gough. Readers who
knew of this homonymic connection of the characters in the
novel with existing Temperance Movement figures would
have assumed that, at least, Joe Gough and Mary Gough
in the novel were White. Frances Harper has intentionally
nuanced the relationship between gender and race to leave
the status of the characters unimportant to making the argument for women's rights and temperance.

    This chapter should be thought of as following logically
from a description of cascading political claims against racial
inequality, where the societal development of the problem of
political mobilization on behalf of a free Black community,
to protect political rights in *Iola Leroy*, discussed in chapter 2,
is followed, in chapter 3, by the requirement that this collective mobilization, described in the novel *Trial and Triumph*,
reference objective measures of equality – some description
external to its formation so as to protect its members from
the inequalities that are developed within. In this chapter, the
role of the individual as someone who can choose, and must

make important political choices with regard to a description of social inequality, is described as necessary to achieve the coherence of collective demands that could continue to challenge existing inequalities in the society at large. In other words, this chapter discusses a novel by Frances Harper that argues for the importance of a personal moral position for making effective collective justice claims in the society.

That this novel was serialized in the midst of the organizational work Harper was doing in the Temperance Movement is, in my opinion, an indication of how she sought to define the work necessary for individuals with regard to the relationship between gender and racial inequality in the society. Temperance was the political vehicle for making sure that political claims for racial and gender justice were, as she describes in her speech from 1866, "all bound up together" (Harper, 1990h, 217).

The plot

Sowing and Reaping begins with a short conversation between two men, in which one of them exclaims at how the owner of a saloon has closed down his premises because his wife was so opposed to the business. Their interlocutor says in response, "Well, I would never let any woman lead me around by the nose. I would let her know that as the living comes by me, the way of getting it is my affair, not hers, as long as she is well provided for." The response to this diatribe is a clear statement of the position that Harper provides as the underlying moral argument of the novel: "All men are not alike, and I confess that I value the peace and happiness of my home more than anything else, and I would not like to engage in any business that was a constant pain to my wife" (Harper, 1994, p. 95). The two discuss the relationship between men and women, but in the context of financial success. And Harper makes clear that the possibility of making money off of the ruined ambitions of others is not acceptable, to women in particular. The assumption here is that men and women have distinct places or roles in society, on the one hand, and, on the other – the assumption espoused by Harper – that there is a relationship to industry that is shared as a family.

This idea of generosity and understanding being developed by the individual allows for the extension of this to others, those outside the family, and therefore describes a collective ambition, as witnessed by one of the interlocutors mentioning that he refused to foreclose on a debt of $500 because he felt sorry for the other person's misfortune. He believes this investment of forbearance and community support will benefit him in the long run, and that he would rather lose the money now and think of it as an investment in the future. Later in the story, in fact, this proves true, as fortunes change and the person, Paul Clifford, who lent the money is paid back by the son at a critical time. The message of generosity and working together to build the resources of the community mirror those relations of comity and exchange in the family, and this is contrasted with the idea of looking always after oneself and defining one's personal interest, rather than community interest.

John Anderson and Paul Clifford, the interlocutors, are characters that the reader follows throughout the novel, beginning when they are young grocers. Eventually, John Anderson shifts away from Clifford, deciding to go into liquor sales and owning fancy clubs; he is ambitious and stops at nothing to succeed, while Paul Clifford refuses to invest in the sale of liquor, even if it is lucrative. Belle Gordon and Jeanette Roland also represent two different choices for women. Belle Gordon refuses the advances of Charles

Romaine, who is becoming a drunkard, while Jeanette Roland falls for the prospect of his wealth and professional potential. Belle Gordon eventually meets Paul Clifford, marries him and lives a contented and fulfilling life, while Jeanette is miserable and suffers. John Anderson eventually dies with the ruins of his family around him.

What is telling, however, is not the juxtapositions of characters, or the subplots, but the way Harper switches between scenes in the novel with men and then women, and then brings them all together. She purposefully weaves together questions of gender roles and equality with the idea of a community that must sustain itself against the raw appeal of wealth, moral dependency, and alcohol addiction. The drive, ambition, and opportunities of a life should be met and constrained by the requirements of constancy and self-control. The seeds of a commitment to a moral life are sown among the thorns, fall by the path and are taken up and lost, or find good nourishing soil and take root.

Harper provides examples in equal part of women and men who lack judgment and perspicacity, even when they are surrounded by those who urge caution. For the characters in the novel, drinking is a sign of a lack of social control, of a desire to too quickly advance or engage in the hubris of mastering an environment that isn't truly theirs to own. Neither men nor women hold a monopoly on the solution to excess desire and willfulness; both bear the capacity to destroy the community, and thus themselves, through bad judgment. The fact that wantonness destroys the person and demoralizes the community, and is then a threat to the capacity of others to build a successful life, makes the problem of drinking not merely personal but social, and definitive of what is possible for a community (Harper, 1994, p. 106).

Harper is explicit, throughout *Sowing and Reaping*, about the importance of a gender equality defined through the work of collective social judgment and individual self-control. At one point she has the paragon of moral constancy, Belle Gordon, say without arrogance:

> And as we sow, so must we reap, and as to saying about young men sowing their wild oats, I think it is full of pernicious license. A young man has no more right to sow his wild oats than a young women. God never made one code of ethics for a man and another for a woman. And it is the duty of all true women to demand of men the same standard of morality they do of women.
>
> (Harper, 1994, p. 103)

For a society that had, a decade earlier, sloughed off the evils of chattel slavery, the idea of the dangers of a lack of self-control, of being enslaved to personal desires, was an important admission of potential culpability for the community. To replace the oppression of an absolute White authority developed in slavery, with a lack of self-control and the absence of social responsibility in drinking or social wantonness was counterintuitive. Freedom must be more than simply the right to do whatever a person desires, and must be grounded in the idea of a common set of ambitions.

In its description of the consequences of social behavior, the novel attempts to provide the reader with the moral agency to succeed in achieving specific social goals, but, because of the historical record that readers would have had at the time of the travels of Frances Harper in the South after the Civil War, the novel was also a description of the achievements of the formerly enslaved in the decade since the end of the War. A thriving town where the population had the leisure to consider the moral cultivation of its population, free from material want, had to be considered aspirational at the time.

Readers of the novel in 1876 could ask themselves, based on the description of the town in the novel: What does the equality of persons demand of us, as Black people (Williams, 2013, p. 28)? Through the actions of her characters, Harper also asks this question today, of us. What will we sow, such that we can reap a harvest that is abundant – so that we can realize that we are all bound up together in one national purpose or destiny? That we are still very much a racially divided nation today must enjoin us to pay close attention to the work of those such as Frances Harper, who wrote this novel about morality and political purpose toward the end of the nineteenth century.

The rigidity of the gender roles that Harper describes, in spite of her description of equal gender culpability, is one that leaves women with few options for deviance and dissent similar to those of the men, however. The moral rectitude that women are expected to demonstrate is for Harper's vision ideally matched by that of the men. Only once does Harper mention in the novel, and then only indirectly, the idea that women might also drink. She does mention women who frequent gambling halls and are prostitutes, but women in the novel are accused not of partaking themselves in debauchery, but of offering drink to their potential partners. From this perspective, women can be thought partially responsible for the moral values of the community, even though, as the opening conversation tells the reader, it is the lack of respect for women that allows for the immorality of the community. That women must also bear the burden of the bad choices that men make is for Harper a powerful message in the novel. How men sow, in the absence of equal political rights, so shall the women reap.

At the time the novel was published, Frances Harper was a widow and had written poems and the short story "The Two Offers," which lauded the independence of single women, while also being supportive of marriage in her writing of the novel *Minnie's Sacrifice*, for example. So, what made things difficult in terms of marriage? Debauchery and drunkenness, because these things lead men to neglect their homes and wives, and in the novel to eventually become ill and die. This was the novel's explicit plot. But what is implied throughout is that it is the absence of an equality of purpose and moral direction shared by both parties to the relationship that causes problems for people. How could the expectations of both husband and wife be the same when women could not vote?

The vote

If women were in fact held to certain social standards, they should also have the right to vote. The 14th Amendment granting all men over 21 the right to vote was ratified in 1868, and the 15th Amendment granting Black men the right to vote was ratified in 1870. The first replaced property with gender as a legal status, since it was no longer possible, since the 13th Amendment in 1865, to enslave people as property except as punishment for a crime. That women could stand in part for the morality of the family meant that they also should be able to participate in the measure of its political development as a component of the community. Anything else was unacceptable, to Harper and many others, and this is evident in the constant measure of morality and social standards by the women throughout the novel. That women were powerless without the vote, and should not be made to rely on the devotion of their husbands to secure their liberty, was stated explicitly and also allegorically in the failure of Jeanette Roland to curb her husband Charles Romaine's appetite for alcohol. The power of the sanctity and reputation of the good home to determine the actions of the men, the constraint on women without the vote in addressing their concern for the social conventions between men and women, the policing of their own moral behaviors, were insufficient to control the political choices of men. Harper writes, for example, when describing the capacity of Jeanette Roland to control the activities of Charles Romaine, that "her power to bind him to the simple attractions of home were as futile as a role of cobwebs to moor a ship to the shore, when it has drifted out and is dashing among the breakers" (Harper, 1994, p. 163).

It is in this context of developing the political organization necessary to secure women's rights that Annette and her mother, Mrs. Gladstone, talk about the importance of the vote for women. They stake out opposite positions on the matter, with Annette disparaging women's post-War agitation for the vote: "Now mother if we women would use our influence with our fathers, brothers, husbands, and sons, could we not have everything we want?" Mrs. Gladstone's response is to suggest that this is insufficient to protect not only the interests of women as a population, but the interests of the society:

> No, my dear we could not, with all our influence we never could have the same sense of responsibility which flows from the possession of power. I want women to possess power as well as influence, I want every Christian woman as she passes a grogshop or liquor saloon, to feel that she has on her heart the burden of responsibility for its existence, I hold my dear that a nation as well as an individual should have a conscience.
>
> (p. 161)

Harper goes on to point out the importance of education for women in order to have the capacity to one day acquire the vote, and how single women, those adults without a male relative, would not otherwise be able to have their needs represented in politics (Harper, 1994, p. 162).

Without the vote, Harper explains, women are unable to pass laws to protect themselves from bad decisions by the men in their lives and in the larger society. Without the vote, the worst thing for a woman to do was to cede what control she had as a single woman to that of a man who was dissipated and unable to control his appetites. The novel is rife with examples of poor judgment with regard to drinking by fathers, brothers, husbands, and sons. Harper provides examples also of women who are dragged down by the drunken dereliction of their husbands, showing that drinking represents for women the most obvious example of the lack of control over their own lives without the vote. What seems on the surface a novel about the dangers of alcoholism is throughout, from this perspective, a call to action for women to strive collectively for the vote.

How do you describe a community where those who provide the moral compass are simply left at home, remaining in the private sphere rather than being able to define the public in a democracy – one where the actions of some are considered of no account, and there is no recourse or institutional capacity with which to determine a different path? As Frances Harper describes it, this is the problem when the man should have steered instead of simply drifting in the currents of his life. This sentiment, expressed throughout Harper's writing, expresses the problem identified most clearly in the novel *Sowing and Reaping*: of trying to determine where this Black community is to go, what they can become, and how to get there, when roughly half of the community is encouraged to ignore the lessons taught by the other half. While this sounds like a harsh judgment, for Frances Harper, having to explain what is to be done to a community forming after enslavement, and for us today, with millions of Black people in prison, there seems no other way to discuss the problem. The political efficacy of Black women was the most important mandate for her generation, and for ours.

The Temperance Movement is used in *Sowing and Reaping* by Harper as a conceptual surrogate – even though it was a real-world commitment that she engaged in throughout the rest of her life – for the issue of how a woman should lead her life, and how her insecurity about her own resources and choices for success was due to the view of gender inequality in a society where women could not vote. That a widow is described as having been made bankrupt upon the death of her husband due to his debts, and that the widow makes the son promise to pay off her remaining creditors isn't a coincidence in the novel but the expression by Harper of a mandate for moral constancy, a description of the true woman, which is then the basis for arguing for the vote for women. That this same thing happened to Harper when, upon the death of her husband, the dairy farm's creditors repossessed her milking equipment gave the example some poignancy and force for the reader at the time.

What were women to do if their husbands decided to go out in public, to drink and gamble away their family's financial assets, squander their political capital, while women remained in a social world constrained to discussions of the household? Harper makes a point of having her characters discuss whether women should handle the finances of the household, or a man, and how a woman could not own property of her own except what was given to her by her father, brother, or son. Through another character, Miss Tabitha, and with phrases that resonate from the American revolution, Harper argues that "We single women who are constantly taxed without being represented, know what it is to see ignorance and corruption striking hands together and

voting away our money for whatever purposes they choose"
(Harper, 1994, p. 162).

This is a feminist political novel, one that also addressed
the relationship between gender and race as a political solution to developing the community of free Blacks a decade
after the War. It is a test of the reader today's own thinking
about racial politics, this trace or implicit racial voice – a call
to race by Frances Harper, someone who was in fact writing
a book about the role of the women in society and the need
for them to have the collective and individual political power
and rights that derive from being able to vote. Could Harper
have written a book about the rights of Black women in contrast to the racism of White women? Yes, this was a subplot
in each of her other three books. So why did she excavate
references to race in just this novel? Because she needed an
interpretative field for the argument for gender progress in
the nation, even as she made a claim about the centrality of
a free Black community to the description of this country
itself. If any are denied political rights, it is not a democratic
society.

Describing race as a context provided by the aims of the
society in question, and the audience and author, allows the
story to demonstrate for us today the subtle pull toward justice of a claim for women's rights that would also include
all women, even as it offers up the possibility of addressing
problems specific to racial inequality. This allows the reader
to consider the problem of gender and class for the Black
community, not a society where race is also an issue. The
novel *Sowing and Reaping* was serialized in a Christian African
American newspaper, and so the readership was supposed to
understand the text as a story without the requirement of
racial difference – a story about themselves, as a community
populated by free people with new aspirations and ambitions
to participate in defining the life of the nation in the 1870s.

In developing the temperance debate within the actions of the novel's characters, Harper provides a frame for how we also think of Black progressivism and conservativism today. The progressive feels that anything that impedes the development of opportunities toward racial justice and equality as a community should be prohibited, while the conservative argues for the importance of allowing individual ambition to supersede the needs of and divisions in the community. The choice between caring for the welfare of others as a description of social justice for the community, and the gratification of individual desires at the expense of the needs and social expectations of others is stark in the novel. At the same time, today there is little discussion of the social requirements of individual moral action with regard to the Black community. Few would see their own social actions as reflecting the larger society, but rather as their own moral perspective divorced from any larger societal implication.

The novel, instead, connects the desires of individuals and their moral choices to collective social outcomes, for families and for the community. The relationships between persons, the individual characters, are each developed with regard only to a concern with providing the characters with clear moral choices. The ability of men to resist consuming alcohol is described as a matter of character, a product of upbringing, an understanding of the personal and community peril that alcoholism represents, and a definition of true manhood. This idea of manhood is described by Harper in stark and unambivalent terms through the contrasts between the characters of the novel – for example, Paul Clifford and John Anderson.

Paul suffers for his obstinacy and refusal to compromise his moral beliefs for personal gain. He is generous in principle when to be so is not to his advantage, and he assists others without stint or hesitation. John Anderson, on the other hand, is described as always looking to get ahead, to do what he needs, regardless of the ethical consequences for others, and describes his morals as being limited to the idea that what is best for himself is best for everyone. John Anderson is going to get his, and if others benefit that is fine, as long as they don't get in his way. Any chance for wealth is to be grasped by him without hesitation.

With these characters, the novel asks the reader also the question of what should be required of men, those who can vote – at least in theory – at the time of the serialization of the novel in the 1870s, to provide for the population of women as a political bloc. As Harper points out, and as she knew from personal experience as a public speaker, a single woman had no socially legitimate means of public expression. The organization of women into marches and engaging in collective action on their own behalf is mentioned only once in the novel, but Harper is clear that even a man such as Paul Clifford, who shares equally the burdens and duties of the household with Belle Gordon upon their marriage, is unable to fully represent a woman's need for equal representation in the polity.

The quandary here for the reader is to decide what is required of men – particularly Black men in the context of when the novel was published – when the men have just established the law that does not allow women to vote. How can Paul Clifford support the needs of Belle socially, and not also do so politically? It is this problem that opens the novel, and the conversation about how a man is supposed to engage with his future wife's ideas about both the world and his own behaviors is, albeit problematically, also a contemporary concern. John Anderson is very clear that his future wife will have no say in what he does outside the immediate physical household.

What begins as a description of the authority of men over

their activities in business is, by the middle of the novel, described as a decision of male social behaviors, such as drinking and gambling or attending church and temperance meetings. The novel attempts to make the case that individual moral choices should be considered as community concerns, as the responsibility not solely of individuals, but of those who provide the opportunities for immorality, whether these come from oppression and hardship, or social encouragement. It is when the destruction of women's lives is caused by things men do as their political representatives – as agents completely out of their control – that Harper raises the problem of the vote for women. In the novel, it is only when women are able to find their voice in social situations outside the home that the question of what rights are required for women's equality can be raised. What is at stake is the wellbeing of the community, of which women are an active part.

As Harper points out, marriage is not a strong enough contract to secure political representation for women. That Harper makes this argument almost 50 years before women could vote should be understood by us as a testament to her perspicacity as a writer and thinker. The argument for temperance should be seen as a strategy used by Harper to make a claim against both men and women in the society for the right of women to vote. That this claim is set against the choices of men and women who are striving for financial stability and wealth, as well as stable and loving relationships, should be interpreted as an effort by Harper to appeal to the sensibilities of a reading public that was concerned with how material success and a moral life were to be balanced. That the ruinous effects of drink on families were a concern for many made its discussion in the novel a suitable topic by which to introduce the importance of the vote for women.

But the problems of morality and community remain a central issue for the Black community today, even if the questions about its future are not framed with regard to voting and drinking. In the novel, Paul Clifford was raised by a mother who was adamant about teaching her son the importance of temperance and right living. He remains steadfast and a good person throughout his life, which is attributed by Harper to this personal maternal care and attention to the needs of the community (Farrar, 2015, p. 54). It is Paul Clifford – and not Charles Romaine, who is without moral character – who falls in love and marries the novel's example of young righteous community activism, Belle Gordon. In this depiction of choices and social outcomes, Frances Harper stands firmly in the camp of those who argue today that the Black mother must provide the moral bulwark against the temptations that otherwise exist for young Black men and women to become involved in behaviors that ruin their capacity to contribute to the effective development of the community. However, the argument made in the novel is not solely about the temptation for people to make bad choices. Harper, in the novel, is trying to make a case for the need for political rights to defend the community against not merely bad actors such as John Anderson, but also collective political oppression in the form of misogyny and racism.

The gender politics in our society still allows men to conceptualize themselves as able and encouraged to remain fettered to a moral life only by choice, rather than by obligation to the community, and to their partners and children. That Paul Clifford lives with Belle Gordon as an equal partner is consistent with Harper's gender ideals, as he not only listens to her but shares the decisions about both household and business with her. What matters within Harper's framework is that Clifford learned as a child to respect women, not just as persons with their own ambitions and ideas, but as a source for moral claims equal to those of men in an environment where there were other competing sources for determining actions.

It is with regard to those institutions and social ideals that exist outside the household that Harper writes, and in this context the vote is the most important available measure of political equality for women. That today women can vote should be weighed against the comprehensive suppression of Black voting into the 1960s. The suppression of Black male voting had begun already in the 1870s when Harper published *Sowing and Reaping*. That this continues as a factor in determining political outcomes today isn't a coincidence, but an important aspect of the construction of racial inequality and gender inequality in the society. In fact, the suppression of the Black vote today acts as did the prohibition of the vote for women until 1920 – as an important constraint on the capacity of both Black people and women to successfully form the community politics that are necessary to address the problems of both gender and racial inequality. It is in this context that we can see the genius of Harper's seemingly conventional description of moral constancy and its linkage to feminist advocacy. She provides recipes for not merely survival and recovery, but cooperative positive development of the community for both women and men (Harper, 1994, pp. 161–2).

The personal is political

Belle Gordon is attracted to Charles Romaine but refuses to marry him because he drinks. She cannot give her heart to someone who is irresponsible with the trust the community has in him. It is important to the story that he is told by Belle exactly why she won't marry him, because this sets up the possibility that he can stop or will control his desires at her request. Can he listen and agree when a woman provides knowledge to him, when it is in his own interests, since he desires her as well? Is he receptive to the collective moral criteria available to them both, or does he lack not only the self-control, but also the will, to fulfill the needs of the community? As we find out, Charles Romaine is not sincere, reliable, or trustworthy with the needs of the community.

His explanation for why Belle refused him is important. Jeanette Roland asks him why he didn't marry Belle Gordon: "But Belle is very kind; she did it all for your own good." He remarks, "Of course she did; my father used to say so when I was a boy, and he corrected me; but it didn't make me enjoy the correction." Jeanette responds by suggesting kindly that, "It is said our best friends are those who show us our faults, and teach us how to correct them" (Harper, 1994, p. 116). Charles actually acknowledges his misplaced priorities, suggesting that the obligation to parents and duties to his wife need not be honored, but instead resented. Rather than affirm the moral criteria for not only friendship but a loving equal relationship, he suggests that he really wants someone to smile when he is around and make conversation, not judge him or demand things from him he isn't willing to give. He describes Belle Gordon thus: "Belle is very good, but somehow her goodness makes a fellow feel uncomfortable. She is what I call distressingly good" (Harper, 1994, p. 115).

"Belle Gordon is a Christian . . . other women might write beautiful poems; she did more. She made her life a thing of brightness and beauty." So writes Harper to describe the main character, on whom the novel's plot depends. Belle believed "that the inner life developed the outer," and ministered to the poor and downtrodden about self-reliance and self-control (Harper, 1994, p. 124). It is this faith that girds her convictions about the relationships to which she commits. Belle Gordon believed that "she was bought with a price" (Harper, 1994, p. 123).

Jeanette Roland is not as discerning, even though she is thrice warned – once by the example of Belle Gordon, her friend; then by Belle directly as to the character that Charles Romaine demonstrates; and then by Charles himself when he says he just wants someone to come home to. She marries Charles in spite of this, only to see him be fired from the law firm where he partnered with his father, and neglect the family so much that his son dies without him at home (Harper, 1994, p. 164). Jeanette Roland doesn't use her moral compass to discern what is necessary, but rather cares about being socially affirmed. Like Charles Romaine, she cares about appearances and immediate personal gratification, rather than the behaviors and ideals that provide for a viable and thriving community. That her child with Charles Romaine dies, there is no inheritance or progeny, no future community derived from this union, is Harper's stark example of what is at stake in not trusting in the moral criteria provided by parents and friends – that which is described as a care for the community.

These two examples of women coming to understand the relationship choices required for their own happiness, and that of the community, are included alongside the description of Paul Clifford's education by his mother when young and the redemption of Joe Gough. Paul Clifford was the son of a widow, whose husband had died from drinking after spending their fortune. Interestingly, Harper provides a description of the characteristics that made Paul's father susceptible to drink. Genial, charismatic, joyous, a wonderful companion at home, the father had as a result been also a great drinking partner at the saloons. Worried about him, his mother saw the same characteristics in the son Paul. So she spoke to him about self-control and the problem of drinking, and, as Harper writes, "In the morning she sowed the seed which she hoped would blossom in time. And bear fruit throughout eternity" (Harper, 1994, p. 99). The mother's ambition proves correct, and Paul is a stalwart and true member of the community, someone who accepts the modest returns from being a grocer rather than the wealth that accrues with liquor sales. Belle and Paul marry after they meet while rescuing Mary and Josiah Gough from the latter's intemperance.

Josiah (Joe) Gough is the husband of Mary Gough, whom Belle Gordon encounters when Mary faints in front of her in the street. Overworked, laboring to feed her children after her husband spends his days out drinking, Mary is dying of sorrow and exhaustion. Mary feels that it is her duty to "cling to her demented husband," and to do what she can to reform him from his drinking (Harper, 1994, p. 129). One day, shortly after having assisted Mary to her apartment, Belle sees that Mary is missing all of her hair. Her husband had cut it off to sell it for money for liquor (Harper, 1994, p. 133). Belle Gordon convinces Joe Gough to go to the Reform club, and while he is there Joe realizes that he can find a way back to Mary and his children: he just needs to, in the sense described by Harper, commit himself again to his own salvation and progress (p. 139). He signs the temperance pledge, reforms his behavior, and finds a job (Harper, 1994, p. 142; Peterson, 1995, p. 317).

The stories of these four younger people are provided in the novel as examples of what Harper means by the individual choices available to successfully develop the Black community. It is Mary and Josiah Gough who allow for a redemptive education of individuals, defined by commitment and constancy in the service of their relationships with others. What allows for Joe's recovery is the subordination of his own immediate desires not only because of the concern for others, but because of a return of a commitment to himself – his own understanding of the moral status that is at stake, his own life as coincident with that of the larger community. That he realizes this fact through the initial public embarrassment experienced in being confronted by Belle Gordon and Paul Clifford is important in Belle and Paul's journey to assist others. Joe is proof of their success.

The public space established as a consequence of personal decisions becomes the marker for assessing the moral condition of the community. Joe Gough's redemption, the work of Belle and Paul, the demonstrated failures over a lifetime of John Anderson, Jeanette Roland, and Charles Romaine – all provide for Frances Harper the measure for the moral success of the society. We don't have to agree today with the novel's message of temperance to understand that the concern with gender inequality in the absence of political rights, and moral character in the context of the promise of material wealth, remain very important to our society.

In the novel, Frances Harper has described her vision of the coming Black community through these relationships of assistance, redemption, and failure. We continue to struggle as a society with assessing the relationship between the personal and the description of community. Harper provides a specific set of instruments to be used when determining how we should act. Not all societal pursuits, not all that is possible for us to accomplish together, result in positive fulfillment. There are some activities that, in our freedom to choose our personal destiny, can result in our destruction. For Frances Harper, drinking alcohol, sexual wantonness, and public debauchery provide a personal path to the corruption of the very public that describes the ideals of the community.

The principle that underlies the identification of these social problems for Harper is a rejection of social activities, such as wealth accumulation without a moral compass, that provide a measure of how we should be distributing resources in the society – one that includes the mandate to correct, rather than accept, descriptions of social inequality. That the principles of the good of society, so to speak, require that individuals demonstrate self-control and the discipline to direct their activities to specific tasks isn't a new idea. In *Sowing and Reaping*, Frances Harper has provided for her readers a description of the social conditions that she believes we must address as a society.

Women in private and in the public

To further develop this understanding of Harper's vision of the personal commitment required to achieve the radical egalitarian vision of community provided by the example of *Iola Leroy*, it is useful to explore the themes in "The Two Offers." This short story was published in the inaugural issue of the *Christian Recorder* in 1859, 17 years before *Sowing and Reaping*.

The plot

"The Two Offers" is a story of two women who make consequential decisions with regard to relationships: one dies as a result of her marriage, and the other survives because, instead of marrying for convenience, she lives with a broken heart. In this piece, published in 1859 when Harper was 34 years old, the author distinguishes between the moral education provided each young woman as they grow up, and the innate human emotional capacity of each as a person to love and care for others. Harper also provides a description of how education about morality in the home, when they are young, determines how men develop their relationships with women.

As in *Sowing and Reaping*, this story presents the home as the first and most important place where individual morality is developed in a society. Harper provides a description of both the role of the mother in the home and what this idea of home must represent in the flourishing of an individual. The mother in any ideal family is described as an artist, a poet who should cultivate in the souls of her children the principles of goodness, beauty, grace, and love so that they can live nobly (Harper, 1994, p. 110). Harper writes throughout of the idea of truth, what it is to be true, and the importance of the truth for a child. This truth includes the ideal of consistency of parental authority – the need for a child to have obedience and duty defined not by chance but by a clear set of instructions and punishments.

To know and live in truth, for the child, in Frances Harper's vision, is to obey parents even if they don't provide for what we call today financial security, and to learn and act with an understanding of grace, beauty, and love. To act from a principle of respect for a constant parental authority, which is defined by a love of the child shown not through material conditions but through moral training, is to bring up a child able to contribute positively to the lives of those they encounter and to develop families that reproduce these values. According to Harper, a child is able to resist the allure of things that aren't good if brought up properly in a true home.

Harper states explicitly that gambling and prostitution are the antithesis of the truth and goodness of the home, and that these places where "unhealthy and unhallowed excitements" made "the well-regulated home" seem tame are problematic (Harper, 1994, p. 112). The home must provide respect for thrift and loyalty, for saving and industry, for limiting the desire for intimacy to the person to whom one is married.

"The Two Offers" follows the lives of Laura Lagrange

and her cousin, Jenette Alston. Laura was raised in a home of material wealth and indulgence, while Jenette was raised without wealth, but with an abundance of parental affection and a sense of goodness. Jenette's father dies without absolving financial debts and her mother is taken advantage of by the creditors. Subsequently, because as a woman she is unable to secure the financial means to sustain the home, Jenette's mother loses everything. Jenette is later, as an adult, able to recover from this early setback, and finds recognition and affirmation as a writer in the world.

Early in her adult life, Jenette falls in love with a man who becomes her "heart's worship," but then he dies and Jenette bears the pain of this loss for the rest of her life: "[A]nd so, pressing back the sobs from her almost breaking heart, like the dying dolphin, whose beauty is borne of its death anguish, her genius gathered strength from suffering and wondrous power and brilliancy from the agony she hid within the desolate chambers of her soul" (Harper, 1994, pp. 107–8). Although Jenette is haunted by this loss, she builds a full professional life and provides support for many in her community, including her cousin Laura.

Throughout her novels, Frances Harper always describes the love of women for particular men, as life partners, in singular terms. None of the heroines, even Iola Leroy who finds her own love of Gresham to be insufficient just because of his incapacity to imagine acknowledging his love of someone Black, demonstrates any interest for any man but the one and true partner. Laura Lagrange, on the other hand, begins the story with two offers for marriage in hand, neither of which she describes as arising from a love she returns. Convenient, acceptable, and for Laura a seemingly necessary solution to the vagaries of her own life, she therefore listens skeptically to the admonishment of her cousin Jenette, who suggests that even the difficulty she has in choosing between them reveals a lack of love and of understanding by her cousin of the consequences and personal importance of marriage as "an affinity of souls or union of hearts" (Harper, 1994, p. 106). Laura marries one of the men, and the central part of the story is comprised of the reader encountering Laura on her death bed, waiting in vain for the footsteps of her absent husband, while Jenette attends at her side. The man whom Laura Lagrange married isn't even given a name, being merely a symbol for the problem of defining what a constant love requires of a person.

Harper describes the husband thus: "In early life, home had been to him a place of ceilings and walls, not a true home, built upon goodness, love and truth . . . it was not the place for the true culture and right development of his soul" (Harper, 1994, p. 110). That Laura was raised spoiled and without obvious hardship counts against not only her ability to judge her own feelings of love and principles, but her capacity to understand the true consequences of marrying where love is not found. In this way, Harper demonstrates the importance of experience and adversity, of striving for something in order to understand its value. What is interesting for us is how this description of personal moral development is not couched in racial terms, and the same racial indeterminacy of characters is offered the reader as, years later, in *Sowing and Reaping*.

What Harper and her audience think of as obviously also including a description of human differences accessible to the African American author and readers of the short story in 1859 is not what we would think of today as reflecting the way we think of racial difference or how we imagine an African American readership today. In other words, we should be very careful to understand that Frances Harper's great success with the short story "The Two Offers" is an admonition to us, and a criticism of how we think of race today. Why would she need to discuss race differently when writing about the problem of temperance and gender inequality to a largely Black audience? The answer we give reveals how we think today of the relationship and definition of gender, race, and class, but doesn't tell us anything about what readers thought in 1859.

In "The Two Offers," Jenette chose independence and loneliness rather than Laura's fate of being tied to a husband who could not reciprocate her affections – someone who was, as Harper writes, "vain and superficial in his character" (Harper, 1994, 109). Harper states quite plainly for the reader that it is better for a woman to be single than yoked in a marriage that leads to a loveless home (Harper, 1994, pp. 110–11). This idea of home is important for Harper, as a refuge and loving place, a place of comfort and joy, and, upon the collapse of her marriage, Laura finds her way back to her parental home, there to die. It should be recalled that what Harper is also intimating with the invocation of single womanhood is that it is better to be without political rights than to suffer from the immorality of oppression – voting for its own sake is not enough. And the drunkenness of the men is proof of this. For Frances Harper, moral choices and progressive politics are what motivate the argument for political rights.

In *Sowing and Reaping*, written almost two decades after "The Two Offers," Harper allows for the husband Joe Gough to reform and demonstrate his dedication to his wife through signing the temperance pledge. He is able to secure a job through the auspices of those in the temperance community, though not one commensurate with his training. This demotion in skills and employment, from accountant to porter, is symbolic for the reader of the damage drinking causes to a person's life. Once a mistake is made, there is the possibility of a redemption that always remains incomplete because of a forgone constancy of purpose, a lost opportunity. Absolution in *Sowing and Reaping* depends on future right action and obedience to the principles of truth and beauty.

Harper clearly portrays the problem of wayward actions and straying from the path of righteousness as something which an individual – and, by intimation, the nation – can only with great difficulty correct (Peterson, 1995, p. 316). And in the novel *Sowing and Reaping*, she describes how the saloon owner John Anderson forces a young child to drink to accustom the child to the effects of alcohol, to build a dependence and future customer for his liquor, just as Charles Romaine is unable to resist the appeal of a drink without then losing himself in dissipation. Once tasted, the effects of drink are forever, in Harper's vision of purity and right action. But in "The Two Offers," the determination of a good man and the judgment of a good woman are not difficult to discover, merely requiring the will to stay the principled course.

That Harper discusses the importance of the role of women as independent and self-actualizing agents, rather than passive recipients of male attention, in this short story, written a decade before the first of her four novels, *Minnie's Sacrifice*, is critical to understanding the complexity with which she portrays the women protagonists in her writing. It is simply not enough in Harper's writing that women find appropriate partners, men able to answer their claims to a loving household and the needs of the community; women also must find fulfillment as persons independently. The mistake that Harper describes Laura Lagrange making in "The Two Offers" is to see herself as defined solely by the offers of marriage and, by extension, the husband she eventually chooses to marry. Harper is explicit, even in this early piece of writing, that there is more to being a woman than

the capacity to marry and provide a loving and devoted companion to a husband. Harper is clear that being a mother
is also only one aspect of what would allow a woman to
find satisfaction and meet the goals of her own life. In this
complex way, she offers for us today an understanding of
how individuals should be perceived as an integral part of a
whole community, a description of equality and freedom in
society – the person is either left to drift or given the direction that it requires to thrive. Frances Harper is making
the claim that the needs of women – of Black women – are
equivalent to those of anyone else in the society, and their
social and political equality is an indication of the society's
political progress.

While bereft of the love of a husband, Jenette Alston is
able to develop a successful career amid acclaim and recognition for her work. She is someone "who accepts her earthly
mission as a gift from God, and strives to walk the path of life
with earnest and unfaltering steps" (Harper, 1994, p. 106).
She advocated for the slave and the fugitive, the hungry and
the poor, and believed that "life was not given her to be frit-
tered away in nonsense or wasted away in trifling pursuits"
(Harper, 1994, p. 114). The new woman was someone, in
Harper's description, who made the decisions necessary to a
life lived only in part for others – someone who also developed themselves, and in doing so also sought to improve
the conditions wherein other persons lived. For the new
woman, the pursuit of principle and right action superseded
the social requirement of marriage for women. As Harper
writes at the end of the story, "true happiness consists not
so much in the fruition of our wishes as in the regulation
of desires and the full development and right culture of our
whole statures" (Harper, 1994, p. 114). Jenette Alston was
not defined at all by the men in her life, except by having
them as friends. The loss of her love motivates her to new

endeavors and pursuits, and she literally improves her life through not being attached to a man.

According to Harper in 1859, it is not merely the form that women require, but the substance – the essence – of political equality, its tangible result in their capacity to make right decisions. It is also a test of citizenship that Jenette can meet. From this perspective, Laura's husband has squandered his political inheritance, the right to make decisions with others about the community. And so, when Laura leaves his home to return to her parents, this is the final condemnation – the loss of his own capacity to determine what is to come.

In this story, therefore, Harper directly takes up the issue of the woman question that concerned the larger society at the time. She does so not only as a published Black woman poet involved in supporting the Underground Railroad with William Still in Philadelphia at the time of the story's publication, but as someone who as a single woman had been making speeches and writing essays to magazines for years on the issue of Abolition. As Frances Foster points out, only Sojourner Truth was also as capable of weathering the social criticism levied at a single woman lecturing to the public (Foster, 1990, p. 13).

That Jenette Alston is described as fulfilling her destiny later in life as a single woman in advocating for the slave and in providing solace to the runaway, the fugitive from a terrible system of oppression, reveals the connection between the gender claims made of both cousins and the pursuit of racial justice. When Harper writes "The true aim of female education should be not a development of one or two, but all the faculties of the human soul, because no perfect womanhood is developed by imperfect culture" (Harper, 1994, p. 109), this is a critique of the institutions wherein women live in 1859, in the United States. That this "imperfect culture" holds the inequality of Black people as given by law, as slaves and as a free population, and that this is inexplicably described within gender role formation is self-evident for the free Black poet and writer Frances Harper. The story is not an appeal to a White audience for a raceless and gendered equality of condition, but, rather, it suggests that women should consider the problems of slavery and of racial injustice as integral to their own struggle for equality.

Laura dies of heartbreak because she is unable to imagine a life outside the conventions defined by the roles of wife and mother. Why wouldn't Laura, once she returns to her parent's home, realize that her marriage and her dead child, her own childhood and her parent's marriage, are simply not enough to encompass the needs of a woman? This story is a powerful rebuttal to the argument that women writers in this period sought to confirm in their novels the social constraints of unequal gendered roles. Frances Harper does exactly the opposite in her short story, suggesting what today would be described as a feminist practice, where the social interstices between the reproduction of gender and racial roles allow for women and Black people to imagine new social descriptions of equality. Jenette is able to find fulfillment in doing the work of racial justice, and in doing so also transgresses the established place provided for the true woman defined by conventional mores and typified by Laura Lagrange. That Harper was herself constantly braving a hostile public, and challenging the expectations of a conventional patriarchal description of what her own life should look like in 1859, adds weight to the narrative of the story (Foster, 1990, p. 12). For both cousins, someone must die for there to be resolution of the gender roles available to them. Loss occasions a break, the potential for something new and unexpected – for Laura, her own death; for Jenette, her own life.

But this artifice of the deaths of men in the story points to the difficulty Harper has in making the independence of women acceptable to readers. Would the righteous and dutiful, loving Paul Clifford in *Sowing and Reaping* accept a Belle Gordon that spoke in public and wrote novels, essays, and poems, as did Harper? At the time of "The Two Offers," the author was herself single, and the story could also be thought of as an attempt to establish a public role for the professional poet and writer, the intellectual and activist – a Black woman named Frances Harper.

Gender and race at home

Today, it is often considered correct to identify race in a written text as simply comprised of a string of words or phrases, the use of specific words, markers in our day of the limits of a conversation about racial injustice and inequality. Beyond these words or phrases, our language and social life are, incorrectly, often argued to be free of racial content and racial political affect. The idea of race that is visible to us when looking back historically to 1859 isn't as apparent when we live within the social concepts of our own time. As a consequence of living our time in thought, most resist the idea today of a thoroughly saturated racial social environment, where this is the difference that defines things everywhere, accepting instead the idea of race being a conscious artifact of a traditional perspective of human differences, a tradition that somehow must be elided or avoided as an inheritance.

The language of implicit bias and diversity arises out of this assumption today of a nearly good enough society with regard to racial inequality. A racist today is someone who uses specific speech or other actions to delineate racial inequality, but this is argued as separate from the idea of racial differences reproduced without this discriminating language. But, of course, race finds definition as a difference throughout

FRANCES E. W. HARPER

our lives, and to limit our corrective actions to those deemed
currently illegal or inappropriate is, for the Black individual,
both frustrating and unfulfilling. There is a past and a future
to which we must attend as well – just as in the case of the
gendered choices of Laura Lagrange and Jenette Alston.

Harper offers a description of how individuals should confront this idea of a social norm that in its paucity can kill, and
which is at the same time insufficient to realize the needs of
individuals. "The Two Offers" provides a lesson in the cost
of accepting constraints on how we define not only gender
roles, but also Whiteness and Blackness, because neither
cousin is identified with markers that we use today to suggest
racial difference. This tension between equality and injustice
– how the two cousins are both equal to the men in their
lives, and yet suffer under gendered social expectations that
require something from men as well as women if they are
to be resolved – is also a conundrum for our description of
racial equality.

Harper was fully aware of the complexities of this equivalence of gender and race in her own person. In 1864, in the
middle of the Civil War, when her husband Fenton Harper
died and she was forced to give up the farm because of debts,
she must have found it hard not to think of the similar fate
ascribed to Jenette's mother in "The Two Offers." Because
race is not identified in the short story in the way that we
do today – in terms of the two cousins being Black, or in
terms of a White person who intrudes on the presumption
of equality of consequence with slurs or explicit prejudice,
or where the race of the men is in question in the story – it
is important that the reader consider how the description of
race was perceived by Harper and readers in her own time,
in contrast with today. The idea of a difference must be first
marked in specific ways, only to be ignored or erased, leaving
only a trace that is both indelible and corrosive, just because

it can no longer be discovered with the social tools that we allow ourselves to use today. How racial difference is reproduced socially in our time shouldn't detract from how we perceive the challenge to a description of gender and racial inequality raised by the short story "The Two Offers."

In the idea of home in "The Two Offers," Harper provides not only a refuge but also a ground, a place where relations are supposedly true and right, from which to build a world of equality. This isn't so much the idea of upbringing as important, as the possibility that something about education when young provides for the development of people who learn to value specific ideas of gender and race – children learn to act as adults within or against the social norms of gender difference that are learned. Harper is clearly appealing to the vanity of her readers when she suggests that teaching the good provides for good citizens. What is it to teach, and is this in contrast or contradiction to the idea of learning? The role of parents in determining the character of their children is decisive in this story. What isn't accessible for parents and the cousins are the conditions for success or failure that exist in the world around the child. That this is obvious when the choices for the cousins are both inadequate doesn't leave the reader with an optimistic perspective on the social change occurring in the society. Rather, we are without the means to address how gender equality should be developed, just as Jenette works to resolve racial injustice only when her own description of gender injustice is a given.

Better he be dead than a husband is the stark mandate for the reader of the story, and, unless mitigated by success, this returns the moral development of the man to the center of the possibility for the growth of women, the needs of the putative White person to the center of the Emancipation of Black people. This dependence of both cousins on male social development and existence leaves the question of what each would do with a male partner, with someone White, who demonstrated constancy of purpose and care?

This is the challenge answered by the partnership of Belle Gordon and Paul Clifford in the claim to a moral purity in *Sowing and Reaping*. However, what is the path of redemption available to women, if in fact women are to provide the moral definition of the community? What should be done about the fixity of the gender roles themselves in the short story and *Sowing and Reaping*, and the requirement that women are supposed to appeal to and act as sources for the morality of men, once political equality is acquired and women can vote? The gender roles seem defined outside of the interpretative frame given in the short story, and so the idea of a man who defines the role of women isn't accessible to criticism. At the same time, though the husband is described, he is absent from the short story, and so the two women are positioned together in a relationship in contrast to the two absent men. It is Jenette who sits at the bedside of Laura, not her husband. Jenette and Laura have conversations, and not with men. They speak about men, and about their roles as women in connection to men, and so the presumption is that they need men to be able to take the measure of their personal development. While Laura's brother suggests that she return home because she is so sad, it is her mother who soothes her. For Frances Harper, it is not clear why men would have to be at the center of a description of the lives of women if in fact women were conducting all or much of the progressive work in the community. What would the role of men be except to constrain the aspirations of the women in their lives?

If we change the perspective slightly and speak of this idea in terms of race, how is the description of the necessity of someone White to the aspirations and definition of Black progress developed? If race implicates parties in a

relationship that is by definition unjust, why is the idea of
the White person required to address the problem of racial
inequality? Could not the measure complexly be a narrative about persons who are also Black, such as in "The Two
Offers?" Why not consider the story to be about women,
and not men at all – about how both women learn that they
can't need men for fulfillment?

In the essay "Enlightened Motherhood," published in
1892, Frances Harper continues the themes of healing
the nation and the idea of humanity that form the basis of
the novel *Iola Leroy*. At the beginning of the essay, Harper
equates everyone Black by describing their purpose in freedom, eliding her own status as having been born free. She
writes: "It is nearly thirty years since an emancipated people
stood on the threshold of a new era" (Harper, 1990c, p. 285).
This single gesture, which is possible because of the process
of Emancipation, is, for those who are Black, world-making
– literally – as it erases the distinctions of condition that she
and others have based on whether they had been enslaved. A
population that was divided between those who were legally
unmarried, illiterate, without knowledge of government or
law – "a homeless race, to be gathered into homes of peace-
ful security and to be instructed how to plant around their
firesides the strongest batteries against the sins that degrade
and the race vices that demoralize" (p. 285) – and those who
were also Black and were free, to build something that must
also be called freedom.

This idea of unity is the focus of the essay, and Harper
outlines what she thinks is required for Black people to
acquire the fruits of this freedom, to realize equality in the
face of very concerted campaigns by White communities in
the South in 1892 to suppress the Black vote and subordinate the Black population anew. Eschewing the idea of the
public, the schools, and the churches as sites for the possible

preservation of the gains that have been achieved, Harper appeals to the Black mother and the sanctity of the home. Whether in a last desperate appeal, or a further encouragement toward racial uplift, Harper finds herself united, across any distinctions of class or former legal status, with other Black women, who in her opinion must rally around the idea of the home, a place that wasn't possible to define for those enslaved but was now to be the basis of a new community.

Of money and fame

In the context of this effort to build a sustainable, thriving Black community, wherein a large part of the population is enslaved, Frances Harper writes in the essay "Our Greatest Want" about a threat posed to this Christian ideal of the good and its fervent pursuit of racial justice in the time of slavery. Published in 1859, in the same year as her short story "The Two Offers," Frances Harper discusses what she argues is the false appeal to community leaders – from merchant to minister – of expediency, exchange, and money to provide for the needs of the community. The social and political equality that financial wealth would afford the free Black community is for Harper insufficient just because it would not bring with it the generosity of spirit and integrity, the earnestness, that is necessary to free those Black people still in bondage.

Harper suggests that the solution is not to participate in the slave economy, generating wealth that can be used to pressure the institutions of slavery themselves, or a boycott of products made by slaves, such as occurred in the North, but instead a commitment to self-sacrifice and helping others. She explains, "We want more soul, a higher cultivation of our spiritual faculties" (Harper, 1990d, p. 103). This essay was published before the Civil War and so Harper could not know that, six years later, slavery would be eliminated as a legal institution in the US. The claim here of trying to find a way to put pressure on the institution through economic means was considered very important.

How could Blacks remain enslaved if those who were free, and their allies, had the wealth to compete for profits? This wasn't a trivial question when the economic engine created by slave labor was able to compete with Northern industries. The economic problem for abolitionists when addressing slavery was a formidable one, and it is easy to be nonchalant since the solution was a Civil War to come, but Frances Harper's contribution to this debate is important for what it tells us about the scope of her interests, and the awareness she had of the problem of economic inequality and the needs of the free Black community for profits and success in the shadow of the competition from Black slave labor.

This matters to us today because Frances Harper expresses a truth that we have a harder time accepting, simply because the description of racial inequality provides for the exceptional status of a few Black people as supposed proof that the system of economic distribution is fair. Harper critiqued the idea put forward by others that it is possible to change the description of racial injustice through economic parity, as though wealth accumulation creates the preconditions for racial equality. Is wealth disparity the reason for racial difference? If not, then why would money provide some semblance of equality of result or consequence in an economic system that continued to exploit Black labor? Harper describes how the community would, at some remove, be trading in the labor of their own people, given that slaves and their production were interwoven as an economic good throughout the US economy. This is a fact that most Black people today who see wealth accumulation as an end in itself – an ideal which Harper is also implicitly critiquing – as a measure of success in the society, don't consider. They don't see that they too are profiting from the impoverishment, incarceration, and depressed living conditions of other Black people.

For each who succeeds, there are many more Black people who do not, in this current model of wealth accumulation as the measure of racial equality. Harper's essay goes further, however, and points out that what is instead to be sought is the sacrifice of wealth and status by those in the community for the development of others. That equality will come not through the social status of some at the expense of the many (in Harper's time, the slaves), but by those who can provide help actively assisting those who need it. The argument, laid out in just two paragraphs, is disturbingly prescient of our own situation today.

What is the measure of racial equality, how would we recognize it, and what will it take to achieve it? For Harper, the solution is not merely collective action, but the commitment of those who would turn their attention not to self-aggrandizement but to the development of the innate capacity for good and truth in everyone. This was a powerful criticism of the commitments of those who were free, and their allies, as they sought to use economic profit and wealth accumulation to change not just the perspective, but the fact, of racial inequality in the country. In some sense, this criticism is too apt and daring for our current situation, where Black elites vie for attention from White economic interests, even as the rest of the Black population remains mired in conditions of economic precarity. That there is currently an industry developed around the problem of Black life and Black social inequality, wherein Black wealth can accumulate, is very similar to what Harper experienced. Then, free Blacks and their allies were generating wealth from the criticism of slavery, as abolitionists, and sought to expand this to a campaign with which to put pressure on the economic sustainability of slavery. Today, the criticism of the conditions for Black life generates a community of people who similarly might consider their own wealth as equivalent to a definition of a "good enough" racial equality. Harper disagrees in principle, and suggests, in the quote above, that racial equality cannot be achieved by economic wealth in a market where the very exploitation of Black people is a good in itself.

Redistributive policies would have to account – as was the problem after the end of slavery – with the existing exploitative relationships and processes that reproduced inequality, even with the infusion of more resources. Throwing money at it won't help, if the money just gets transferred to others immediately. This situation requires people who are willing to risk themselves and their livelihood to bring Black people out of their condition. She writes, "We have millions of our race in the prison house of slavery, but have we yet a single Moses in freedom, and if we had who among us would be led by him?" (Harper, 1990d, p. 103).

Frances Harper references Moses in this situation because he turns away from personal wealth and acclaim to suffer with those who were enslaved. And then Harper writes something in the essay that goes straight to the heart of the current racial dilemma in the US:

> When we have a race of men who the blood stained government cannot tempt or flatter, who would sternly refuse every office in the nation's gift, from a president down to a tide-waiter, until she shook her hands from complicity in the guilt of cradle plundering and man stealing, then for us the foundations of an historic character will have been laid.
>
> (Harper, 1990d, p. 104)

This is a perfect example of how she relies on Christianity for the basis of her own political commitments, but it is a

Christianity that would eschew wealth for freedom, and exist-ing definitions of a good enough equality for the redemption of racial justice. Frances Harper offers too radical a prescrip-tion for a US today that continues to require racial inequality as the engine for economic growth.

In reading Harper's works, we do not need to reject or ignore her Christian moral code but, instead, to ask our-selves, by way of contrast, what our own morality requires of a government and the community that is trying to address racial inequality. What is required of the individual beyond personal success and wealth, in the service of improving the conditions for Black people in the US? For many, this ques-tion today would seem nonsensical and even insulting, as they would say that their own success is in fact a measure of the advancement of the Black population as a whole. But it is easy to see in this answer that what is achieved is not racial equality for Black people but individual social, economic, or political parity with those they interact with. The problem of racial inequality would persist beyond the individual in this sense – the immediate experience of the individual's success would obscure the reality, and, as a result, racial inequality would persist in the larger society. That this success would come in part at the expense of others is something that Harper takes issue with through the rejection by Moses of his life as a prince, when the accumulation of wealth is seen as an end in itself, taken as a measure of parity with White people in the society – one that abandons the cause of justice for Black people as a whole.

But at the expense of which others? How accountable is Frances Harper in 1859 to those who are Black and formerly enslaved? There must have been a substantial difference in social standing between the Black slave and the free Black person, particularly in a situation where the slave had previ-ously to account for their presence anywhere to an owner or those with the authority to decide on their actions. How free was a slave in their interaction with other Black people, slave or free? The relationship of exploitation was one of ownership, and so slaves could be tasked with anything available to a human being to accomplish. The money earned by a slave was the property of the owner, which meant that a slave had no earning capacity that necessarily devolved to them. Today, because of Hollywood, we usually think of slaves as working the fields, but slavery was a status and someone could be an accountant, a blacksmith or saddler, or an artist, for example, and be a slave. The majority of the slaves in the country were employed in the plantation economy, so most slaves would have been relegated to tasks that involved production in that economy and supporting the living conditions of the Master or Mistress. While violence was used often on slaves and without any expectation of repercussions for the owner, it was the systematic institutional processes of control and discipline that allowed for slavery to exploit human beings.

We have to be careful today, when this status seems so distant, in the sense of Emancipation being so long ago, to not reduce the Black slave in our imagination to a thing, or an object, but to understand that, for Frances Harper, slaves were people that she knew. They had no capacity for avoiding the system that bonded them for life, except escape and running away, but that didn't mean that they weren't present in other ways socially. This means that there was a difference between free Black people earning money and exploiting the system in place that allowed for the enslavement of people, though exploiting it indirectly, and the slave's ability to accumulate money from this relationship. Unless otherwise indicated, a slave earned money or other resources for the owner. And they worked with no social expectation by the owners of personal gratification. Of course, that is not how humans exist in the world – we find something of meaning in whatever we do consistently. What Frances Harper was referring to in her speech was the situation in which free Black people knew that there was no remuneration or benefit for slaves in being slaves, and so there was no necessary connection between free Black wealth accumulation and Abolition.

While this problem of male dependence, as we have seen, was later addressed in the relationships between persons in Frances Harper's novels – for example, in *Sowing and Reaping* – it is useful to consider briefly a short story written by Harper where the moral development of the always absent man is the central concern.

Conclusion

Moral choices

In a short piece of fantasy, "Shalmanezer: Prince of Cosman," published in *Sketches of a Southern Life* (1886), Frances Harper explicitly defines the moral life of a man. The prince Shalmanezer is approaching manhood and has inherited wealth, physical strength, and beauty (pp. 33–46). Harper describes him literally thinking about what he should do with this inheritance when he is approached by the personifications of Desire, Pleasure, Wealth, and Fame. After greeting Desire with enthusiasm, Shalmanezer is available to the blandishments in turn of Pleasure, Wealth, and Fame, only to subsequently collapse due to moral dissipation. Peace arrives and, with Self Denial, provides the necessary transfusion of purpose to revive the prince from the moral consequences of his actions. His death is avoided only through the intervention of his own will to moderate the influence of Desire.

As mentioned above, only Mr. Gough in *Sowing and*

Reaping demonstrates a similar resolve in Harper's fiction – the possibility of redemption after the male individual has failed to uphold moral standards. That Joe (John) Gough was a real-life person connects the ideas described in the novel to the argument for a transformative redemptive practice made in the political activism of the Temperance Movement. That Harper is centering the novel around the idea of gender inequality and the right to vote, in addition to the idea of the moral choices people make, allows us to consider the possibility that what we do as individuals matters to the larger conditions of a community or society. Harper provides the reader with an argument not for a specific recipe for moral righteousness, but for how to develop the character of a community through personal agency. The fallen and the uplifted each exist alongside one another, and this is enough for Harper. There are no acts of redemption that are not always singular and the work of the individual, a requirement to account for one's own actions rather than attend too closely to a concern for the immorality of others. That there is a limit to what can be done as a person for others is in this way developed as a constraint on the Christian ethos being advocated for by Harper.

The implication throughout Harper's work is that the moderation of personal desire provides what is possible, but is insufficient to address the issues of gender and racial injustice. Shalmanezer's own qualities provide for his vulnerability to temptation. Without beauty and wealth, it is implied, he would not suffer from the possibility of desire. Fame, the adulation of the crowd, is a commensurate desire only through his capacity to meet its demand, climbing the challenging mountain as a feat before onlookers. Prowess and excellence goad him to the precipice of a soul that is unredeemable. Such was the fate in Harper's novels of men who do not obey the demands of conscience and engage in right action. But what is interesting is how Shalmanezer is presumed an innocent, a child who must learn not by parental instruction but by personal trial and error. The male moral journey as a model for determining right action is distinct therefore for Harper from the perspective of the woman assessing the suitability of a man as a partner for love and marriage, where constancy and forthrightness, truth and beauty, are required by her at all times.

Personal growth, such as is also evinced by Iola Leroy in the novel of that name, is here explicitly developed as a journey required for a moral life – a test of resolve and self-denial. The requirement that is placed by others, what women require of men, is less important for self-preservation and moral constancy than observing and reining in one's own desires. That this is observed by Harper in the moderation and care with which Gresham proposes to Iola, as a White man, in *Iola Leroy* is important, just as is the fulfillment that Jenette receives from her work once the man upon whom she bestowed her love dies in "The Two Offers."

Harper is very clear that personal beliefs are important as a condition for personal excellence of character, but they do not directly impact the problem of equality that persists outside the relationships in question. The treatment of women and Blacks, for example as social categories, in the 1870s when "Salmanezer" was published, would provide the constraints as well on his relationships. We could envision a situation in which the description of gender and race would prohibit all contact or associations except for specific interactions, where right behavior or love would be so constrained in this context as to limit the capacity of a relationship to develop. Anti-miscegenation statutes and violence directed to preventing certain relationships would be examples of this. The story of Shalmanezer represents the formal limits for Harper of personal redemption, but leaves the question of larger societal descriptions of social difference unaddressed. It is with this perspective that we can now turn in the next chapter to consider the serial novel *Minnie's Sacrifice*.

The lesson to be taken from *Sowing and Reaping*, "The Two Offers," and "Shalmanezer: Prince of Cosman," for us today, is that there is no better, more valuable measure of sacrifice called for than to offer the talents and moral life of our persons on behalf of the Black community. In their need and for us, for the country and the community, the women have often borne the brunt of the harm and neglect that Black people have experienced, even as they have been unable to claim a gender equality that is necessary for the successful development of a moral society. That these works by Frances Harper discussed in this chapter bring us closer to understanding what is required of each of us individually today is the most rewarding thing that they could accomplish. However, there are several elements of these works that are worth noting.

Of the women

The descriptions of the women and men, and their fate, change over Harper's writing career. In "The Two Offers," Laura Lagrange must die, and in *Minnie's Sacrifice*, which will be discussed in the next chapter, Minnie dies, but, by the 1870s, the death of the women is no longer the central theme of Harper's writing. Instead, those women who die rely solely on a dependent relationship with men, but those who do not, survive, and are defined as carrying the future of the community onward through their actions. In *Sowing and Reaping*, Mary Gough faints on the street but recovers through the attention of Belle Gordon, only to fall ill with depression again through the actions of her husband. But

210 FRANCES E. W. HARPER

Mary's death, which Belle Gordon announces as possible, is rejected by Belle as unacceptable.

There is a refusal to die for the men and their actions any longer in *Trial and Triumph* – a refusal to be dependent on others for their moral character, for the good of the community. This individual commitment to the community becomes the definition of a successful life by the time we read *Iola Leroy*. A child dies in *Sowing and Reaping*, and John Anderson and his son die in ways that are described by Harper as terrible and the result of uncontrolled avarice and dissolution. But the women are no longer required to be passive and waiting on the actions of men. Instead, they must find other ways to continue to address the problems of this imperfect community.

In *Trial and Triumph*, Lucy, the mother, dies, as does the younger sister Gracie in *Iola Leroy*, but both are described as victims of men who serve as examples of what women should not do in their relationship to men: a man who refused to be a husband; and a father who relied on another man, his cousin, instead of placing his faith in the capacity of the women to sustain the community. Lucy's death provides the main plot line in the novel, and Gracie's death in *Iola Leroy* is as a helpless child victim, a sacrifice that doesn't seem to alter the plot at all. The symbolic death of Gracie represents the loss of hope in a coming community, brought on by the mother's enslavement. Their deaths motivate those who live to further action in the novels.

By the 1880s and 1890s, Harper refuses in her fiction to allow men to fully define the world that women create for themselves and the community. The importance of the professional career of Jenette in 1859 in "The Two Offers" is also evident in 1892, when, in *Iola Leroy*, Iola suggests that she will write a book about the need for progress for the Black community, and in the actions of Lucille Delany, who is described as an active participant in public gatherings and fulfills the mission of community development as a teacher. In *Trial and Triumph*, Annette's loss of love doesn't cause her death but, instead, motivates her to leave the town, making way for her to become the educator at the center of a thriving community.

What we see is the progressive development of the role of women in the Black community in the fiction of Frances Harper. This refiguring of what is imagined for Black women, their capacity not only to heal the figurative wounds caused by slavery but to educate to achieve and sustain the aspirations for the future community, was one of Harper's most important contributions to the readers in her day, and for us. She provides a description of the African American community in the 1870s, 1880s, and 1890s, which is not merely struggling, but capable of answering the charge before it and able to thrive if conditions are favorable.

Harper has described the Black woman feminist scholar activist. She has in her fiction given voice to roles for Black women as leaders and architects not just of the moral claims in the community, but of the vision for how it needs to develop socially, economically, and politically. The work of Black women provides the structure and direction for the work of the community, even as men assist and participate as equal partners in fulfilling their ambitions.

It is Marie, Iola Leroy's mother, who, after all the heartbreak she has experienced, leaves the intellectual gathering near the end of the novel – where many including Iola have presented papers, read poems, and discussed the future of the race – and says to Robert Johnson, her brother, with regard to the value of these gatherings, "I would gladly welcome such a conference at any time. I think such meetings would be so helpful to our young people" (Harper, 1892, p. 261). Her approval defines the aspirations of the community. It is Marie Leroy, who survives rather than dies after being remanded back into slavery, who now can observe as her children work to make the world a better place for the Black community.

5

Minnie's Sacrifice and the Poetic License

Politics

The previous chapters have explored some of Frances Harper's novels with the purpose of developing her ideas about gender and racial inequality into a coherent politics, to give the reader a sense of the many different examples and arguments that she provides in her later works for a radical egalitarianism. What I have wanted was to, first, give a description of the political vision in *Iola Leroy*; and then how Frances Harper perceived the idea of community, and the requirements of equality that must define political progress, in *Trial and Triumph*; and, finally, in *Sowing and Reaping*, "The Two Offers," and early fiction, how Frances Harper conceived of the individual who could contribute to this holistic definition of social progress and justice.

Now I would like to consider what Frances Harper thought was the problem in the society that a person, the community, and the society had to address as a cohesive plan for progress. How did she perceive the social challenges that people faced, considering that she already saw the natural moral equality of all human beings as a fact of the society? How did she conceptualize the solution to inequality and the terrible examples of injustice in her own time? This chapter will consider Harper's earliest novel, *Minnie's Sacrifice*, as well as her poetry and speeches. We know, because of the work of recovery done by researchers in the last four decades, that Frances Harper was one of the most important poets of her generation, bringing her words to thousands across the country in a time when regular communication was through journals and newspapers distributed by post, train, and ship. Her published poetry was widely read and she was incredibly popular (Boyd, 1994, p. 77). Harper would often give a reading of her poetry at her public speaking events, where her poetry books were also on sale. Not only was she an accomplished public speaker, but she would give lectures, often, throughout her lifetime. Her talks were both insightful and important artifacts of the political concerns of the time (Boyd, 1994; Foster, 1990). In this chapter my aim is to bring these various sources together into a discussion of what the political meant for Frances Harper.

Minnie's Sacrifice

Minnie's Sacrifice is the first of Frances Harper's novels, and was serialized in the *Christian Recorder* in 1868–9. It was written a few years after the end of the War, after Harper had made several speaking trips through the Southern states, collecting stories as well as learning about conditions in the region. We know from newspaper accounts and her own letters to friends in the North that Harper was a successful public speaker as she traveled throughout the areas devastated by the conflict, where traditions of the enslavement of Black people had been overturned only through the military defeat of the slave owners. In her writings about the conditions she encountered, Harper speaks of the terrible needs of the formerly enslaved, both for resources and for an education, and of the need to define the promise of what freedom would provide for them. Her speeches often were to the newly freed, but also to racially mixed crowds of women and to the public at large.

The period after the Civil War was in the nation no longer a time for the language of Abolition but one for the language of possibilities, of compromise and reconciliation. The destruction of the Southern region in the War and the Emancipation of the slaves had already meted out a form of revenge on those who had rebelled. What was required, instead, was a message of peace, prosperity, and new potential. To provide everyone with a sense of the possibilities atten-dant on the description of racial equality on offer required that Frances Harper speak about the needs of the impover-ished and deprived Black people to their former Masters. She had to speak as an appeal not to their common humanity, but to the dangers to political stability of neglecting the newly freed and the need for economic recovery. Her talks were on the need to educate the freed persons so they could be productive on their own, could manage their affairs without assistance, and could contribute to the welfare of others.

It is important for us today to understand the acumen it must have been required on her part to shift from the argu-ment for a fiery Abolitionism before the War to a politics of reconciliation and racial uplift afterwards. Frances Harper wrote her speeches and provided the political context and sense of expectation for her audience at the talks. She was speaking often to those who, just a year or a few years before, had been on the other side of the War from those in her

Movement, to those who had owned slaves, and to the formerly enslaved, in a society that at the time was still reeling from the invasion of the Northern Army, the migration of freed slaves, and the collapse of the regional economy. And she had been born a free Black woman. Most former slaves could not read, and the poverty must have been overwhelming. Few if any of her audience had ever encountered a free Black person with her presence and mien.

To embark on this speaking tour was a powerful ambition for a person to pursue, even though the engagements were arranged alongside speeches by others, and it represented a difficult task even if she had considerable experience with public speaking. She was joined in this ambition by many others – Sojourner Truth and Harriet Tubman, for example – who also went South after the War to help the formerly enslaved. This series of journeys through the region meant that she was brought face to face with a wide range of environments in which people lived within the region, and gained considerable experience with conditions after the War. She also taught for a time, and organized assistance to freed persons as a part of her lengthy tours in the South. Frances Harper's missives to newspapers in the North during her travels were also an important source of information for readers. It is this experience with the South after the Civil War that Harper brought to not only her novel *Minnie's Sacrifice* but also her poetry in the period. Harper was a poet and writer, and these experiences were the muse for her literary work at the time.

The plot

In *Minnie's Sacrifice*, two young children grow to adulthood in separate families not knowing they are Black, only to have this legacy revealed to each in dramatic circumstances. Louis Le Croix was raised by his sister and grandmother, the one White and the other Black, and his White owner father adopted him. Louis grew up not knowing that he was in fact Black, that his adoptive father was his real father, or that the servant was in fact his grandmother. This secret of racial intermixing was kept in the family without Louis knowing, providing a contrast to the standard narrative at the time – of the child of the White slaveowner and a Black slave being kept in the slave quarters and raised as a slave.

For the readers of the *Christian Recorder*, the most pernicious of personal tragedies associated with the idea of racial difference was the callous alignment of phenotype with cultural inferiority. When this was made the object of enslavement, the problem was compounded, with the process of ownership allowing for the development of the terms of this inferiority in the relationship between the parties involved. This description of race, through the institution of slavery, as capable of sundering even family ties, violating the conditions for a faithful intimate love between a husband and wife, and forcing a parent to cast off their own children as their property to sell in the market, was the subject of the first pages of the novel. If such conditions were possible, the description of race that allowed for enslavement was an idea that violated the requirements for family, community, and society. This idea had no future, and the Civil War that had occurred and taken so many lives was therefore, for the reader in 1868, a tragic yet expected outcome from such a fundamental violation of moral principles.

The novel opens with the grandmother, Miriam, sitting next to the dead body of her daughter, Agnes, who had been the intimate slave mistress of the White owner. A few pages later the White owner does not reveal any remorse at the death of a woman he was intimate with, and Camilla, his

White daughter, demonstrates little sadness at the death of what is for her only another slave. When Camilla arrives at the cabin, she expresses that she didn't even know that Agnes had a baby, but she does respond to the tears of the older mother grieving the loss of her child (Harper, 1994, p. 4). Camilla exclaims that she was so distraught at the thought of Miriam grieving the loss of her child that she was willing to forgo her dinner – that she had to come to the cabin straight away. This callous affect by the owner's daughter at the dead body of another human being, who measures her affections for the person of Miriam in terms of having to miss her dinner, reveals the truth of how the ownership of slaves perverted human relationships. Yet, in the story, Camilla is considered someone who was always kind, and her journey to self-awareness as someone White who allowed for racial injustice to persist around her is an important aspect of the story.

Upon discovering that the baby is pale with fair skin and golden curly hair, Camilla exclaims that it is beautiful and it is a pity such a child must be raised as a slave. The reader knows that Camilla is in fact the sister of the child, which provides the perspective necessary to understand the hubris in the idea of race and hypodescent by blood. Her own father is also the child's father, and, as she says, unwittingly, "He is just as white as I am" (Harper, 1994, p. 4). She speaks of the beauty of the child, since it shows no evidence of racial admixture. Miriam points out that he is still, after all, a slave, in spite of his fair appearance. Camilla vows to save the baby from being a slave, by having her father pretend it is in fact the baby of a friend of his who has died. She insists to her father he should adopt the child as his own and send him to school in the North. The reader shares a moment of gallows humor with the father at this suggestion, since the child is in fact his, and he could now officially adopt his biological son as his foster son under his daughter's scheme. The caul of race forces this complex artifice on both father and daughter, while the slaves, including the child's grandmother, are silent about the truth. Camilla succeeds in her plan, and the child, Louis, is raised as White, sent north for schooling, and left unaware of his racial heritage until he is an adult. Through her description of these circumstances, Frances Harper asks the reader to consider how we define family and what we are willing to countenance for achieving our goals.

Seen from one perspective, Louis's story could not have been well received before the Emancipation of the slaves, since it asks readers to accept that, like the undocumented today in US society, the law still provides for the existence of those who refuse or don't accept conventions that are unjust. The story suggests that persons respond to inequalities and injustices by trying to develop alternative productive and satisfying lives, and that having a law doesn't make it right – or even likely – that people will obey. Louis isn't White, so the narrative is provocative by presenting the possibility that a White family would assist a child in passing rather than engage in the usual suspicion that Black people are trying to pretend to be White. That Louis could refuse this racial accommodation as an adult is a reversal of the claim to White superiority that remains popular today, and Frances Harper knew this. The story is therefore more than merely one of how some found their calling after the War in helping Black people in the South, and suffered for it. Harper is trying to have the reader understand – by way of an exercise in thinking through the problem of concealment, secrecy, and social conventions – that being Black isn't a difference that should make a difference for family and the society.

Parallel to this manipulation of the existing racial system of social classification on behalf of Louis and his family, Frances Harper also provides a study of how Whiteness is

defined through the process of developing social relationships. Camilla and her father struggle not with thinking of
Louis as like them, but in discovering how their relationship
to the child is connected to the politics of Abolitionism and
the experience of the slave. As slave owners, they still own
slaves who have to be silent about the racial status of Louis,
and the grandmother has to return to the field to work, with
her dead daughter lying in the cabin and the baby being
tended by "an aged woman who was too old to work in the
fields, but not entirely past service." Harper is writing here
from the perspective of the White slave owners, to make a
point about how the father of the child and Camilla both
think of Black people at the beginning of the novel.

By the end of Camilla's journey in the novel she is no
longer the person who in those first pages could complain of
missing her dinner because a slave had died. While the novel
includes a rape and lynching as acts of violence, these are
turning points in a journey toward an understanding of the
place of race in their lives that all of the characters share. It is
a rare novel, and one published in serialized form to be read
aloud in a parlor, saloon, or cabin in 1868. It asks readers to
think about how both White and Black people learn how to
define racial justice and equality together.

Minnie Le Grange had the misfortune as a small child of
looking exactly like her White owner, her father. The White
Mistress on the plantation is publicly embarrassed when
Minnie is mistaken by a visitor for one of her own children.
The public humiliation she experiences at the wayward life
of her husband in this moment is too great, and she punishes
the child for embodying this evidence of his indiscretion.
Minnie's mother Eve is simply too valuable a seamstress to
be sold, however, so her father arranges the means to have
the child smuggled to the North and adopted by a White
Quaker family as one of their own. Through this journey,

Minnie becomes White. The trader the father relies upon is an old college mate, a Black man who has passed throughout his life as a White person. Harper offers this character as an example of how common such circumstances are and of the impossibility of applying any criteria for racial difference, since it is just punitive, and not natural or right.

In framing the actions of the Mistress as precipitating Minnie's journey and the plot of the novel, Frances Harper provides again a description of how Whiteness is experienced – the idea of what it is to be an owner of others because you are White. In addition to going into detail about the Mistress and her cruelty toward Black slaves, Harper describes how her mother was even worse, beating slaves constantly, and denying a slave access to her husband just to demonstrate her authority to do so. The implication that the older Mistress was keeping the wife and husband apart because she was trying to eliminate a rival, and was intimate with the Black husband whenever she so wished to be, is clear in the novel. This detail is provided so the reader understands that what the Master did in raping slaves was also accomplished by the Mistresses. The fact of slavery and the idea of racial inferiority allowed for this predation to be described as unfortunate, but also acceptable if kept secret – as though this would be secret from the slaves. In fact, in the narrative, Harper reveals these details of the current and past Mistresses through a conversation among the slaves in the kitchen. Throughout the novel, Harper provides the reader with a shifting of voices, from White to Black perspectives, about the problem that racial inequality and injustice create for the characters and the readers of the novel.

After being raised with a White Quaker family in the North, Minnie discovers that she is Black when her mother approaches her on the street, having come north to find her. There is a moment early in the novel when the father explains to his wife, Georgette, how he sold Minnie, and pretends to have gotten a good price for her, when in fact he has spent a great deal to secure her freedom and the pearls he gives to his wife. He then walks out of the wife's parlor and into the room where Ellen, Minnie's mother, sits awaiting news of what has happened. He fulfills his promise of not selling his own daughter and has a likeness made of Minnie at Ellen's request, so that she may eventually find her.

The father has sent Minnie away from the system of slavery, but not as someone Black; instead, acknowledging the racism in the North, he wants her to be brought up as White. For the reader in 1868, this recognition in the story, by the father, of the importance of sending the child north as White and not as a freed Black person is Harper's means of criticizing, first, slavery as an institution, for what it allows in the treatment of human beings, and, second, the problem of how racial inferiority as an idea underlies all social relations throughout the nation. For the Northern reader of the *Christian Recorder*, this decision, written by a famous abolitionist author, to have the child – and the trader as well – pass as White was an admission that Whites all understand the price of racial oppression to be too great for their own families to bear. They were not oblivious to the racial injustice being meted out upon Black people in the North. This is reintroduced as an idea when Minnie is revealed as Black later, when her mother finds her in the North. Her schoolmates are described as having an argument about whether her being Black matters, to them and to their school. The implication of Blackness being a stain or blight upon the social status of all involved who are White in the Northern school is explicit.

In this detailed work, Frances Harper provides us with a study of how racial differences are developed and maintained, as well as the social costs for both White and Black people of adhering to this idea of a public difference and a personal equality. The scene early in the novel of the Master traveling from one room to the other after sending Minnie away, walking from the place for his wife and to that reserved for the slave – reproducing in his journey the arc of his continued abuse of both Ellen and the wife, on terms based on their gender, racial, and slave status – makes a powerful impression on the reader. These scenes accurately and symbolically reveal how racial injustice and gender politics come together for each of the characters. To one woman, he gives pearls bought supposedly from the sale of the person whom they both know is his child. Harper uses Georgette's perspective to state: "what mattered it to her if every jewel cost a heart throb, and if the whole set were bought with the price of blood?" (Harper, 1994, p. 21). And to the other woman, his slave, he provides the future means to find her lost daughter.

But the father has given up his child because of the system of racial oppression that he accepts. This implication, according to Harper, is the emotional price of a Whiteness they must now claim and own, as they once owned other persons. And he does accept these conditions of a Whiteness that allows him to sexually assault Ellen, part with his child, and refuse to acknowledge his own relationship to her in public. Minnie can't be one of the family, and neither can Ellen. Love doesn't exist between the husband, the Master, and his two women partners, and Harper makes it plain that this is the price of the social system by which race is defined. In an appeal to the consciences of White men, the contradictions and compromises required by them to maintain this system are laid bare in these scenes. It is again a rare moment in literature – we don't often read today about the costs to White men of the system of racial injustice that persists.

Minnie and Louis meet in the North and are immediately

taken by one another, but they only fall in love once they discover their shared racial heritage. Louis is a frequent visitor in the South because he doesn't know of his racial background. He is a Secessionist, and is described as a true White Southerner in his belief in the morality of Black slavery. Just before he joins the Southern Army, his White sister Camilla and the Black slave Miriam, who is – unbeknown to him – his grandmother, reveal his true patrimony. This is only done at the last minute, and only to avoid Louis fighting against himself, against the idea of racial equality that he represents for his family and the reader.

In an important scene, Frances Harper switches between the voice of Camilla and that of Miriam, mid-sentence, symbolizing Louis's passing back into Blackness from being White. Only Miriam, as someone Black, could speak the truth. For his sister Camilla to have done so would be to reproduce the wound of racial inferiority. It would have been to put him in his place, a possibility that the reader has known was always threatened by the father's casual reference to Camilla not having the patience to take her commitment to the conversion of the child from a slave seriously. If Camilla had not persisted over the years in her heart's desire, Louis would have simply been remanded back into slavery, moved from one room to another in the plantation house. Now, as he is about to fight against the North and the cause of Black people, Camilla and Miriam must tell him who he is, or risk losing the justice of that fight forever. For both – and this points to the political development of Camilla in the context of racial justice – there was a limit to what the system of racial inferiority could allow Louis to do. He could be socially contemptuous of Black people, he could castigate others and argue against the cause of racial equality, but he couldn't be allowed to fight against the very emancipatory politics that had freed him. It is a powerful scene. As Camilla says, "'Because,' – and she hesitated. Just then Miriam took up the unfinished sentence, ' – because to join the secesh is to raise your hands against your own race'" (Harper, 1994, p. 59).

Rather than join the Southern Army, Louis must now flee north to freedom. Over the journey north, Harper has Louis receive help from slaves, in several touching and symbolic scenes of their personal sacrifice on his behalf, leading him to question his beliefs about racial inferiority. One slave, for example, cuts his own feet so the blood will lead the blood-hounds away from Louis and onto his path instead (Harper, 1994, p. 64). Because he looks White, Louis must announce his intentions to flee north to those he encounters – he must identify himself as someone not just deserting, but also Black. The repetition of the journey north as someone Black now, in contrast to when he could travel freely as someone White, for Louis and the reader, completes his transformation across the literal color line. As Harper writes, "But at last Louis got beyond the borders of the confederacy, and stood once more on free soil, appreciating that section as he had never done before" (Harper, 1994, p. 65). For the reader, Harper suggests the requirement for each of us is a similar journey, but one that brings us into contact with both the experience of racial injustice and the understanding of our own culpability in its definition. It is this sense of implication for both Louis and Minnie, now that they are Black, that requires that Louis fight for the Northern Army, and that both at the end of the War return to the South to teach and organize freed people to secure their rights.

Minnie and Louis marry, and Louis joins the Union Army and fights in the War. After the War, they settle in the South, as Whites try to take back political control of the region. Before the couple leaves, however, they talk one last time with Camilla, in a scene that should be thought of as

evidence of how Frances Harper hopes the reader can reconcile the competing ideas of Whiteness and Blackness. Camilla
explains how, during the War, those Whites who lived in
the South and were loyal to the Union were "ostracized and
abused," and the men were assaulted and sometimes killed.
She asks them why they intend to go into the rural Southern
towns and assist the newly freed, saying that if she were them
she would remain in the North. She explains that "You and
Louis are nearer the white race and the colored. Why should
you prefer the one to the other?" (Harper, 1994, p. 72).

But it is precisely the experience of having been White –
the both of them – and now being Black that reveals their own
necessary social commitments. Camilla's inability to imagine
herself as Black – as anything but White – is what commits
her to the idea of racial political equality, but not the same
comprehensive racial social equality that Minnie and Louis
understand. As Minnie says, she decided "that I would live out
my own individuality and do for my race, as a colored woman,
what I never could accomplish as a White woman" (Harper,
1994, p. 72). Camilla cannot truly understand this idea of
racial equality – as though race doesn't matter, isn't real.

Camilla's difficulty is not because she is White, but because
she refuses to allow herself to consider what it means, for
her Whiteness, to be Black. She denies her own implication
even as she castigates those who see Black people as inferior. This is revealed by the relationships that she has with
her former slaves at the plantation. They have become the
help, in the absence of slavery. This isn't the same thing as,
in Louis's words, "to be known by our character, and not
by our color; to be permitted to take whatever position in
society we are fitted to fill" (Harper, 1994, p. 73). To determine the measure of human beings in the absence of racial
difference – how are we to come to a description of this?
Frances Harper offers us as readers today two possibilities.

The first is that developed in the attempt by freed Black people in the novel to strive to achieve parity of purpose and ambition with others, through uplift, education, and right moral action. The second is that described by the actions of Louis and Minnie, who sacrifice their own possibility of social equality by refusing to pass as White.

Because this is actually what is happening, in their journey from being White to being Black, both Louis and Minnie demonstrate the process of "baptism by fire and blood" whereby someone could come to understand the arbitrariness of racial designations. Simply living as a Black or White person within the confines of existing racial politics isn't enough. The person has to understand their experience of the social ambiguity and uncertain ambivalences of supposed fixed racial designations as motivating a challenge to what race means. They have to become an activist, a person trying to use individual or collective action to change the description of racial inequality that is pervasive in their environment. The first perspective suggests that there are fixed standards by which to measure social progress; the second understands this idea as something developed with others, an equality of result that is found together.

This distinction is present in the description of how Camilla, at the novel's end, is able to entertain Minnie as a social equal, even though she is Black, and begins to understand the journey toward a social justice required of her as well, after the Civil War. That each has very different destinies at the end of the novel reveals a politics of racial equality that Camilla refuses as well. She does not risk the social authority on the plantation that describes her own Whiteness by joining Louis and Minnie in their activism and teaching.

Upon settling in their new town, Minnie teaches and takes care of the needs of local people, while Louis enjoins local freed peoples to organize and participate in politics, and vote. In the novel, the couple is an iconic example of selfless dedication to the needs of the freed people, who are largely full of hope, as well as defining for the reader the possibilities in allowing Black political control of the region (Harper, 1994, pp. 83–5). Their struggle is set in the very moment when Black men were being denied the vote across the country. The loss of the vote, once granted, is devastating to their local community.

The collapse of the opportunities for Black freed people to succeed in building the new community leads to a conversation in which Minnie argues that women need the vote as well, and that this would make it harder for White people to control the resources and laws that impact the Black community (Harper, 1994, pp. 78–9). It is in this moment, in 1868–9, that Frances Harper states what is to remain her perspective on the measure of racial equality. Minnie says, "I think, Louis, that basing our rights on the ground of our common humanity is the only true foundation for national peace and durability. If you would have the government strong and enduring you should entrench it in the hearts of both men and women" (Harper, 1994, p. 79).

In the essay titled "A Factor in Human Progress," published in 1885, Harper clearly lays out her personal vision of what is required to address the problem of race and gender inequality. The ideas are not framed as such, as the topic of the essay concerns the purpose of an education and the question of what is to be done to support education for the Black population. She describes the need for lifting the Black population as a whole out of desperate circumstances and observes that the problem is not whether education can be provided, but what this population is to do with the education. What should this newly consolidated free people do with their potential, 20 years after the end of the Civil

War? Harper is clear that this is not just a problem of education, of providing resources and knowledge. As she puts it, "Knowledge is power" (Harper, 1990a, p. 275).

But knowledge is also dangerous just for that reason, in the hands of those who would abuse its privilege. Harper identifies the solution to inequality as moral training, alongside whatever influence the home, school, and church provide for individuals. The question she wants us to ask of education is: "What will it help us do for others?" The educated person should be a "moral athlete, armed for glorious strife, ready to win on hotly contested fields new battles for humanity" (Harper, 1990a, p. 276). Harper describes the possibility of an equality to come as being through self-sacrifice and self-surrender, the capacity of a people to deny their immediate needs for the satisfaction of the wants of others, to nurture and heal the suffering of others.

She provides an example of a school teacher in the South among the newly freed, who complains of lacking suitable society, and suggests that instead the teacher ask how she might improve those around her, to make of their community something worthy of a higher moral standard (Harper, 1990a, p. 280). Turning back to lift up those nearby is a difficult task, requiring a change in the moral standard of the entire community. It is just because of the plight of the newly freed and oppressed Black person that we should gather them up and give them assistance. Who better to aid, and to teach, than those in desperate need? This is the message, and defines the role that Harper personally has in the national movements. At 60 years of age, she is not in the field starting schools in the Southern countryside. Instead, she is engaged in delivering organizational support, resources to be used by others on the ground. Her role is to provide the vision and confidence for a new generation.

What should be the goal of education? In 1885, this

was as crucial a question for the Black population as it is today. Do you teach bright young children how to do specific jobs that are available, requiring as little thought and initiative as possible, or do you teach them how to think critically about society and their community, to understand the nature of the good and the just? Do you teach about the reasons for the law and government, about education and the economy, about the reasons for the War, and how the marketplace works, or only how to read and write their name and to complete a ledger, and manage their household tasks? What is the purpose of an education? This was a crucial question that also required an understanding of what the goals of the community were – how Black people were to be included in the economic, political, and social life of the nation. The answer for Harper is that the Black community, and Black women, must strive to understand their relationship to other people, to understand who they are as a people in the nation, given their history and what they hope to accomplish.

In *Minnie's Sacrifice*, published in 1868–9, Minnie is killed shortly after beginning to teach in the community, lynched by a mob. Louis mourns her and dedicates his life to the cause for which they both lived, the improvement of the conditions for the free Black people. The failure of the promise of racial equality is therein juxtaposed in her death with that of Laura Lagrange's in "The Two Offers," published ten years before, and discussed briefly here in the previous chapter. The meaning of that story of two women and their choices in love and life takes on new meaning in the context of the death of Minnie. In "The Two Offers," the death of the literal promise of love for Jenette allows her to develop as an important contributor to the society; for Frances Harper, the issue is not matrimony or the choice of partner as the most important decision by the individual, but instead whether individuals in their lives can form the right moral behavior conducive to the thriving of the society. Whether single or married, what matters is to consistently act with the moral character that allows for others to benefit, to allow for the creation of innovative and important contributions by others.

The neglect by the husband of Laura in "The Two Offers" caused a fatal mourning for the lost chance, a relationship impossible to countenance. Not only does the child die, but so does Laura, and thus the inheritance of possibility is lost. He represented not simply an immoral choice, but the inability to establish a viable society because of the actions of both partners. Instead of being a moral tale of individual loss and the choices of partners that a woman can make, the story can be considered an allegory about what is required for the society to meet the demands of the future – what individuals must do to contribute positively to the society. The short story is, in 1859, remarkable for what it demands of the society, not merely what it asks of the individual. If what is possible, given the terms for social activity, isn't sufficient, the individual will die, and others can cause the end of hope – the literal deaths of the children.

And, of course, this same disassociation from right action, a justice impossible to establish, "causes" Minnie's death by a White lynch mob after the War, in *Minnie's Sacrifice*. As readers, we find ourselves shocked not because of the death of a Black woman at the hands of a lynch mob – a rare event in literature – but at the futility of the work that Minnie and Louis engage in, and how it is simply not enough to secure their own welfare. Hope dies, even though Louis soldiers on. And Frances Harper is willing to suggest, by providing this example of lynching, that, if a solution to White collective violence isn't found immediately, the democratic possibilities attendant on the creation of a newly freed people, the promise of a just nation made to those who had been enslaved, will have been made in vain.

Written after Harper had completed a speaking tour through the South after the War, the book *Minnie's Sacrifice* is rife with details of the lives of the newly freed Black people, with stories of the violence they experienced as slaves during the War, and their poverty and need to make sense of their new reality in the years that followed Emancipation. There are several pages of testimony by former slaves to their faith in what the future will bring, now that they are free, and a description of the importance of the education that Minnie provides, in domestic training as well as literacy, which will in time uplift the entire community. Minnie's presence and willingness to assist them demonstrates the goodness of a humanity that otherwise has been terribly represented in the actions of slave owners and the new organization, the Ku Klux Klan.

In this, the closest of all of Harper's works to an anthropological study of the conditions that existed immediately after the War in the region, the situation described in the South is daunting. There is an air of desperation and violence that permeates the novel, and when Minnie dies, the reader had expected Louis to die instead because of the resistance of Whites to the organization of Black male voting in the region. After her death, Louis has to be content with seeing the community celebrate what she meant to them, and that they honor her sacrifice for them, for what might still be possible when the novel was written in 1868. We know from our vantage point in history that, in fact, Frances Harper's prescience was accurate, and, by the time of the publishing of *Iola Leroy* in 1892, there was little to hope for by way of resistance to the new violently oppressive regime that described White political authority.

In the postscript of *Minnie's Sacrifice* that the author writes directly to the reader, Frances Harper says:

> The lesson of Minnie's sacrifice is this, that it is braver to suffer with one's own branch of the human race – to feel, that the weaker and the more despised they are, the closer we will cling to them, for the sake of helping them, than to attempt to creep out of all identity with them in their feebleness, for the sake of mere personal advantages, and to do this at the expense of self-respect and true manhood, and a truly dignified womanhood.
>
> (Harper, 1994, pp. 91–2)

There is, in these words by Harper, no escape from the responsibility to oneself and to the racial justice that is possible, if only a person is willing to sacrifice the security that comes from accepting the conditions of racial inferiority.

The poetry of a people

In *Minnie's Sacrifice*, Harper understands the importance of the characters of Minnie and Louis for the nation, and what they represent for the reader (Griffin, 2001, p. 310). Their struggle is Harper's way of refuting arguments made by Whites at the time as to the inability of freed Blacks to manage and address their newfound rights responsibly (Robbins, 2004, pp. 182–3). Minnie's death is a harbinger, a prophetic warning of the violence that has become possible. To address the energy and enthusiasm that Black people now have after the War, for building a new world – to define with others a new community in which everyone can participate, no matter whether former slave or free, from North or South – is not enough. The post-War world requires that we also expect something new and different from those who have been defined as White, as a corollary to how Black people have been described during slavery and as free in the North. The idea of racial difference itself, how it should be thought of as a problem, was at stake. It was simply not enough to hope and work hard, to understand the plight of other Black people. It was just as important to the future to find a way to attenuate and challenge the idea of a Whiteness that had to preserve itself through a social idea of Black inferiority – an idea of Whiteness that could then successfully reimagine and reinstitute a racist politics after the War.

Readers of the *Christian Recorder* in 1868–9 would have been very aware of the problem of racism in the North. The newspaper, as the organ of the AME church, was itself a key component in the collective definition of Black social progress in the North. At the same time, the Emancipation of the slaves and end of the War left potentially unaddressed the problem of the racism that allowed for a Whiteness capable of enslaving other persons. It is the central tenet of Frances Harper's life's work – and that of Frederick Douglass, Martin Delany, Ida B. Wells, and Sojourner Truth – that to solve the problem of racism required that the social definition of Whiteness be directly challenged. This is why we see the constant development in Harper's novels of those who are Black but otherwise look White, the depiction of literary circles, the generosity of former slaves to the Whites they encounter, rather than the display of an anger and bitterness that itself could describe a threat of violence.

It is as though everyone Black in Harper's novels has been eagerly waiting the chance to prove their worth and capacity to contribute as equals in a new national racial unity. There is a continuous offering to the reader, Black or White, of the idea of racial equality as a description of class politics – and, centrally, gender politics. It was clear to the reader of all of Harper's novels that she thought the answer for the nation was in the hands of Black women, their sustenance and uplift. Without the tools to erode the idea of a Whiteness that demands Black inferiority, the reader of *Minnie's Sacrifice* is brought face to face with the possibility of the violence of the lynch mob as the future description of White social potential.

In response to this threat, in *Minnie's Sacrifice* Frances Harper offers us a counter-proposal, another way to think about what race is to mean for those who are White after the War. She develops the character Camilla in such a way that her personal limitations in changing and adjusting to the idea of racial equality after the War are obvious. But it is also clear that, in the retelling of the Moses story, as Camilla spares Louis from his fate as a slave, for a time, Harper is also offering a more complex script for us to follow in pursuit of racial equality. In 1869, Harper also published her long blank-verse book of poetry, *Moses: A Story of the Nile*.

Imagine a poet on the stage lecturing, sometimes twice a day, about the evils of slavery, the need for temperance, the costs and obligations of freedom, and the rights of women. Is it so hard to imagine that someone with a poet's heart would also write novels and essays whose plots and themes were poignant and urgent? Or that a poet would offer her art to a people enslaved and then free, writing both for a current crisis and for the promise of a better future? Frances Harper was first a poet, and remained a poet throughout her life. It is in her poetry that we find the political, her description of what should be done.

The poems are the closest thing that we have to her speaking to us directly, and often the poems were meant to be read aloud. Frances Harper used her poems, usually in pamphlets, handed out to the audience for a small cost or for free, to explore with her audience the inner life that we have, individually, as a community, and as a nation. She brought poetry to the people and gave them back their words. In this, she demonstrated for us the responsibility that we should have to ourselves and to others.

In *Moses*, Frances Harper changes the relationships between Moses and the women in his life from that of the biblical story. Charmian, who rescues Moses, is described, as is Camilla in *Minnie's Sacrifice* in relation to Louis, as loving him, saying that he is "Doubly mine: as such I claimed thee then, as such I claim thee now" (Graham, 1988, p. 39; Harper, 1993, p. 137). The poem allows Harper to bring in the voices and perspectives of the women who sustain the ambition of Moses and the people (Johnson, 2016, p. 56). It also allows her to tell the story of the relationship between Black and White women that must be developed to sustain the politics of racial justice (Rutkowski, 2008, p. 92). The poem, like the biblical story of the life of Moses, considers the dilemma that a people consolidated on the basis of their oppression must face when free to choose how they will live. But Harper's focus on the threat faced by Black people and the desire to reconcile with racial inequality reveals the precarity of the lives of Black people in the immediate post-War years. At each obstacle, some beseech Moses to return to the land of Egypt and slavery, even as he must ask God for another miracle to keep their faith in the journey. In the poem, Harper describes, first, Moses' resistance to the conditions of slavery, and then the years of preparation required to become that person who can ask God on behalf of his people to free the slaves.

Two figures in Frances Harper's other writings represented real-world Moseses: Harriet Tubman, whom she knew; and President Abraham Lincoln, whom she never met. But the poem is focused not on the rescuing of the slaves by an individual, but rather on the capacity for a people to come together through their faith and to overcome obstacles to their salvation. In this interpretation, it is a poem about the difficulty of collective action, even as it lauds the importance of developing leaders capable of providing moral probity.

Women provide the conscience and the context for the moral choices for both Pharaoh and Moses early on. But the poem, in this way, lifts up the idea that social equality, with regard to both race and gender, must be developed. Moses listens to Charmian – his mother – and his sister, Miriam. Miriam sings a song of deliverance on behalf of the people brought to salvation by Moses.

Pharaoh gathers his men in council and listens as they plan to wage war against those seeking only to flee, which is for Harper important as a statement of the intransigence of loss for these men. They cannot simply let those whom they owned leave; they demand for their due the obedience of others, even if doing so threatens their own lives. The description of Pharaoh's forces pursuing the escaping slaves into the risen sea reveals their refusal to accept the power of the Hebrew God in contrast to their own, and implies their conviction that who they are as Egyptians is defined by their capacity to enslave others.

The contrast between relationships of domination, and those that define the freedom to develop a human capacity for love, trust, and the good, are described here in mortal terms (Harper, 1993, p. 141). To the flouting of the mandate to kill Moses as a child, and the initial rescue by Charmian in the reeds of the river, are joined the perspective of Miriam upon watching the death of the Pharaoh's forces in the sea. As Harper writes, "She saw His choosing 'twixt Israel's pain and sorrow / And Egypt's pomp and pride" (Graham, 1988, p. 60), and Miriam bursts out in song. Deliverance is at hand, and now comes the difficult journey to describe the freedom so hard won – a time of a golden calf, and the curse of slavery upon their souls.

But it is the moment between Miriam and Camilla in *Minnie's Sacrifice* when they reveal Louis's true racial inheritance that establishes the politics of racial reconciliation and redemption available to Camilla, and also to Charmian in *Moses* (Rutkowski, 2008, pp. 94–5). Both are described as necessary to rescue and assist in the survival of the benighted and outcast, and this description supports the idea that Whiteness itself does not eliminate the capacity for right action. What matters is that each allow their own roles to be taken up for criticism by Black people, they acknowledge their responsibility to those who have suffered great harm. This racial complicity, in an approach that may seem too generous today, does not preclude mutual acceptance and love between persons. In fact, it is in *Minnie's Sacrifice* that Frances Harper provides the only reference to an interracial relationship, briefly described in the novel through a conversation between Louis and the White man who married a Black woman. It is only in the context of this description of responsibility by Whites that the man is able to safely acknowledge that one is White and the other is Black (Harper, 1994, pp. 79–80).

Harper describes in these characters the requirements of a personal protest or counter-claim against the complicity that is defined socially for Camilla, in the indolence and comfort of the social position that racial inequality allows her. The Secessionist description of Whiteness provides nothing that Camilla wants, once she understands the problem of racial injustice both through the journey she takes with her father, and her developing relationship to Louis. His progress literally redeems her from captivity in a worldview where racial inequality is both just and true. When she joins with Miriam in freeing Louis from the deception necessary to save him from slavery, by revealing to him his true self, she is freed as well from the burdens of a Whiteness that Dr. Gresham in *Iola Leroy*, for example, could not leave behind, as a value worth preserving.

But it is in this context that we can see the powerful statement to readers of the poem *Moses*, when Harper admonishes the newly free, writing: "when the chains were shaken from their limbs, / They failed to strike the impress from their souls" (Graham, 1988, p. 63). The inability to find the courage to fight for the definition of their newfound freedom, to make something of their nation, led the people of Moses to lose a generation to the desert. This is what causes the death of Minnie – the inadequate response by the Black community to the violence of the Klan. It is hard not to consider this as both prophecy and warning by Harper because of what she had observed in the years she had traveled the South since the end of the Civil War. That she could provide admonishment to a population to which she had devoted much of her life's work at that point is also a public statement as to how difficult things were, how dire, and the urgent need for encouragement for a people that were united only in opposition to something now past. Without the courage to take the kingdom offered, they were to lose it all.

The reference to re-enslavement was not real and was not possible, but was a limit – the reference to which Harper felt all must listen. If not slavery, what was to come? How should Black people seize their destiny as a people? What we find today, over 150 years after this poem was published, is that not one, but many, generations have passed, and still the destiny of the nation is as a place where racial injustice is a defining feature, integral to how we define the courage of a people. Where is the land of freedom now? Harper, in the poem, suggests that it lies right before the Black people, ready for the taking, if only by their children, those born out of slavery and free of the condition that, she writes, "frets through nerve / And flesh and eats into the weary soul" (p. 63). She concludes with the observation that, while the previous generation "died / With broader freedom on their lips," God has reserved the heritage for their "Little ones" – the promise of a home.

Nation building

The poems that Frances Harper writes in the decades following the end of the Civil War, about the obligations that this newfound freedom demands of the nation, are considered some of the most important in her oeuvre. *Moses of the Nile*, the six poems chronicling the life of Aunt Chloe, and the poem "The Slave Mother" establish the parameters for a not yet discovered country. As cautionary tale, admonition, and strategic missive, these poems also demonstrate the understanding by Harper of the very difficult and dangerous path ahead for a country where racial slavery had been defeated, and yet there remained an open wound that had to be healed for all involved. As we now know, those who had been enslaved could not develop a new authority and social condition through which to claim racial equality. Instead, the purview of local government in the South was allowed to develop through conditions for extra-legal violence and a desire by the defeated to recover their economic and political authority.

While ostensibly about the cost of slavery to individuals and the nation, each of these poems considers the price of freedom, the strategies and sacrifices occasioned by what had proven in the years after the War, for Harper and those fighting for racial equality, to be no easy fight. Instead, what occurred was a massive and comprehensive collective struggle by many distinct and often opposing constituencies to define the ambition of what was really for Black people a potentially new country. Who now, in the decades after the War, would answer the question for the nation of what it means to have been a Black slave or to have been born free?

What is often ignored in a discussion of Reconstruction and the development of Jim Crow society in the South is not only the perspective and promise, but also the fears and concerns, that Black people saw in this environment. Harper provides an important record in her poetry of how Black people sought to define the possible, in spite of the dangers of violent reprisals, both unregulated and expected. The lessons in the poems speak directly to those concerned today about what has happened more than 50 years after the conflagration in US society that was the Civil Rights Movement; what Black people can do still to secure a yet unachievable equality, the description of the possible in the midst of the current reimagining of a singular White nation that seems to also be on offer. What is required of Harper's readers – a definition of what it means to still be White, and to decide how the fact that someone is Black allows for both solidarity and compromise – is true today for us as well.

What we find in the novel and the poem is a provocation of the idea of a Whiteness that must be held on to – in death, as with the Pharaoh's army and the sea, and as a bystander to the lynching of Minnie. What Harper suggests is a road in the future that was not taken in the rise of Jim Crow and separate-but-equal legislation in the aftermath of *Plessy* v. *Ferguson*. Harper's understanding of the failure to realize, in the years between the novels and the poem, the promise of this provocation of Whiteness explains why *Iola Leroy* is a text focusing solely on the retrenchment of a Black life where it becomes its own goal. There is no hope in *Iola Leroy*, only the knowledge of a struggle that will continue, a progress made in spite of what exists to limit Black equality. In *Minnie's Sacrifice* and *Moses*, Frances Harper is appealing to a possibility. What if, in fact, those who were White and slave owners could learn to live alongside Black people as social and political equals?

It might have seemed to Frances Harper, because of the incredible promise that freeing the slaves had created, that victory could also be had in the conditions whereby someone such as Camilla with Louis, and in her description of Charmian with Moses, could relinquish any claim on the destiny of Black people. At the same time, this was a poet who had braved the impoverished war-torn Southern states immediately after the War, and her experience prior to the War in the North had not been without hardship. She must have known the leap of faith she was asking of someone such as Camilla, who, in refusing the claims on Black people made by Whiteness, could themselves be harmed. It was not simply a matter of giving up slavery as the means of economic growth, but to release from an enforced social inferiority a group of people that could compete for goods and ambitions in the society.

Love was not enough, and that was the central dilemma in both *Minnie's Sacrifice* and *Moses*. The personal decisions of individuals were not enough to defend the population from the actions of a collective demand for a Whiteness able to terrorize other people into submission. Rather, what Frances Harper suggests is that the very range of instruments used to produce White superiority, from slavery and scientific racism to informal expectations of social segregation and housing covenants, defined as a concept something for which the individual White person could not account. In other words, though White, the person could no more halt the processes of racial differentiation than they could if they were Black.

The conception of racial difference was a collective

distinction, and so could never be successfully removed from the social descriptions of persons, only mitigated locally through individual decisions of love, self-effacement, sacrifice, and generosity. What was required was, instead, something that wasn't only personal but also required cooperation – something that would measure itself against the idea of collective inequality. The instrument to hold in common with other people was religious faith, for Frances Harper and many other African Americans in her lifetime.

But this description of Christian faith was, as Frances Foster points out, militant in its articulation (Foster, 1993, p. 149). Frances Harper admonished her readers to join together to not just resist the erosion of what equal rights they were able to secure, but also to find new purpose in joining together – to describe a political motivation beyond the end of slavery. This is a huge ambition, as it suggests that the target for the politics that fed the Abolitionist Movement was not "just" slavery, but also to diminish or eliminate the practices of racial inferiority in the United States as a nation. This is a very different collectivizing enterprise than to engage in five years of Civil War and witness the deaths of millions of people. But it is also something that would require a similar degree of coordination of purpose.

A Black faith

This concern to develop a common basis for mobilizing against racial inferiority was conceptualized by Frances Harper and all others in the Black community through the only social narrative that a Black person could assume everyone would be familiar with. This was the idea of a Christianity which, even for those who eschewed its moral and practical mandates in their own lives, was ever present as a common social language (Boyd, 1994, pp. 169–70). As Frances Harper alludes to in her poem "Aunt Chloe," when learning to read, often the text that made the most sense to be able to read was the Bible, which many former slaves would have had contact with through their owners (Graham, 1988, pp. 127–8).

For many slaves, the only pretext for regularly meeting as a group that was acceptable to their owners was Christian worship. Except for possibly schooling and work, the only other place where a large group of African Americans publicly gather on a regular basis today is every Sunday in a Christian church. When, in the novel *Iola Leroy*, Frances Harper provides for, first, a conversation about the state of the War among slaves in the marketplace, the next scene is the religious gathering, where the slaves plot their escape under the guise of worship. In the novel, this is not only promoted by their owners, but viewed as providing solace for their political condition. In the use of language to express slave resistance with coded words, and then the use of their faith to bind them together in a scheme to collectively leave their enslavement, Harper establishes through *Iola Leroy* a description of how slaves resisted their captivity with the social tools readily available and reasonably safe for them.

In *Minnie's Sacrifice*, Harper also provides a common language of Christian faith between former slaves as they discuss with Minnie how they make sense of their situation (Harper, 1994, pp. 83–4). This social tradition of collective meanings, regardless of regular church attendance, was also evident in Frances Harper's free Black population, as we can see from even a cursory glance at her first published book of poems in the latter half of the 1840s, *Forest Leaves*. In *Forest Leaves*, the assumption is that readers are able to understand and see their own moral and ethical concerns reflected in the biblical references and religious language of the poems.

In "Haman and Mordecai," Harper refigures the biblical Esther's heroism in confronting King Xerxes about the plot of Haman to have the Jews, her people, killed. Haman arrives:

> For full of pride and wrath,
> To his fell purpose true,
> He vow'd that from his path
> Should perish ev'ry Jew
>
> (Ortner, 2015)

Following this, Harper describes the signal mark of Esther's call to action:

> Then woman's voice arose
> In deep impassion'd prayer,
> Her fragile heart grew strong
> 'I was nervings of despair

With the power of a woman's heroism – someone with courage from her conviction and faith – Esther provides the perfect model for the young Frances Harper and the hope for her own future career as a poet and writer:

> And Haman met the fate
> He'd for Mordecai decreed,
> And from his cruel fate
> The captive Jews are freed
>
> (Ortner, 2015, p. 9)

But this also should be thought by us today as an appeal to an audience that could exist, a community to come that Harper is bringing into conscious existence, with which these narratives of resistance, struggle, and the description of personal victory are shared.

An example of this assumption and development of a shared language for the condition of Black people in the society, of a struggle in common across both the enslaved and the free in the 1840s, for Frances Harper, is given by the poem "Ethiopia," first published in *Forest Leaves*, and later included in her second collection of poems published in 1854, entitled *Poems on Miscellaneous Subjects*. The poem was also published in *Frederick Douglass' Paper* on August 25, 1855. The poem opens with "Yes, Ethiopia shall stretch her bleeding hands abroad, / Her cry of agony will reach the burning throne of God." Only in a collective appeal to justice will the perfidy of slavery and the slave catcher end for Black people, and, at the poem's end, the appeal to forming a collective sensibility, as Ethiopians, is made directly to the audience (Ortner, 2015, pp. 2–3).

In the same vein, in *Forest Leaves*, Frances Harper continues to build the audience's understanding of a shared language of rights and justice on behalf of Black people, slavery, and biblical scripture in "Bible Defense of Slavery." In this poem, the claim is made that Christians cannot uphold the values of slavery without pasting over or concealing the terrible treatment of people as slaves. As she writes, "Remember slavery's cruel hands make heathens at your doors" (Ortner, 2015, p. 18). This refutation of the Christian defense of slavery is important as a statement by Frances Harper. Already in the late 1840s, she conceives of a Christian religious faith in opposition to that which slave owners sought to propagate to their slaves. This difference in biblical scriptural use by slave owners and Black people is pronounced in the poetry of Frances Harper. But it is the shared language of community building, of referencing a specific understanding and knowledge of morals and ethics, a politics, that justifies the biblical allusions for Harper. For what else would she reach to to allow for a common cause between slave and free African American?

When discussing the place of Christianity in the poetry of Frances Harper, Katherine Bassard points out that we should distinguish between the literal and superficial readings of the Bible performed by slave owners, who brought a notion of natural Black inferiority to their reading of scripture, and the politics of restoration or retrieval that Harper and other African Americans used to refute the idea of Black inferiority (Bassard, 2007). The impetus behind the type of Christology that Frances Harper developed in her poems, speeches, and novels allows for a common Christian purpose to be defined, explicitly against the idea of racial differences as immutable and definitive of moral and ethical categories. Instead, what Harper sought was a language with which to restore and confirm the audience's faith in the scriptural message in the Bible, as something held in common.

In the poem *Moses*, for example, Harper uses the Bible to disclose to her readers the possibilities in their own lives, of an ethics of social practices, in prayer, but also in their common appropriation of the text to make sense of their lives (Bassard, 2007). This community would constantly reaffirm itself in the readings of *Moses*, the public readings of the poem, and the hermeneutics of scriptural appropriation that would develop as a result within this audience.

Harper provides more complexity to the definition of a Black Christian life after the Civil War than she does in *Moses* and in *Minnie's Sacrifice*, in the poems about Aunt Chloe. Comprising six sequential poems, "Aunt Chloe," "The Deliverance," "Aunt Chloe's Politics," "Learning to Read," "Church Building," and "Reunion" were all published in 1872, in *Sketches of Southern Life*. The first poem opens with Chloe finding out her children are to be sold to pay the debts owed by the plantation upon the death of the Master. Her cousin Milly commiserates, explaining that:

Oh! Chloe, I knows how you feel,
'Cause I'se been through it all;
I thought my poor heart would break,
When master sold my Saul

(Graham, 1988, p. 117)

In her grief, Chloe stops eating and wastes away. When she is near death, Uncle Jacob, an older Black man, chides her and tells her to acquire faith instead. He explains:

Just take your burden
To the blessed Master's feet;
I takes all my trouble, Chloe,
Right unto the mercy-seat

(Graham, 1988, p. 118)

Chloe starts to pray and finds solace in her faith.

How should we respond to the sundering of relationships that can't be recovered? Harper offers the analogy of death, of a permanent loss, for Chloe, in the sale of her two boys, but that isn't enough. The slave could not concede the loss of family without giving too much authority to the Mistress, whose power over the life and death of a slave was total. To grant that same authority over the relationships of love and care that were developed between parents and their children was to do the impossible. It was simply untenable to accept the intervention of the authority of the owner into the relationships that slaves developed between themselves. It is this realization of an inviolability of the capacity to form relationships in spite of, and not because of, the presence of the authority of an owner, Mistress or Master, that gives the slave their humanity back.

This is also the relationship – that of family – wherein, for Frances Harper, the equality of humanity promised in biblical scripture was revealed. The indelible social bonds between family members and loved ones were immune from the cruelties of racism – in their essence, if not in practice. The slave is, for Harper and for her audience at the time, therefore, never socially dead, merely politically excised, as are women in the period of US history in which Harper was alive, because they could not vote. Why adopt as our view today the totalizing perspective of slavery that a White owner would have: that their perspective on what a slave could want is all that there is, that every want of a slave is merely the owner's desire? Black people have always been just like White people, and the irony is that every White owner knew this fact of a common humanity.

It has become a strange self-fulfilling fiction of our supposed social progress today that argues that, alongside the presence of free Black people – a writer as talented as Frances Harper, a speaker as voluble as Sojourner Truth, and a will as strong as that possessed by Harriet Tubman – White people thought of their slaves as nothing but those humans who could be, because of social and legal instruments, kept in bondage. That the science of racial difference was being developed in experiments on slaves and free Black people in this period doesn't obviate the fact that the call to prove a scientific difference was deemed necessary (Owens, 2018). In spite of, and because of, the equality of humanity across the racial divide, this arbitrary but required color line – the use of the new scientific method to definitively prove a difference that was necessary – became an obsession. But this shouldn't confuse us today as to the importance of the continual social and political mobilization by Whites necessary to keep Black people in their supposed natural place. The fact that oppression was required to achieve a supposed White superiority was the basic proof of a human equality, one that everyone understood to exist. Certainly, Frances

Harper never doubted her own equality with those people around her.

As a result of this constant social pressure toward reconciling social oppression with the fact of human equality across the idea of racial difference, the acquisition of political equality for Black people was a dangerous threat to White social superiority. The new political equality would have proved fatal to the ambition to perpetuate the idea of Whiteness as a measure of democratic citizenship in the United States, if not for the violence and retraction of rights in the decades after the War.

This problem of a loss of political rights in the decade following the Civil War in the poem by Harper is described as analogous to the loss of family by Chloe. This is important for what it says about the idea of progress toward racial equality we should entertain today, and how, without a consistent rights-based politics, the Black community is unable to sustain an effective response against those who collectively continue to define a supposedly necessary Black inferiority. For Chloe in "Aunt Chloe," the problem is not reconciling the loss of her sons with her capacity to make good on an escape or their death, but surviving with the faintest of hope that she might see them again. If there was a way, it would happen, so long as she believed in that possibility, and that something greater than the work of the Mistress and herself was operating on their collective destiny.

This is what Uncle Jacob offered Chloe with the turn toward Christian scripture – the belief in something beyond the authority of the Mistress, something that would make it right, would redeem the loss of family, in this life or the next. This is – similar to the poem "Haman and Mordecai," but with Chloe present throughout – a story about a Black woman and her perspective on the events of slavery and the War, which centers that experience in the argument for Black political rights. This message is, for example, also applicable to those who await the return to public society of those imprisoned today in the era of mass incarceration, as a hope sustained by faith in the possible reunification of family and reaffirmed social ties.

The power of prayer

When we think of incarceration today as equivalent to a captivity resembling slavery, we should think of this as a problem in how racial inferiority is defined through both practices. Why did someone remain on a plantation instead of fleeing north or into the surrounding countryside? Why it was possible to enslave people is a question that has more to do with individual human beings and the description of what they accept as given and normal, what can be imposed upon them and what cannot, or how the structures of the labor-form itself mandate a specific set of actions by the slave. For example, cabins and the big house, field work in contrast to servitude in the kitchens or rooms of the main house, defined what was asked of a slave and what was not. Ownership of a slave did not make everything possible for the owner.

The original readers of "Aunt Chloe" would not think, just because it was possible to sell Chloe's children, that it was therefore in the Mistress' power to do anything she wished with her. And in that fact lies Chloe's future redemption and the possibility of her freedom. In the same context, the imprisoned do have rights against the institution of imprisonment itself, and the sentencing and parole systems allow for individual decisions to matter. What is interesting is how the current system of mass incarceration has been permitted to develop as a response to the fear of racial equality – as a

response to the threat posed by the institution of Black political equality in the 1960s.

In the next poem in the series, "The Deliverance," Chloe's
Mistress and her kind-hearted son, Mister Thomas, speak of
the coming War. Thomas is determined to fight, arguing
that the battle will be quickly won. Chloe expresses the opinion to the reader not only that she believes he is fighting on
the wrong side, but that slavery is at stake in the War. She
says, in an echo of her own pain at the loss of her boys, "How
old Mistus feels the sting, / For the parting of your children
/ Is a mighty dreadful thing" (Graham, 1988, p. 121). Here
Harper makes an equivalence that for the reader in 1872,
after the deaths occasioned by the Civil War, would resonate
strongly. As in war, so it was for the slave – it was impossible to stop the loss of a child. The Mistress may also get
her child back, and will pray for that, as does Chloe for the
return of her boys. That Mister Thomas is kind and takes
the side of the weak in conflicts makes his eagerness to fight
a symptom for the reader of the sordid corrupting nature
of slavery and mastery, and, more pointedly, the pernicious
consequence of the idea of racial inequality.

The slaves pray instead for the War and slavery to end,
and:

> Mistus prayed up in the parlor,
> That the Secesh all might win;
> We were praying in the cabins,
> Wanting freedom to begin

(Graham, 1988, p. 121)

Chloe and the other slaves watch the demeanor of the
Mistress to determine the changing outcome of the War,
and Uncle Jacob, referring to the need for faith in the midst
of the terrible uncertainty of the Civil War, says "Children

don't forget to pray; / The darkest time of morning is just 'fore the break of day" (Graham, 1988, p. 122).

Suddenly, the Northern army is camped outside the plantation. The slaves have a jubilee, and celebrate Lincoln and the end of the War, but the Mistress is heartbroken at losing her slaves. But freedom isn't easy. After the initial euphoria, Chloe points out:

> But we soon got used to freedom,
> Though the way at first was rough;
> But we weathered through the tempest,
> For slavery made us tough
>
> (Graham, 1988, p. 123)

Lincoln is killed and Harper writes of the grief experienced by Chloe and the slaves at this terrible loss. Lincoln's vice president, Andrew Johnson, becomes president and, instead of being a Moses, helping the Black population, he lets the former confederates take back their authority over the land. When Johnson loses the subsequent election, Chloe says:

> but now we have a President,
> And if I was a man
> I'd vote for him for breaking up
> The wicked Ku-Klux Klan
>
> (Graham, 1988, p. 124)

Harper goes on to describe through Chloe's voice the politics of the day, of White men asking Black men to sell their vote. She mockingly describes that some do, for three sticks of candy, for meat and flour, rations, and for sand disguised as sugar. Chloe describes how the men reacted when the women scolded them for selling their votes:

And I would think he felt quite cheap
For voting the wrong side;
And when Aunt Kitty scolded him,
He just stood up and cried

(Graham, 1988, p. 125)

Another woman made sure her husband voted correctly, threatening him with being turned out if he didn't vote as she wanted. Chloe credits her fellow "women radicals" with winning the election even though they couldn't vote (Graham, 1988, p. 126). That this problem of the erosion of Black political rights exists today shouldn't have us ignore the difference that Frances Harper must address in the poem. Black women cannot vote, only the men can vote, and so a conversation between the men and women in the Black community, parallel to that about temperance and public social activity and the home elsewhere in Harper's writing, was important in Harper's perspective to the capacity to develop a Black community that could resist the encroachment of newly acquired political rights after the War. Today, in this context, we can see the importance to limiting the political efficacy of a unified Black community interest by refusing the return of voting rights to the victims of the policy of mass incarceration of Black people.

But Harper also has Chloe discuss the good men who vote to support the needs of the community and can't be bought. As she says:

And we've got lots of other men
Who rally round the cause,
And go for holding up the hands
That gave us equal laws

(Graham, 1988, p. 126)

The relationship between Black women and men and the vote as a vehicle for advancing the needs of the new community of freed people is explicit in the poem. That the Black vote is opposed by the actions of the KKK is a given for Harper and her readers. Faced with the purchasing of votes and violent intimidation, some type of resolute commitment by Black people to the idea of a community was necessary. Who would they turn to when the new president, after Lincoln's assassination, doesn't protect Black people when the former Rebels take what they want from the newly freed Black people?

The next short poem is "Aunt Chloe's Politics," where Harper has Chloe discuss how ugly politics are, and how dishonest the politicians: "Now I don't believe in looking / Honest people in the face, / And saying when you're doing wrong, / That I haven't sold my race" (Graham, 1988, p. 127). The problem with this betrayal of the community by some Black men is that both White and Black people depend on the resources that good government provides, and so, as Harper points out, when the money for a school isn't there, all the children suffer. But the attention to schooling is crucial in the period after the War, for poor Whites as well as Blacks. This is the recipe, according to Harper, for how to succeed in developing an active and thriving society, in spite of the corruption and violence levied against this idea of a new Black community.

And in the next poem, "Learning to Read," Chloe describes first how slaves did various things to learn to read in spite of it being forbidden, because, as she said, "Knowledge did'nt agree with slavery – / 'T would make us all too wise" (Graham, 1988, p. 127). But Chloe learns to read because the teachers came down from the North and ignored the sneers and frowns of the Rebels. Learning to read the Bible was important to her:

So I got a pair of glasses,
And straight to work I went,
And never stopped till I could read
The hymns and Testament

(Graham, 1988, p. 128)

The Bible, of course, was the one book that was readily available to everyone, and so the need for a common text, a community of ideas and possibilities, was satisfied in reading its pages. It should be remembered here that, at the time, Black print culture was thriving so that, in addition to the Bible, every Black person in the society had access to newspapers, magazines, broadsides, and of course short books, and prints of essays and poems such as those published by Frances Harper. That interpretation and messaging were different between persons was less important than the capacity that texts had of finding a language of morality in common. Thus, Harper's use of scripture in her poems, and the advancement of a literary ambition that she advocated for the community, was an important contribution to the idea of a Black society (Peterson, 1995). In the end of the poem, as a result of her acquired literacy, Chloe gets a cabin and lives alone and independent.

In the next poem, "Church Building," Chloe describes how the community builds a meeting place, a church, by collecting money from everyone, in spite of their poverty. Uncle Jacob, who saved her life so long ago and is the pillar of Christian faith for the community, gives the first message in the church and then dies, blessing them. In this piece, Harper offers an idyll of Christian activism, where everyone finds their faith together. This poem is followed by "Reunion," where Chloe reunites with one of her long-lost sons and finds out about the other, who is married and has a child of his own. In her joy, Chloe remarks that now the Mistress has no power to tear them apart, and says:

> I'm richer now than Mistus,
> Because I have got my son;
> And Mister Thomas he is dead,
> And she's got nary one
>
> (Graham, 1988, p. 129)

Chloe then suggests that the son should write to his brother to come visit, and she will expand the cabin to house everyone. Her hope is that he will come and she will be reunited with both sons, so she can then die in peace. The rewards of the Christian faith that Harper describes are a house and family reunited, where the mother is able to live out her remaining years in peace. The particular Christian faith of the Mistress – one that ordered obedience to White people as the highest priority of the slave, and attempted to define a White superiority – isn't rewarded in the poem, and the positions of Mistress and slave are reversed after the War, as Chloe points out. The slave owner and slave have reaped what they have sown.

The common struggle

Frances Harper provided more complex scriptural readings than the audience would have heard in a sermon in churches. Based on the character in Harriet Beecher Stowe's novel *Uncle Tom's Cabin*, "Eliza Harris" is a poem about a young mother fleeing to freedom, across a frozen river, with her child in her arms. In this piece, Harper evokes the mother's fear of the slave catcher with his gun and baying bloodhounds. She describes the mother, torn between the refusal to subject her child to the horrors of slavery and the risk involved in attempting escape: "Oh! Poverty, danger, and death she can brave, / For the child of her love is no longer a slave!" (Graham, 1988, p. 6). Harper's words reveal the capacity of a mother to do what is required, to live or to die by her own hand, in the context of a nation that was otherwise indifferent. The condemnation of slavery was for Harper both immediate and personal. That she knew slaves in Baltimore, New York, and Ohio, and understood intimately the nature of the promise of succor for Blacks in the North, is obvious. And yet the possibility of fugitivity was for Harper infinitely better than the defiled and degraded condition of slavery.

We too often think today of slavery as something similar to captivity, where the captured has a value beyond simply their possession, but in fact slavery was a state of abjection within which anything was permitted of the owner. That some desires proved impossible to fulfill didn't necessarily stop the owner from trying. The slave catcher could and did wound or kill Black slaves rather than let them escape. "Better dead than free" was also the phrase on the lips of the Master, as he set loose the bloodhounds that could hunt down their prey. To flee, for the slave, was thus to risk everything, for there was no penalty for violence inflicted on them other than that of destroying merchandise.

That much more was actually at risk for everyone involved in slavery as an institution, and that shame and guilt existed as a wound, was for Frances Harper a too easily forgotten condition of slavery: "Where bondage and torture, where the scourge and the drains, / Have plac'd on our banner indelible stains" (Graham, 1988, p. 7). But Harper provides an accounting in this poem of the moral cost of building a nation upon "the shrieks of despair, and the bay of the hound." What terrible event, the reader thinks, would force a mother to brave the ice of a frozen river with her child in her arms? What would force us to do so, if not something terrifying and cruel? For Harper, this doom is the caul of slavery for the child, what the mother knows of a life in bondage, of their child's life to come when sold away from her.

Harper offers the reader hope, in spite of the palpable danger and fear of discovery that the reader shares with the fleeing slaves. Without hope, why would the mother run? Without a place of succor, a reprieve or redoubt, what is the point of harboring nobility and purpose, of asking for mercy? Rather, as Harper puts it:

> Oh! How shall I speak of my proud country's shame,
> Of the stains on her glory, how give them their name?
> How say that her banner in mockery waves –
> Her star spangled banner – o'er a million slaves?
>
> (Graham, 1988, p. 6)

This idea of a necessary hope as a demand for the freedom from slavery, a claim upon the nation itself, is rousing and powerful in the poem "Eliza Harris." The plight of Eliza Harris as she learns her child is to be sold away, and the language of fawn and hound to signify the human slave and owner, would have been familiar to readers of the novel. In setting the story of Eliza Harris' escape to verse, Frances Harper places her own art within the narrative of the abolitionist themes of that novel (Turner, 2007).

"Eliza Harris" was published in 1853 in *Fredrick Douglass' Paper*, and was included in Frances Harper's book *Poems on Miscellaneous Subjects* (1854). Not only would the poem have garnered attention due to its association with the popular novel and its poignant theme of the runaway mother and child, but Harper could use the scene to criticize the events occurring within a nation that lauded itself on the sanctity of the relationship between mother and child. Harper's words in "Eliza Harris" reveal how there remains something not yet addressed in the capacity of this nation to harm others.

What shame devolves onto us if we, instead of imagining a frozen river that is assayed only with great risk to the mother and child, today speak of a wall on the other side of the Rio Grande river to keep out those who must seek refuge across the border in the US? Rather than meet the arrivals with blankets and safety, we arrest them, or they drown unaided. And to then separate the parents and child at the border upon apprehension by US authorities – don't these ideas evoke some of the trepidation and ambivalence readers of this poem would have felt in 1853, when White Americans were as divided on the issue of slavery as they are today on the issue of immigration? Could we not also speak about the problem today of racial inequality in a way that doesn't allow us to accept certain conditions as either normal or just?

The threat of losing her child causes Eliza Harris to flee across the river in the middle of winter. How do we account for why a parent would travel hundreds, perhaps thousands, of miles to the US border with a child, and brave the currents of the river, only to drown, the child in their arms? There is too similar a cause today – the refusal to acknowledge a responsibility for the actions of another, the knowledge that we have prompted the flight and danger, the fear. I use the case here of immigration, but this could easily apply to the problems of homelessness, incarceration, and abject poverty across the United States. Frances Harper's poem "Eliza Harris" resonates for us today because it speaks of our own anxieties, our guilt. We have not solved in the Unites States this problem of a violence for which no one claims responsibility – a form of collective violence with no individual culprit or perpetrator.

What we don't get from reading Frances Harper's work is the reassurance that personal relationships are enough, that family is the normative basis for equality or justice. As much as Harper provides a description of the struggle to create and maintain a relationship with other persons – particularly between Black women and Black men – this isn't itself the basis for individual excellence or perfection. She doesn't perceive the individual who is fulfilled in their relationships as the definition of equality, or as the reference to be used to assess the justice of a society. Instead, it is clear that Frances Harper sought a combination of equal individual rights and collective rights against the conditions experienced by persons in the society. She did not hold a view that marriage would realize social equality for women, or that interracial relationships would bring about racial equality.

In the poem "The Fugitive's Wife" Frances Harper provides the reader with the perspective of the wife who realizes that, in order for him to survive, her husband must run away and leave her and their children in slavery. According to the speaker, a love lost is better than the conditions of slavery, and she berates the husband for his timidity of conviction. That she would want him alive and therefore free, rather than with her for a time and dead, seems to the reader both obvious and a terrible responsibility for her to shoulder. But this is an argument for the privileging of individual rights and protections over the comforts and affirmations of family and community that exist in any social condition. Where is the slave Master, the owner who is responsible for this terrible choice, as the partners embrace one another and tears fall from the husband's eyes? We anticipate the arrival of the Master at any moment, cutting off his escape.

Just as in "Eliza Harris," the reader watches as the husband dashes to freedom – here, the reader adopts the perspective of the wife herself, and Harper places the reader

in the position of knowing they will remain behind, as the
husband braves the dangers of escape. How should the wife
feel, abandoned and yet knowing that there was no other
choice – that for her own love's sake he must flee, and in
doing so the one thing that gave her joy was taken from her.
As Harper writes, "It was my sad and weary lot to toil in
slavery, / but one thing cheered my lowly cot – / My husband was with me" (Graham, 1988, p. 19). This is not said
pathetically, but resignedly, as though now with his impending absence the drudgery of her life, the loss experienced by
her own enslavement, was confirmed.

What would it be like, to say goodbye to your beloved
not because of their death or for a trip somewhere for a few
days, but because of their need to flee to the land of freedom,
to secure their own safety – realizing that you would never
know what had happened to them? To leave the plantation
was purposefully fraught, as the runaway must be caught and
punished, or the entire system of slavery would collapse. The
uncertainty of being a slave was not knowing what was going
to happen next. The poem captures this uncertainty, and the
reader shares this terror:

And in his eyes a gloomy night of anguish and despair; –
I gazed upon their troubled light,
to read the meaning there.
He strained me to his heaving heart –
My own beat wild with fear;
I knew not, but I sadly felt
There might be evil near

(Graham, 1988, p. 19)

That the poem leaves open, and emotionally raw for the
reader, the inability to perhaps ever know the destiny of
the choice to leave the social conditions that exist at home,

because of the threat of violence or loss to come, is important. What Harper is trying to offer the audience is an understanding of how precarious life as a slave was – so much so that it was not possible to sustain social bonds. The violation of human social bonding and the inability to be safe – this is a violation of individual human rights.

That Harper provides for an intersectional perspective for the reader when the narrator complains of the fragile emotional state of men, who are unable to handle the grief and pain that women must, is expected and welcome. In that he must flee, and she must stay, there is a subtle reproach that hints of their love in these words: "He vainly strove to cast aside the tears that feel like rain:— / Too frail indeed is manly pride, to strive from grief and pain" (Graham, 1988, p. 19). The terms of the husband's departure are waived in the poem for an end that signals the responsibility and burden for those who must remain in slavery – a woman's lot, but also that of a mother. "'Bear not,' I cried, 'unto your grave, / The yoke you've born since birth; / No longer live a helpless slave, / The meanest thing on earth!'" Similar to "Eliza Harris," "The Fugitive's Wife" relies for its poignancy on the impossibility of sustaining in slavery the relationships that humans require to have meaningful lives. The threat of selling the child and the loss of the spouse, and his abandonment of the wife and child, mirror what occurs in the novel *Uncle Tom's Cabin* between George and Eliza Harris, and starkly demonstrate for Harper's readers how slavery makes of the slave owner someone who does not value the norms of family and home, that their ownership of other persons is itself purposefully inhumane in character and design. The hypocrisy of slavery as requiring the destruction of the slave family to provide for the profits necessary to sustain the family of the owner are here demonstrated in bold relief.

The poem "The Slave Auction" likewise addresses the problem of individual rights in the context of racial injustice – the sordid economic scheme of selling people away from their loved ones and families. Young girls cry in distress as they are sold as their mothers look on ignored, a wife watches as her husband is bartered away, and men are gathered along with children to be sold. Harper then expresses what this loss must feel like, what this sale would do to a person who must watch their loved one traded for coin:

> Ye who have laid your love to rest,
> And wept above their lifeless clay,
> Know not the anguish of the breast,
> Whose lov'd are rudely torn away.

> Ye may not know how desolate
> Are bosoms rudely forced to part,
> And how a dull and heavy weight
> Will press the life-drops from the heart

(p. 10)

The onlooker here is in the audience of the auction house itself, as Frances Harper may have experienced as a free Black person, but also as someone reading the poem and White would experience this sale. The poem addresses the very idea of buying family members – of selling someone's child, a husband, and a wife – and what that would mean for those who lost a loved one to the market, the pity and anguish of being helpless to avoid their fate, and what this would mean for a person, to have their love pressed out of them by the weight of this loss.

Harper does not occupy the perspective of the sold, the lost ones, those who fled or were given away. This is not because the condition where someone would be sold or flee to an all but certain death was unknown to Frances Harper. Instead, I think this is because to occupy that perspective of loss is to admit to a failure of a volitional capacity that is itself shameful to the person. This is the moment of absolute loss, of having their own rights taken away, on the auction block or in the separation from those whom they love. There is no speech or voice that could account for the loss of independence this position describes. Yes, we talk of the individual slave today in terms of the freedom of the fugitive, but forget the people left behind; and we speak of the adversity overcome upon being sold down the river, but not of those who remain, bereft.

We record the speeches of the convicted in the courthouse, or the last words of the person about to be put to death by the state. But we don't know how to occupy that location of helplessness and the absence of rights upon which these descriptions depend. It is this moment that slavery and a host of other practices that deny human rights create within the society. It is this that Harper abjures in the poem, and asks the reader to consider as a terrible cost that society has created for everyone.

Taken together, these poems represent an appeal to the humanity of the reader, asking what sort of person could see love as expendable, its denial as something from which to profit. This dramatic imagery purposefully appeals to the reader for sympathy not only for the families of the slaves, but for their own humanity. These poems seek a redemptive spirit or thought from the reader, a weakening in their resolve to continue the practices that cause such suffering in others as fellow humans (Johnson, 2016, p. 147). Why do we create a social position that it is impossible for a human to occupy and not be wounded? This subject is particular to Harper, and assessing the poems requires that the readers consider what it means for them to participate in actions

– even if from a distance of 1,000 miles – that would have as their consequence the dissolution of all social relationships. Our implication in these actions is clear – because of the vantage point afforded us in each scene, we watch passively as society reproduces the conditions of inequality and injustice.

To some extent these poems also ask the free Black reader at the time to consider the burdens that they have had to bear, as individuals and as a people, and to show mercy for the effects of this trauma on those who have been enslaved and are now fugitives. From this perspective, the poems reflect the events occurring for readers in the society at the time of their publication. In 1853, after the Fugitive Slave Act of 1850, escaped slaves, and those who were accused of being fugitives from a justice that was as pernicious and wrong as it was capricious, were vulnerable to recapture, and all Black people in the North had to consider what slavery and freedom meant for them.

To be born free was not now a certainty of political status, something that would allow for a false pride of place in this context, but instead a status that had to be earned through securing the rights and freedom of others, by harboring and aiding the escaped slaves. The Act, in effect, mobilized the free Black population in the North, in self-interest if for nothing else. It should be remembered, as well, that Frances Harper was increasingly involved in abolitionist work at the time of the publication of these poems, and with good reason. The events described in the poems as occurring in the South were a consequence now brought home to the North by the Law of 1850.

Today, the ideas of fugitivity and humanity presented in the poems force a reckoning with the responsibility that we have to those seeking refuge in our country. Those who require our succor upon their return from prison, the asylum seeker and the purposefully forgotten, because they confirm the violence and impossibility of the individual condition within our society, demand our attention and assistance.

6

Conclusion: Of Poems and Politics

In 1864, Frances Harper penned the poem "Bury Me in a Free Land" as a call to action for those fighting against the South in the Civil War. Originally published in the *Liberator*, and often cited by those rallying against slavery at the time, the poem takes the perspective of someone who refuses to rest until slavery is defeated, and who thereby galvanizes everyone else to do the same (Graham, 1988, p. 93). A paean to those who have died in a land where slavery continues to cast its shadow, Harper describes the restlessness, the refusal to acquiesce, and the anguish of those who must watch over a land that bears the coffle gang, mothers crying in despair as their babies are torn from their arms, the baying of bloodhounds as they seize their prey, and the young women sold away for pleasure. The poem intimates that the fight against slavery is a noble cause, that there is no higher calling than victory, for even in death slavery continues to haunt the land.

The speaker frames the poem with the signal refusal to be

buried in a country where such a thing is possible. Why, in death, would she want to oversee the suffering of a people through the blight of slavery? The sacred rites at the end of a life have to be important, to honor the life of the individual, and for someone of Frances Harper's public visibility to refuse burial in the country not just for herself, but for everyone fighting the cause of slavery, is powerful condemnation. The opening promise of a sacrifice, lives lost to history in humble graves without recognition, if slavery is not defeated, offers her own reputation and life to the cause. What is to be the measure of a life Harper asks, what honor, if slavery is not defeated in their lifetime?

The words "Make it among earth's humblest graves, / But not in a land where men are slaves" are followed at the end of the poem by lines that mark the honor that would be accrued by someone laid to rest in a country where slavery had been defeated:

I ask no monument, proud and high,
To arrest the gaze of the passer-by;
All that my yearning spirit craves,
Is bury me not in a land of slaves

(Graham, 1988, p. 93)

In the middle of the bloody struggle of the Civil War, what better legacy for the soldier than to know that their life's sacrifice had defeated slavery and freed the land? In these words, Frances Harper honors those whose death has not been in vain; she promises an epitaph worthy of their sacrifice.

Much is made today of a historical juxtaposition between the enslaved and the free, and the responsibility, of those who could, to fight against the suffering that slavery caused throughout the country. "Bury Me in a Free Land" offers a message for the reader about the responsibility that freedom from slavery allows, and prompts us to consider: What should our legacy be today? What is the collective responsibility to address the conditions under which people live in this country? It is not enough simply to say, "At least we are no longer enslaved." How are we supposed to account for the differences between the enslaved and the free, if the suffering of a people continues? The nobility of which Harper writes, of that particular freedom's struggle, has passed more than 150 years ago.

The questions remain salient: How should we honor the noble dead – what have we made of the freedom for which so many sacrificed? What is the description of the land in which we still live, but a place of suffering and woe? What is required of our poets and writers, to muster us for the cause of racial justice? These questions are the basis of the rousing call to action of "Words of the Hour" (1871). In the poem, Frances Harper ardently appeals to the Northern victors not to abandon the lands of the South, not before the victory is won over slavery. She writes:

> The minion of a baffled wrong
> Are marshalling their clan,
> Rise up, rise up, enchanted North!
> And strike for God and man
>
> (Graham, 1988, p. 103)

She goes on to claim that the vanquished Secessionists have only changed their name, that they have hidden in plain sight, ready to strike back and regain their lost control over Black people. She writes, "And o'er the ruin'd auction-block / Erect the common school":

> To wipe from labor's branded brow
> The curse that shames the land;

And teach the freedman how to wield
The ballot in his hand

(Graham, 1988, p. 103)

Worried about the inability to secure voting rights, safety from increasing violence, and the gradual abdication of their victory, Harper tries to rouse the North to the danger inherent in leaving the Southern region uncontrolled or in ceding control once again to the very forces of the Secessionists in the interests of political expediency or a lack of will to support Black Emancipation. It wasn't enough, as we see in this call to heroism and nobility of purpose on behalf of Black people in the South. The danger may seem obvious to someone whose struggle is in trying to define how to distance themselves from a violent and supposedly superior concept of Whiteness, but for Black people after the War the collective politics they held in common was not explicitly directed at the problem of social inequality, but, instead, political inequality. With the rights question settled temporary for Black men, it proved difficult to find a suitable claim to mobilize all Black people to fight for equality. Faith provided that. Lynchings provided that. An activist faith was the social glue whereby it was possible to imagine these experiences as a common problem.

Frances Harper crafts a poem in 1874 chronicling the dreadful consequences of not being able to escape slavery. The price that Eliza Harris threatened to pay, but did not, in the imagination of Harriet Beecher Stowe was in real life exacted in the tragedy of Margaret Garner, described in the poem "The Slave Mother." Here, the reader observes the desperate plight of the mother with her four children as she makes her way across the Ohio River to freedom. Following her, instead of allowing her the freedom the crossing should have provided if not for the Fugitive Slave Act of 1850, is the federal marshals' approach in the poem, and she says:

If the Ohio cannot save,
I will do a deed for freedom,
Shalt find each child a grave.
I will save my precious children
From their darkly threatened doom,
I will hew the path to freedom
Through the portals of the tomb

(p. 30)

She then takes a knife and kills her daughter, before the catchers stop her from killing the other children. This retelling in 1874 serves as a warning to the reader of not merely the cost in human lives that slavery brought with it, but how the laws could be used to pervert the cause of justice and freedom.

Almost 20 years after the actual tragedy of Margaret Garner took place, Harper provides a lesson for the reader in what they are fighting to prevent – a catastrophe whose prohibition must remain a condition of the community. This condition is, however, defined by the refusal to compromise with those who would enslave others. "The Slave Mother" addresses the consequences of the willingness of the North, after the War, long after the event took place, to withdraw their troops from the South, allowing the former slave owners and White interests to recover their authority over Black people and the land. In 1874, when the poem was published, this willingness to compromise with the defeated White political and economic interests at the expense of the freed people was taking shape. Frances Harper is reminding readers about the consequences of compromise, of the Fugitive Slave Act of 1850, and the moral cost of acceding to the demands of Southern White interests (Johnson, 2016, pp. 66–70). It would not be enough.

Mourning

In *Idylls of the Bible*, published in 1901, Frances Harper therefore mourns a nation. In a new version of *Moses: A Story of the Nile*, Harper attempts to remind the reader of the promised land – the yet unattainable life of a community free from fear and injustice. The poem is prophetic, a call of admonishment as well as to action; the reader understands their complicity in the failure to achieve that their current condition represents. White collective politics has reduced the ambitions of Black people in the country to claims of individual accomplishment and greed. Told to only act within the parameters set by a demand that White people are always superior in status and condition, the Black person can allow their own social status to reflect their proximity to specific White people. As sycophants to, and parasitic on, the limits provided by this measure of racial difference, a Black elite makes excuses and silences their internal critics – of which, Harper was one. Rather than seek out what is possible if the idea of racial difference is rejected, some hold fast to the idea of a distinction that can make a difference to their own fortunes. This comes at the expense of all others, and giving lip service only to the idea of racial justice. These individuals, and this perspective on the inevitability of racial difference, a refusal of the promise of racial equality in deed but not in word, provide an apology for the actions of those who sacrifice advocates of racial justice.

For Harper, the late 1890s and early 1900s must have been a bitter sad pill to swallow, as the new generation of writers eschewed a claim to political rights for a recognition from Whites of their literary prowess. That Black people were always important to the nation, and the economy, should be remembered. Therefore, what was at issue was the politics of distribution and authority, not whether Black people mattered. How, not whether, Black life was to matter with regard to the idea of racial difference was at issue. For Harper, in these last published poems of her lifetime, we see the attention given to the definition of the community after the disaster. No longer is there a call to action in the poems, but rather a concession – individual and collective – to the sacrifices that have been made for the survival of all the rest of us.

In "The Ragged Stocking," a man acknowledges the sanctity of the pledge to right action, in the tattered stocking of a child. After the child's death, he continually fortifies himself against partaking of the pleasures of drink and excesses of immoderate desire, by remembering the price paid by someone else. A price to warrant obedience, the death of Jesus – this is what Harper reminds the reader of in "Christ's Entry into Jerusalem" (Harper, 2010 [1901], pp. 48–50, 53–62). But what the reader doesn't get in these poems is the optimism and call to arms of the poems Harper wrote before the War and in its immediate aftermath. Instead, the poems in this collection read more like those poems Harper published during the War – full of foreboding and explicitly speaking of sorrow and death. For Frances Harper everything in 1901 pointed to a political struggle for Black people similar to that during the War. But this time there were few White people willing to fight alongside Blacks for their common vision of an equal nation.

The reader: the call to conscience

In her poems, Frances Harper allows us in. These allow us to be the closest we will get to how she imagined the world around her and what she wanted out of life. They appear as the inexpensive chapbook, the pamphlet, published in news-papers, sold at her lectures or, given away for free, recited, and comprised of real and imagined events, fictions, and scripture. Foster explains how poets had to understand their audience and, in order to achieve a large readership for their work, had to meet the audience where they were (Foster, 1993, p. 149). She explains how Harper achieved this, by using the popular-cultural references and descriptions of real-world events that her audience would know of. The language was familiar. As McGill suggests, Harper's poems informed the audience for her lectures, and her lectures sup-ported her poetry; where she went, so did the pamphlets and chapbooks (McGill, 2012, p. 67).

The difficulty for a reader of Harper's poetry today is in remembering not what she was trying to do, but how she was trying to do it, how she was able to reach the people. For us, the distance between our time and hers is too great to reproduce all the aspects of a speech or lecture by Harper, but we can understand serialized fiction novels repeating and riffing off poetry, and these offering the audience for her speeches and lectures a rehearsal or the return of an argu-ment or idea. Her zeal and generous skill at communicating her ideas would not only impress listeners, but also inspire them. They would be caught up in the event itself, the pag-eantry of the fully literary world she would bring with her. Harper's own erudition and poise as a person would be the best advertisement for her message of morality and striving together to pursue the highest of ideals. But, for all the work of providing a public within which we might gather, Frances Harper was immensely private as an individual. This we can see from the poems, where there is a distance maintained between the reader and the author. There are some things she didn't write about, verses she didn't put down for us, that would give us today a better sense of the person and not merely the poet and writer, the lecturer and activist. Harper was one of the preeminent activists of her generation – someone who built up what today we would call a brand, which was extremely effective.

There was nothing simple about the knowledge that Frances Harper wanted to convey to the world – about the importance of living a Christian life as a free Black woman, about the necessary relationship between gender and race, and about the challenge posed to us as a society by the possibility of both Black slavery and freedom, and the refusal to give the vote to women. In these chapters, the reader has been afforded only the briefest glimpse of what Harper produced and contributed to our society, as an organizer, an orator, a novelist, an essayist, and a poet. It is not only that she lived what today we would describe as a full life, but also that she dedicated that life to the power of the pen and the word. Her poems and lectures stirred the hearts and minds of many, for almost 50 years. This was an individual who traveled to the most desperate areas of the country, lecturing and talking with people about what could be done about the racism and misogyny they experienced in their lives – what they should do to find a brighter coming of the day. Frances Harper was someone who was steadily lauded, looked for to speak to the public, and sought out for her wisdom. This keen sense of political strategy is evident with even a cursory glance at her poems and speeches, but it is the novels that rock us back on our heels, just because of their courage and insight.

What at first seems to be too melodramatic for the modern reader – the death of women from heartbreak, the refusal to find love again upon the death of a potential partner, the reference to Jesus on the cross and the inconstancy of the disciples – is a statement about the impossibility of developing a democratic society where persons have to rely on their relationships with others for their political voice. If to be a woman is to be described socially through the relationship one has with men, if the expectation is to always be available for the desires and attentions of men, this delineates a basic rights problem that Harper sought to bring to public awareness. As a free Black woman, how was she to find a public voice, the means by which to express her ideas and potentially change the minds of those around her about the rights due to women and Black people? Harper was, in this important sense, a consummate democratic citizen, someone who worked around formidable obstacles to her political expression to deliver a message about the rights due to those in the society.

That she was supposedly turned away at first as a participant in the Underground Railroad because she was born free and a single woman – literally an unknown, by the definitions of her society – was typical of the problem that Harper faced in bringing her ideas to the public. The finding of fault, the criticism she received, the denigration of her person and ambition – she knew well such public and social descriptions of women. In spite of this she persisted, and from the perspective we would have on someone like her today, each first, each success, was hard won and required great courage. In considering her writing, the concepts she brings to our understanding, it is important to try and think through what the experience must have been like to be surrounded by White abolitionists, giving speeches and living with them in Maine in the 1850s. What being the first woman hired as a faculty member at Ohio Seminary would have lent to her sense of the problems with the rights of women, and the cost of freedom and slavery for Black people in the country. It is easy to say, for us now, that the passage of the Fugitive Slave Law in 1850 and then the Act in Maryland in 1853, making her unable to return to the state of her birth without risking being enslaved, were what wakened her to the dangers of being a free Black person in the society. But this is to diminish her own understanding of the life she was living.

What we instead record in her first speeches and writings are the work of someone who had, her entire life, a keen sense of what was thought impossible and inappropriate – who, as an orphan, as a servant in a household to White people, and as a precocious student in her uncle's school, was always having to accept charity and generosity, and the requirements placed on her by others.

Did she understand the risks of being a free Black girl, and then a young woman living in Baltimore in the 1820s, 1830s, and 1840s – this individual who went on to write four longer novels, many books of verse, and would give speeches to great acclaim for decades? This future elite national organizer of civil rights in the last decades of the nineteenth century? Would you suspect that someone with this in her future would be, when young, a formidable intellect and demonstrate the creative spirit that would make of her situation a cause, her own personal ambition? Of course.

Harper was one of the most important public intellectuals of her generation, in a life that included not just the social respect and public acknowledgment of Frederick Douglass, Sojourner Truth, Ida B. Wells, and Harriet Tubman, but also those of Susan B. Anthony, Lucretia Mott, and Frances Willard. Who was the young Frances Harper then – in Baltimore, Ohio, Massachusetts, Pennsylvania, New York, and Maine – if not a person who had something always to give to the world, and determined that she would find a way in her life to do so? What we have in her work, in all its complex formats and cadences, is a record of our democratic life as a nation from just before the Civil War to the turn of the new century. This is a gift that we should have done more to preserve, but we now know that this is exactly why this preservation wasn't accomplished. We owe the recovery of her writings to the patient and exhausting diligence of several researchers – to persons who understood, better than others, the importance of the work of Black people to the democratic aspirations of this country.

The cause of slavery was lost as it was begun. That a society, a country, could have been built on slave labor isn't shocking today; it is what the United States is as a nation. The inheritance of this problem should define our national politics, and it does. But it wasn't a problem for a large proportion of the population in the United States in Frances Harper's day. And the refusal today to acknowledge that it was enough to cause a Civil War – that the plight of Black people, as slave and free, could cause the country to go to war with itself – is testament to the difficulty Frances Harper would have had convincing those around her of the importance of abolishing slavery in the 1850s.

What Harper's writing demands of us today is the reassessment of how we think of race and gender as political concepts. In publishing *Forest Leaves*, her first book of verse, in the late 1840s in her twenties, and her activism in the 1850s, the publication of the second book of verse in 1854, and "The Two Offers" in 1859, Harper's writing prior to the Civil War asks the reader to consider racial and gender equality as the very definition of democracy. Race and gender equality are what we mean by democracy. Their description, then and now, is the measure of our democratic polity. Frances Harper, in spite of all of her work, died without being able to vote in a national election for president. She was always free, but spent much of her life around those who had been enslaved. To measure our democratic polity instead only by the writings of a Thomas Jefferson, a Ralph Waldo Emerson, or Walt Whitman, begs the question of why we would need to avoid the writing of someone who is a Black woman – what is the important work that we do in eliding the writings of not just Frances Harper but so very many others? We should all focus our research attention on the work of recovering our democratic voice, and find value in the writings of those who, in a concrete way, made it possible for all of us to be here and to do the work that we do.

What we learn from the writing of Frances Harper is that the pacing of a racial politics in this country is wrong. In the 1860s and 1870s, it was already possible to talk of the problem of interracial relationships in terms that are contemporary. The professional Black woman, the public speaker, the writer, was already a fact in the lives of those in the community, and everyone in the country. In the 1850s, it was already important to distinguish between whether someone was primarily concerned with race or gender in their writing, and the portrayal of an intersectional understanding of people's lives was evident in the writings of Frances Harper, as it was in the decades that followed. The raw, real politics of gender and race organizational work was well rehearsed throughout her life and had been by the Black women who had come before her. What is new today, for us, is this problem of recovering the understanding of how much work has already been done, of relearning what was lost to the violence, the lynchings, the imprisonments, the deaths by starvation and neglect, the abusive health care, the brutal silencing by partners and the public, and the force of racism, or what Harper describes as "public opinion." We must recover the democratic voice in this country.

We should be humbled, not arrogant, when we read the poems and novels that, at first, with our problematic politics of race and gender, seem naïve, or too colorful – too much, excessive, or too little, not serious enough, badly written and constructed. If we have read and written more ourselves; we should be more discerning, however. And, if we have not, we should pay attention not to what is wrong in her work, in our opinion, but what it allows – what it asks of us if we read it in the best light, on a brighter day.

What this means is that we need to ask ourselves what it is that we are refusing by considering the purposeful language of this incredibly popular democratic activist poet, public speaker, and novelist to be inadequate to the needs of our democratic politics today. This is still the America of Frances Harper. To pretend otherwise is to have decided that Black women, that Black people, and that women don't matter to our past or future. But this would mean we aren't a democracy except in name, and instead something where to be a woman and to be Black are thought problems, questions still for others to consider at great length – but only once they complete more important business.

When we read *Iola Leroy*, the lucidity of the text is disarming, the glib insertion of references to real-world events, of phrases and ideas written by other writers – the riffing on the writing of Harriet Jacobs, for example, or *Clotel*, the simulated academic seminar, the argument in the student dorm room and the dangers of street life, are too much to absorb for most today as a criticism of our democratic politics (Brown, 2003; Cutter, 1999, p. 153). But *Iola Leroy* was written 23 years after *Minnie's Sacrifice*, and the description of interracial relationships and the sacrifice required of the public woman, the voice of the slave and the free Black person had changed in that time. The belief in 1869 that it was possible to do the work in the South of political organizing on behalf of the Black vote and community development had evaporated by 1892, because of the abandonment of the Black South by the federal government, and the successful organization instead of violence as a call to White exclusiveness, and the absence of the law when lynchings occurred. There was almost no recourse for Black people in the law by 1892, and so *Iola Leroy* suggests for us how race develops as a politics over two decades, from the necessary dangerous sacrifice of the Black woman to encompass the figure of the Black teacher and writer dedicated to bringing knowledge of the requirements of democracy to the community. The radical egalitarianism of *Iola Leroy* is disarming, literally, in our time, just because we have become so complicit and appreciative of the generosity of those who, in their acceptance of racial inequality, deign to provide some exceptions to the rule of Black inferiority. To those of us who accept these spoils, Frances Harper would speak, as she does in *Trial and Triumph*, about the false promises of the blandishments of money and social fame.

We should not be optimistic today about the racial future of this country, once we pay closer attention to the message about how it was impossible to appeal to an implacable social description of Whiteness in the actions and words of both the cousin Lorraine and Dr. Latrobe (Ernest, 1995, p. 202). It is not that Dr. Gresham isn't real enough, or is a cheap imitation of what is required for Iola Leroy to fall in love. There is no talk in *Iola Leroy* of her needing a male partner either for fulfillment or to do good works in the community. Dr. Gresham is the limit, for Harper, of the White liberal voice. And the turn away from interracial relationships (where are the interracial friendships with White women in the novel?) is disheartening for the future, as is the fact that we today are possibly relieved at the failure of these relationships. That Dr. Gresham can't work through how to live with Iola speaks to the persistence of racial social segregation today, which, as Harper clearly shows, is an overt sign of a racial description of difference in the society.

The writings of Frances Harper reveal a failure of the work by Black people to successfully prevent the consolidation of a White exclusionary politics after the War. By the turn of the century, her own words predict the fate of her own writings and career, the obscuring and near-loss of her work through over 60 years of future neglect. To ignore this literary contribution is to refuse the voice that sustains and nurtures, to deny the importance of Iola Leroy and her work in the Northern Army camp, the democratic politics that has allowed Black people and women to survive vicious racial and misogynist suppression throughout the country's history and, in the 1890s, still believe in the possibility of a democratic nation. It was not only Martin Luther King, Jr., who brought about the Civil Rights Movement in the 1960s, nor was it the sole interest and intent of White liberals – it was the work also of Black women. This we do know. And the recovery of the words of Frances Harper allows us to understand how this work occurred in her lifetime – how Black women not only participated within the Abolitionist Movement, but pressured the public to consider the consequences of slavery as they lectured, wrote, and organized after the War to try and build a new country (Boyd, 1994; Carby, 1989; Christian, 1980; Foster, 1993).

That this vision of what was possible failed to materialize was not the fault of Frances Harper, but of those whose personal interests, ideas of Black community politics, and description of race and gender equality did not allow for an effective resistance to the steady consolidation of White political interests. May we find the necessary wisdom and courage today to realize the possibilities of democracy in this country through our understanding of the work of Frances Harper.

Bibliography

Angelou, M. (2015) *The Complete Poetry*. New York: Random House.

Bacon, J. (2007) *Freedom's Journal: The First African-American Newspaper*. Lanham, Md.: Lexington Books.

Bassard, K. C. (2007) "Private Interpretations: The Defense of Slavery, Nineteenth-Century Hermeneutics, and the Poetry of Frances E. W. Harper" in R. Lundin (ed.) *There Before Us: Religion, Literature, and Culture from Emerson to Wendell Berry*. Grand Rapids: William B. Eerdmans Publishing Company.

Baumgartner, K. (2019) *In Pursuit of Knowledge: Black Women and Educational Activism in Antebellum America*. New York University Press.

Bell, D. (2018) *Faces at the Bottom of the Well: The Permanence of Racism*. New York: Basic Books.

Bennett, M. (2005) *Democratic Discourses: The Radical Abolition Movement and Antebellum American Literature*. New Brunswick: Rutgers University Press.

Bethel, E. R. (1997) *The Roots of African-American Identity: Memory and History in Antebellum Free Communities*. New York: St. Martin's Press.

Boyd, M. J. (1994) *Discarded Legacy: Politics and Poetics in the Life of Frances E. W. Harper, 1825–1911*. Detroit: Wayne State University Press.

Brooks, C. M. (2018) "Reconsidering Politics in the Study of American Abolitionists," *Journal of the Civil War Era*, 8(2), pp. 291–317.

Brown, W. W. (2003) *Clotel: or The President's Daughter*. London: Penguin Classics.

Bruce, D. D. (1989) *Black American Writing from the Nadir: The Evolution of a Literary Tradition, 1877–1915*. Baton Rouge: Louisiana State University Press.

Carby, H. (1989) *Reconstructing Womanhood: The Emergence of the Afro-American Woman Novelist*. New York: Oxford University Press.

Christian, B. (1980) *Black Women Novelists: The Development of a Tradition, 1892–1976*. Westport: Greenwood Press.

Cohen, W. (1991) *At Freedom's Edge: Black Mobility and the Southern White Quest for Racial Control, 1861–1915*. Baton Rouge: Louisiana State University Press.

Collier-Thomas, B. (1997) "Frances Ellen Watkins Harper: Abolitionist and Feminist Reformer, 1825–1911" in A. Gordan (ed.) *African American Women and the Vote, 1837–1965*. Amherst: University of Massachusetts Press, pp. 41–65.

Connor, K. R. (1994) *Conversations and Visions in the Writings of African-American Women*. Knoxville: University of Tennessee Press.

Cutter, M. J. (1999) *Unruly Tongue: Identity and Voice in American Women's Writing, 1850–1930*. Jackson: University Press of Mississippi.

Delany, M. R. (2017) *Blake; or, The Huts of America*. Cambridge, Mass.: Harvard University Press.

Dudden, F. E. (2011) *Fighting Change: The Struggle over Woman Suffrage and Black Suffrage in Reconstruction America*. New York: Oxford University Press.

Ernest, J. (1995) *Resistance and Reformation in Nineteenth-Century African-American Literature: Brown, Wilson, Jacobs, Delany, Douglass, and Harper*. Jackson: University of Mississippi Press.

Ernest, J. (2004) *Liberation Historiography: African American Writers and the Challenge of History, 1794–1861*. Chapel Hill: University of North Carolina Press.

Farrar, S. (2015) "Maternity and Black Women's Citizenship in Frances Watkins Harper's Early Poetry and Late Prose," *MELUS*, 40(1), pp. 52–75.

Faulkner, C. (2004) *Women's Radical Reconstruction: The Freedmen's Aid Movement*. Philadelphia: University of Pennsylvania Press.

Field, C. T. (2015) "Frances E. W. Harper and the Politics of Intellectual Maturity" in M. E. Bay, F. J. Griffin, and M. S. Jones (eds.) *Toward an Intellectual History of Black Women*. Chapel Hill: University of North Carolina Press, pp. 110–29.

Field, K. (2018) *Growing Up with the Country: Family, Race, and Nation after the Civil War*. New Haven: Yale University Press.

Fields, B. J. (1985) *Slavery and Freedom on the Middle Ground: Maryland during the Nineteenth Century.* New Haven: Yale University Press.

Fisher, R. R. (2008) "Remnants of Memory: Testimony and Being in Frances E. W. Harper's Sketches of Southern Life," *ESQ: A Journal of the American Renaissance*, 54(1–4), pp. 55–74.

Foreman, P. G. (2009) *Activist Sentiments: Reading Black Women in the Nineteenth Century.* Chicago: University of Illinois Press.

Foster, F. S. (1979) *Witnessing Slavery: The Development of Antebellum Slave Narratives.* Westport: Greenwood Press.

Foster, F. S. (1990) *A Brighter Coming Day: A Frances Ellen Watkins Harper Reader.* New York: The Feminist Press at The City University of New York.

Foster, F. S. (1993) *Written by Herself: Literary Production by African American Women, 1746–1892.* Indianapolis: Indiana University Press.

Foster, F. S. (ed.) (1994) *Minnie's Sacrifice, Sowing and Reaping, Trial and Triumph: Three Rediscovered Novels by Frances E. W. Harper.* Boston: Beacon Press.

Foster, F. S. (ed.) (2008) *Love and Marriage in Early African America.* Boston: Northeastern University Press.

Foster, F. S. (ed.) (2010) *'Til Death or Distance Do Us Part: Love and Marriage in African America.* New York: Oxford University Press.

Fulton, D. S. (2007) "Sowing Seeds in an Untilled Field: Temperance and Race, Indeterminacy and Recovery in Frances E. W. Harper's *Sowing and Reaping*," *Legacy*, 24(2), pp. 207–24.

Gardner, E. (2012) "Sowing and Reaping: A 'New' Chapter from Frances Ellen Watkins Harper's Second Novel," *Common-Place: The Interactive Journal of Early American Life*, 13(1).

Giddings, P. (1984) *When and Where I Enter: The Impact of Black Women on Race and Sex in America.* New York: Bantam Books.

Gordon, A. (1997) *African American Women and the Vote, 1837–1965.* Amherst: University of Massachusetts Press.

Graham, M. (ed.) (1988) *Complete Poems of Frances E. Harper.* New York: Oxford University Press.

Griffin, F. J. (2001) "*Minnie's Sacrifice*: Frances Ellen Watkins Harper's Narrative of Citizenship" in D. M. Bauer and P. Gould (eds.) *The Cambridge Companion to Nineteenth-Century American Women's Writing.* Cambridge University Press, pp. 308–19.

Harper, F. W. (1892) *Iola Leroy, Or Shadows Uplifted.* 3rd edn. Boston: James H. Earle.

Harper, F. W. (1990a) "A Factor in Human Progress," in F. S.

Foster (ed.) *A Brighter Coming Day: A Frances Ellen Watkins Harper Reader*. New York: The Feminist Press at The City University of New York, pp. 275–80.

Harper, F. W. (1990b) "Christianity" in F. S. Foster (ed.) *A Brighter Coming Day: A Frances Ellen Watkins Harper Reader*. New York: The Feminist Press at The City University of New York, pp. 96–9.

Harper, F. W. (1990c) "Enlightened Motherhood" in F. S. Foster (ed.) *A Brighter Coming Day: A Frances Ellen Watkins Harper Reader*. New York: The Feminist Press at The City University of New York, pp. 285–92.

Harper, F. W. (1990d) "Our Greatest Want" in F. S. Foster (ed.) *A Brighter Coming Day: A Frances Ellen Watkins Harper Reader*. New York: The Feminist Press at The City University of New York, pp. 102–4.

Harper, F. W. (1990e) "Shalmanezer, Prince of Cosman" in F. S. Foster (ed.) *A Brighter Coming Day: A Frances Ellen Watkins Harper Reader*. New York: The Feminist Press at The City University of New York, pp. 295–302.

Harper, F. W. (1990f) "The Great Problem to Be Solved" in F. S. Foster (ed.) *A Brighter Coming Day: A Frances Ellen Watkins Harper Reader*. New York: The Feminist Press at The City University of New York, pp. 219–22.

Harper, F. W. (1990g) "The Two Offers" in F. S. Foster (ed.) *A Brighter Coming Day: A Frances Ellen Watkins Harper Reader*. New York: The Feminist Press at The City University of New York, pp. 105–14.

Harper, F. W. (1990h) "We Are All Bound Up Together" in F. S. Foster (ed.) *A Brighter Coming Day: A Frances Ellen Watkins Harper Reader*. New York: The Feminist Press at The City University of New York, pp. 217–19.

Harper, F. W. (1994) *Minnie's Sacrifice, Sowing and Reaping, Trial and Triumph*. Ed. F. S. Foster. Boston: Beacon Press.

Harper, F. W. (2010 [1901]) *Idylls of the Bible (1901)*. Lavergne, Tenn.: Kessinger Publishing.

Harris, T. (1997) "What Women? What Canon? African American Women and the Canon" in J. C. Reeseman (ed.) *Speaking the Other Self: American Women Writers*. Athens: University of Georgia Press, pp. 90–5.

Higginbotham, E. B. (1993) *Righteous Discontent: The Women's Movement in the Black Baptist Church, 1880–1920*. Cambridge, Mass.: Harvard University Press.

Hubbard, D. (ed.) (2005) *Recovered Writers / Recovered Texts: Race, Class, and Gender in Black Women's Literature*. Knoxville: University of Tennessee Press.

Hunter, T. W. (1997) *To 'Joy My Freedom: Southern Black Women's Lives and Labors after the Civil War*. Cambridge Mass.: Harvard University Press.

Hunter, T. W. (2017) *Bound in Wedlock: Slave and Free Black Marriage in the Nineteenth Century*. Cambridge, Mass.: The Belknap Press of Harvard University Press.

Jarrett, G. (2011) *Representing the Race: A New Political History of African American Literature*. New York: New York University Press.

Jeffrey, J. R. (1998) *The Great Silent Army of Abolitionism: Ordinary Women in the Antislavery Movement*. Chapel Hill: University of North Carolina Press.

Johnson, W. D. (2016) *Antebellum Women's Poetry: A Rhetoric of Sentiment*. Carbondale: Southern Illinois Press.

Jones, M. S. (2007) *All Bound Up Together: The Woman Question in African American Public Culture, 1830–1900*. Chapel Hill: University of North Carolina Press.

Kilson, M. (2014) *Transformation of the African American Intelligentsia, 1880–2012*. Cambridge, Mass.: Harvard University Press.

Loewenberg, B. and Bogin, R. (1976) *Black Women in Nineteenth-Century American Life: Their Words, Their Thoughts, Their Feelings*. University Park: Pennsylvania State University Press.

Logan, S. W. (ed.) (1995) *With Pen and Voice: A Critical Anthology of Nineteenth-Century African-American Women*. Carbondale: Southern Illinois University Press.

Logan, S. W. (1999) *"We Are Coming": The Persuasive Discourse of Nineteenth-Century Black Women*. Carbondale: Southern Illinois University Press.

McDaneld, J. (2015) "Harper, Historiography, and the Race/Gender Opposition in Feminism," *Signs: Journal of Women in Culture and Society*, 40(2), pp. 393–415.

McGill, M. L. (2012) "Frances Ellen Watkins Harper and the Circuits of Abolitionist Poetry," in L. L. Cohen and J. A. Stein (eds.) *Early African American Print Culture*. Philadelphia: University of Pennsylvania Press.

McGill, M. L. (2016) "'Presentiments,'" *Common-Place: The Interactive Journal of Early American Life*, 16(2).

McHenry, E. (2002) *Forgotten Realms: Recovering the Lost History of*

African American Literary Societies. Durham: Duke University Press.

Morgan, J. L. (2004) *Laboring Women: Reproduction and Gender in New World Slavery*. Philadelphia: University of Pennsylvania Press.

Mossell, N. F. (2010 [1894]) *The Work of the Afro-American Woman*. Whitefish, Mont.: Kissinger Publishing.

Nell, W. (2019) *Colored Americans in the Wars of 1776 and 1812*. Glasgow: Good Press.

Ortner, J. (2015) "Lost No More: Frances Ellen Watkins Harper's Forest Leaves," *Common-Place: The Interactive Journal of Early American Life*, 15(4).

Owens, D. C. (2018) *Medical Bondage: Race, Gender, and the Origins of American Gynecology*. Athens: University of Georgia Press.

Painter, N. I. (1994) "'Representing Truth,'" *The Journal of American History*, 81(2), pp. 472–3.

Painter, N. I. (1996) *Sojourner Truth: A Life, A Symbol*. New York: W. W. Norton & Co.

Parker, A. M. (2010) *Articulating Rights: Nineteenth-Century American Women on Race, Reform, and the State*. DeKalb: Northern Illinois University Press.

Peterson, C. (1993) "'Doers of the Word': Theorizing African-American Writers in the Antebellum North," in J. W. Warren (ed.) *The (Other) American Traditions: Nineteenth-Century American Writers*. New Brunswick: Rutgers University Press.

Peterson, C. (1995) *"Doers of the Word": African American Speakers and Writers in the North (1830-1880)*. New Brunswick: Rutgers University Press.

Peterson, C. (1997) "Reconstructing the Nation: Frances Harper, Charlotte Forten, and the Racial Politics of Periodical Publication," *Proceedings of the American Antiquarian Society*, 107(2), pp. 301–34.

Peterson, C. L. (2016) "Searching for Frances," *Common-Place: The Interactive Journal of Early American Life*, 16(2).

Plessy v. *Ferguson* (1896) 163 US 537.

Reynolds, D. and Rosenthal, D. J. (eds.) (1997) *The Serpent in the Cup: Temperance in American Literature*. Amherst: University of Massachusetts Press.

Richardson, M. (ed.) (1987) *Maria W. Stewart: America's First Black Woman Political Writer, Essays and Speeches*. Indianapolis: Indiana University Press.

Robbins, S. (2004) *Managing Literacy, Mothering America: Women's*

Narratives on Reading and Writing in the Nineteenth Century. University of Pittsburgh Press.

Rosenthal, D. (1997) "Deracialized Discourse: Temperance and Racial Ambiguity in Harper's 'The Two Offers' and *Sowing and Reaping*," in D. Reynolds and D. Rosenthal (eds.) *The Serpent in the Cup: Temperance in American Literature.* Amherst: University of Massachusetts Press.

Rutkowski, A. (2008) "Leaving the Good Mother: Frances E. W. Harper, Lydia Maria Child, and the Literary Politics of Reconstruction," *Legacy*, 25(1), pp. 83–104.

Salerno, B. (2005) *Sister Societies: Women's Antislavery Organizations in Antebellum America.* DeKalb: Northern Illinois University Press.

Sinha, M. (2016a) *The Slave's Cause: A History of Abolition.* New Haven: Yale University Press.

Sinha, M. (2016b) "The Other Frances Ellen Watkins Harper," *Common-Place: The Interactive Journal of Early American Life*, 16(2).

Spires, D. (2019) *The Practice of Citizenship: Black Politics and Print Culture in the Early United States.* Philadelphia: University of Pennsylvania Press.

Stancliff, M. (2011) *Frances Ellen Watkins Harper: African American Reform Rhetoric and the Rise of a Modern Nation State.* New York: Routledge.

Sterling, D. (1997) *We Are Your Sisters: Black Women in the Nineteenth Century.* New York: W. W. Norton.

Stewart, C. L. (2018) *Temperance and Cosmopolitanism: African American Reformers in the Atlantic World.* University Park: Pennsylvania University Press.

Still, W. (1872) *The Underground Railroad: A Record of Facts, Authentic Narratives, Letters, Etc., Narrating the Hardships Hair-breadth Escapes and Death Struggles of the Slaves in their Efforts for Freedom, as Related by Themselves and Other, or Witnessed by the Author, together with Sketches of some of the Largest Stockholders, and Most Liberal Aiders and Advisers of the Road.* Philadelphia: Porter & Coates.

Tate, C. (1992) *Domestic Allegories of Political Desire: The Black Heroine's Text at the Turn of the Century.* New York: Oxford University Press.

Terborg-Penn, R. (1998) *African American Women in the Struggle for the Vote, 1850–1920.* Indianapolis: Indiana University Press.

Tetrault, L. (2014) *The Myth of Seneca Falls: Memory and the Women's*

Suffrage Movement, 1848–1898. Chapel Hill: University of North Carolina Press.

Turner, P. A. (2007) "The Rise and Fall of Eliza Harris: From Novel to Tom Shows to Quilts" in *Uncle Tom's Cabin & American Culture: A Multi-Media Archive*. University of Virginia.

Walker, A. (2003) *Meridian*. San Diego: Harcourt Publishers.

Warren, J. W. (ed.) (1993) *The (Other) American Traditions: Nineteenth-Century Women Writers*. New Brunswick: Rutgers University Press.

Washington, M. (2015) "Frances Ellen Watkins: Family Legacy and Antebellum Activism," *The Journal of African American History*, 100(1), pp. 59–86.

Wells, I. B. (2016) *Southern Horrors and Other Writings: The Anti-Lynching Campaign of Ida B. Wells, 1892–1900*. Ed. J. J. Royster. Boston: Bedford / St. Martin's.

Williams, A. N. (2013) *Dividing Lines: Class Anxiety and Postbellum Black Fiction*. Ann Arbor: University of Michigan Press.

Williams, A. N. (2014) "Frances Watkins (Harper), Harriet Tubman and the Rhetoric of Single Blessedness," *Meridians*, 12(2), pp. 99–122.

Yee, S. J. (1992) *Black Women Abolitionists: A Study in Activism, 1828–1860*. Knoxville: University of Tennessee Press.

Index